AN INTRODUCTION
TO THE THEOLOGY
OF ALBRECHT RITSCHL

by
David L. Mueller

THE WESTMINSTER PRESS
Philadelphia

PUBLISHED BY THE WESTMINSTER PRESS®
PHILADELPHIA, PENNSYLVANIA

PRINTED IN THE UNITED STATES OF AMERICA

Preface

THIS STUDY OF ALBRECHT RITSCHL grows out of my interest in the history of Protestant theology. Like many other persons now engaged in teaching theology in seminaries and universities, I received my theological training at a time when neo-orthodoxy dominated theological education. Interest in this movement led to intensive involvement with the theology of Karl Barth. Further reflection precipitated a renewed engagement with the theology of the nineteenth century apart from which Barth's pilgrimage and contemporary theology cannot be understood.

The theology of Ritschl and his followers played a decisive role in German theology from about 1875 until 1910. Wilhelm Herrmann, the teacher of both Barth and Bultmann, was strongly influenced by Ritschl and represents one link between Ritschl and the dialectical theology that developed after World War I. Though Barth is not unappreciative of certain trends in Herrmann and in the theology of the nineteenth century, he has very little good to say for Ritschl. This accounts in part for the lack of attention accorded Ritschl during the period of Barth's ascendancy. However, with the current renewal of interest in the theology of the nineteenth century, Ritschl is also receiving a new hearing. He is deserving of this attention because, next to Schleiermacher, he is the most significant theologian of the last half of the nineteenth century in Germany. His influence extended to England, Scotland, and the United States, and his thought represents an important link between the theology of the nineteenth century and that of the twentieth century.

This book is an analysis of Ritschl's theology in the light of his doctrine of justification and reconciliation, including both its presuppositions and consequences. Most secondary interpretations have been relegated to the notes. In the final chapter, I have evaluated both the strengths and the weaknesses of Ritschl's system and have tried to see something of his relevance for contemporary theological discussion.

I am grateful to the trustees and administration of the Southern Baptist Theological Seminary in Louisville, Kentucky, for granting me a sabbatical leave in order to undertake this research at Yale Divinity School in 1965–1966. Courtesies extended by the faculty and staff of the Divinity School helped to make the year profitable. A special word of thanks is due Prof. Hans W. Frei of Yale University for helpful counsel during my research. Dean Robert E. Cushman of Duke Divinity School first awakened my interest in the theology of the nineteenth century and in matters epistemological. John Gustavson, my graduate assistant, and his wife typed the first draft of this manuscript and Dr. Ronald Deering and Mr. Gustavson have read the manuscript and made helpful suggestions. Mrs. Leo T. Crismon has gone beyond the call of duty in typing the final draft. Finally, I am indebted to my wife for encouragement and assistance along the way.

This book is dedicated to my parents to whom I owe much. My father, William A. Mueller, was the first to guide me in theological matters and he has followed this project with a fatherly interest.

I have utilized extant translations of Ritschl's works where available, even though they could be improved at points. Responsibility for all other translations from German titles is mine.

D. L. M.

Louisville, Kentucky

Contents

Introduction

RITSCHL'S SIGNIFICANCE AND INFLUENCE

Perhaps no theologian of the nineteenth century experienced so significant a period of dominant influence upon Protestant theology and the life of the church and an equally radical eclipse as did Albrecht Ritschl. Yet many interpreters of modern theology regard him as the most important Protestant theologian of the last century after Schleiermacher. The great church historian, Adolf von Harnack, who stood within the orbit of Ritschl's influence and was for a time a leading exponent of Ritschlianism, spoke of him as one of the modern "Church Fathers." Harnack even predicted that in Ritschl "lies the future direction of Protestantism."[1] This prophecy proved false, but it must be remembered that Ritschl and his school held sway within Protestantism in Germany during the four decades from 1875 until about 1918.

Writing in 1935, Horst Stephan could say: "Hardly any theological figure of the nineteenth century has been brushed aside in such contemptuous fashion by the newer theological movements of the twentieth century than Albrecht Ritschl."[2] Yet before this occurred, beginning about 1910, Ritschlianism had spread from Germany and the Continent to England and America, and there it influenced theology and the church during the first quarter of this century. Walter Rauschenbusch, the prophet of the social gospel in America, was shaped by the Ritschlian theology and particularly its understanding of the Kingdom of God. In surveying the impact of Ritschl and his school in 1897, James Orr designated the following theologians within the Ritschlian camp: Wilhelm Herrmann in Marburg; A. Harnack and J. Kaftan in Berlin; Gottschick and Th. Häring in Tübingen; Kattenbusch in Bonn; Schultz and Schürer in Göttingen; and Wendt in Jena. Indeed, so marked was Ritschl's influence within the theological faculties of German universities in the latter part of the nineteenth century that some critics accused him of using questionable tactics in placing his disciples in chairs of theology.[3] It is perhaps closer to the truth to say that Ritschl regarded it his duty to encourage and promote his promising protégés so that their careers might be facilitated. Harnack remarks that Ritschl advised his pupils to "trust in God, keep your powder dry, and write textbooks!"[4]

The most decisive factor giving rise to Ritschl's influence is the way in which his theological viewpoint provided the context and matrix within which theological discussion and research were carried out in the late nineteenth and early twentieth centuries. Ritschl's methodological starting point with the Biblical witness to the historical figure of Jesus and his redemptive activity struck a responsive chord in the last quarter of the nineteenth century. It was an age in which both speculative theology in the tradition of German idealism and radical and negative theology of men such as D. F. Strauss and Ludwig Feuerbach were under attack. Moreover, though more pedantic and less philosophically acute than Schleiermacher, Ritschl's theology was more Biblically and historically oriented than that of the former. During his long teaching career, Ritschl lectured in New Testament studies, patristics, historical theology, "comparative symbolics," and dogmatics and theological ethics, although during the years in Göttingen (1864–1889) his concentration lay in the area of dogmatics and theological ethics. It has often been observed that though Ritschl made significant contributions to each of the above disciplines and especially to patristics, Reformation theology, and dogmatics, his influence on succeeding generations lay more in his comprehensive theological perspective and the manner in which he was able to combine this with the historicocritical approach than with his historical and systematic conclusions per se.

The testimony of Karl Holl, distinguished Reformation scholar, to the significance of Ritschl is typical of many of his generation. Writing on December 28, 1914, to his friend, Adolph Schlatter, whose *Christliche Ethik* he had just read, Holl enters this caveat:

> You must allow me to take exception at one point. Two ideas which you express so powerfully, namely, that the individual in all his faith and willing stands within the community of faith, and secondly, that one is never related to God in such a way that one can forget the world—these are ideas which Ritschl stressed and on account of which he has been terribly vilified.[5]

In a letter dated January 8, 1920, Holl once again comes to Ritschl's defense in the face of Schlatter's rather negative appraisal:

> That which Ritschl *intended* was not as far removed from your own concerns as you seem to think. . . . When I reflect that Ritschl intended to make Christ central even as do you, that he opposed perfectionism because of his endorsement of a right understanding of justification, that

he comprehended the role of the will in religion and always stressed its significance, that he held that all religious virtues are related to the community of faith—then I find many points of contact between you.[6]

Holl concludes this letter with a statement of indebtedness to Ritschl:

> At all events, at the time when Ritschl's theology appeared to offer me a solution, I was not hindered from taking Christianity seriously. In addition to Schleiermacher and Biedermann, Ritschl's theology . . . was actually the bridge which enabled many to recover their Christian faith.[7]

These reminiscences may serve to remind our generation, which tends to forget its past heritage too readily, of something of Ritschl's importance as one of the fountainheads of modern theology. The words of H. R. Mackintosh in 1937 concerning Ritschl are also true: "Ritschl at the moment belongs, like Tennyson, to the 'middle distance,' too far for gratitude, too near for reverence. He is behind a passing cloud to-day."[8] In the conclusion of this study, we may entertain the question whether the cloud covering the theology of Ritschl has passed from view enabling us to evaluate his contribution more equitably.

It would be instructive to give attention here to Ritschl's life and theological development, but this would lead us too far afield.[9] It must suffice to point in a general way to the broad spectrum of influences that molded his thought. In the course of our analysis, more specific references to the foregoing will be made. A major difficulty confronting the interpreter of Ritschl lies in the fact that he was influenced decisively by the Scriptures, his understanding of the history of the church, and the history of theology and of philosophy. A review of the more immediate intellectual forces shaping his thought would include virtually all the movements that gave rise to the development of the modern mind. He was nurtured in the theology of the Reformation, especially that of Lutheranism; he was knowledgeable concerning Protestant orthodoxy and its demise in the face of the overwhelming tide of the Enlightenment; he was attracted to Kant's ethics and to certain forms of Neo-Kantianism; for a time he was an adherent of the philosophical perspective of German idealism as it came to expression in Hegel and especially in F. C. Baur and the Tübingen School; he rejected the latter and both the radical left wing Hegelianism of Strauss and Feuerbach and the orthodox speculative Hegelianism of the right during his own lifetime; at many points he engaged the theology of Schleiermacher and his impact on the theology of the nineteenth century. In addition, we must recall his continuing involvement with the theology of the Reformation as it came to expression in various movements in nineteenth-century Germany such as Lutheran confessionalism and Lutheran Pietism—neither of which he could acknowledge as the legitimate extension of the intention of the Reformers.

It is not surprising, therefore, that virtually all analyses of Ritschl's thought note the complexity of the intellectual milieu in which he sought to develop a viable theology. This also accounts for the radical divergence of opinion in the interpretation of Ritschl; some see him as an apologetic theologian mirroring the *Zeitgeist,* while others depict him as cognizant of all currents but captive to none. Hermann Timm pictures the seeming impasse with which Ritschl was confronted in attempting to construct and establish his own theological system.

> After he had destroyed the speculative system of truth [i.e., German idealism] with his own hands, he was forced to renew the search for a scientific system in which theology and philosophy, faith in God and knowledge of the world, dogmatic theology and history could be united.[10]

Where is one to turn if one rejects the great philosophicotheological synthesis of Hegel on the one hand, and the theologicophilosophical synthesis of Schleiermacher on the other? That was Ritschl's dilemma.

Two references of a biographical nature must suffice in this brief introduction. Ritschl provides us with a revealing autobiographical statement in 1844 concerning his choice of a vocation. Ritschl was almost twenty-two years old; he had completed his theological studies at Bonn and Halle and stood at the threshold of a long and distinguished teaching career.

> I turned to the study of theology not solely on account of the child's tendency to follow in his father's footsteps, but rather because of a speculative bent which wished to comprehend the highest which had become meaningful to me both by virtue of religious and theological impressions received and also through my historical and philosophical interests. Although the choice of a discipline of study is a venture whose success cannot be anticipated in advance, I have never regretted to this point my decision to study theology. I have given myself to this science with complete abandon.[11]

The final statement is a description of Ritschl's personality and temperament by his son and biographer, Otto Ritschl, which serves to bring certain aspects of his life and work into focus.

> Ritschl was a man of one mold. The spiritual and intellectual stimulations which he experienced and the impressions which influenced the formation of his character and his perspective on life were appropriated by virtue of the uniqueness of his individual gifts in such a way that inner contradictions in his person were ruled out. Thus the picture of his life is simple, clear and pure. He was a strong personality marked by self-control; his will was energetic and purposive; his knowledge was acute and focused upon that which was real, and his feelings were directed toward reaching and appropriating that which was truly worthwhile in

human existence. The content of his life was determined by his vocation; in it he sought only the honor of Him whom he knew as his sustainer. His total energies were dedicated to this end. Other spheres of human life were measured against this norm. He always ordered them according to the ideal manifested to him in the person of Christ and the kingdom of God. The fact that he did this ever more consistently in the course of the years led to a restriction of the wider interests which characterized him in earlier days. Even his understanding of different types of individuals and intellectual perspectives suffered on account of his concentration upon his own goals and striving. Like every other strong personality, he offended many; upon others to whom he was bound by similarity of viewpoint and aspiration, he exercised an even greater power of attraction.[12]

CHARACTERISTIC EMPHASES

Before we give attention to Ritschl's doctrine of justification and reconciliation, some perspective may be provided by singling out certain emphases characterizing his theology as a whole. Though Otto Ritschl may be accused of overlooking certain weaknesses of his father's thought, his designation of the following presuppositions and emphases is both accurate and concise.[13]

First, Ritschl always viewed his theology in the context of the church and pursued it for the benefit of the church. His concern to train pastors and teachers for service in the Evangelical Church coincides with the practical orientation of his theology. Second, he established a clear distinction between religion and theology. The Christian religion has to do primarily with a practical mode of life or piety distinguishing Christians and the church. Theology, on the other hand, is the theoretical delineation of the Christian religion. Third, Ritschl acknowledged that theology could make formal use of philosophy (logic, epistemology) and psychology in theological construction, but he opposed the use of any philosophical metaphysic as the basis upon which a natural religion or theology might be constructed. Fourth, he held that statements of faith are direct value judgments that lead Christians to estimate the contents of faith grounded in divine revelation to be of greater worth than all other values. By contrast, the theoretical construction of theology is accompanied by value judgments only in that the theologian presupposes a prior commitment to the Christian religion as the highest of all values.

Fifth, in Ritschl's view Jesus Christ is the complete revelation of God, his Father, and through him there come to be those who trust in God's forgiving grace and providential care. The content of the divine revelation acknowledged in faith is an objective "given"; it does not come into existence by virtue of man's subjective illusions. However, God's revelation is

comprehended fully only when it is appropriated subjectively through be-lieving trust, thereby becoming the basis for present blessedness and the source of a life lived effectively in the service of God. Sixth, Ritschl main-tained that the Christian community did not come into existence solely through the work of Christ completed in his death, but must be seen as a result of his earthly ministry as the founder of the church and the Kingdom of God upon earth. Consequently, the Christian religion cannot be compre-hended from the proclamation of Jesus alone, but must be seen coming to fulfillment in the rise of the church, which is already present in Jesus' earliest disciples.

Seventh, he emphasized that dogmatics must develop a unified Christian *Weltanschauung* within the perspective of the church reconciled to God through Christ. Eighth, for Ritschl, religion is not to be conceived mystically as the relationship of the individual to God; rather, it is a circle determined by three points, namely, God, the world, and man. Within Christianity, this trinity is seen in terms of God, Christ, and the church, and within the latter the individual Christian is drawn to Christ and through him to God. Ninth, he held that the idea of the Kingdom of God or of the divine sovereignty is the central concept that comprehends all the relationships of the Christian to God, the world, and his fellowman. For Ritschl, the idea of the Kingdom of God involves two related matters. On the one hand, it is the highest good, participation in which constitutes divine Sonship and spiritual Lordship over the world; on the other hand, it is simultaneously the ethical ideal of the Christian community in the light of which, and toward which, the obedient activity of the community is to be directed. In this way, Chris-tianity is analogous to an ellipse with two foci, the first representing the experience of God's redemptive love and the second, the corresponding human activity of love to neighbor.

Tenth, in Ritschl's thought the distinction between the religious and the ethical conceptions of the nature of the church is significant. Conceived in religious terms, the church is the work of God maintained through the proclaimed Word of God and the Sacraments. The ethical conception of the church is independent of the former and has to do with man's activity directed toward God through prayer and toward man in common deeds of service. Both serve to maintain the sense of community. Eleventh, God's action upon man cannot be perceived if man is regarded as passive, but only in the light of his corresponding reaction and activity. In keeping with this presupposition, Ritschl held that God's justification of the sinner had to be viewed by the church as a synthetic judgment of God inasmuch as man is passive with respect to it. Insofar as the believer within the church acknowledges God's judgment as the surety of his own justification, it becomes the regulator of his Christian self-consciousness. The divine forgiveness of sins is identical in content to justification and involves the removal of the guilt separating the sinner from God. Thus it becomes possible for the believer to exercise trust rather than mistrust in the Word of God. In the light of this presupposition, justification is viewed as subjectively effectual in man's reconciliation with God.

But reconciliation is attested more fully in man's volitional and emotional response indicating that he no longer strives against God, but trusts confidently in him. In the religious sphere, this attitude is seen in the exercise of Christian piety through trust in God, faith in divine providence, humility, and prayer directed toward God arising out of gratitude. In the ethical sphere, man's reconciliation is evidenced in obedience to the law of love of neighbor which becomes possible in the faithful fulfillment of one's vocation. The freedom to do the good essential in these religious and ethical activities is always correlated with man's dependence upon God.

Finally, Ritschl made creative use of the basic religious and ethical concepts of Luther and the confessional symbols. The conception of Christian perfection and the *Lebensideal* which Ritschl found implicit in them provided the basis for his own development of the ideal Protestant style of life —a *Lebensführung* qualitatively different from the monastic ideal of Catholicism. As a result, Ritschl disapproved of any confusion of the original Reformation *Lebensideal* with that of Roman Catholicism, and this stance explains his rejection of Pietism as an essentially Catholic aberration.

The Theological Method
of Albrecht Ritschl

THE PROBLEM OF DOGMATIC PROLEGOMENA

Although Ritschl's early publications growing out of his Biblical and historical research involved him in a continuing dialogue with contemporary philosophers, church historians, and theologians as well as with those farther removed from his day, the task of clarifying his own theological method became most acute as he embarked on the writing of his magnum opus on *Justification and Reconciliation*, which appeared in its first edition during the years 1870–1874. The fullest explication of his methodology was reserved for the introductions to Vols. II and III of this trilogy, and it underwent modifications in later editions. In a letter written in March, 1871, Ritschl makes the following lament: "I have experienced once again how unsatisfying all of these so-called methodological (*Principienfragen*) questions are."[1] In another letter from the same period, he confides to Holtzmann in much the same manner: "The people who occupy themselves continually with questions of prolegomena concerning the subjective locus or place of religion, revelation in general, miracle, and the place of dogmatic method are really only in the court of the Gentiles and keep themselves removed from the presence of God."[2] Nevertheless, he struggled to frame a succinct statement of his methodology in these volumes and felt upon its completion that he had achieved his objective.[3]

Yet he maintained that "Christianity as a religion is neutral with respect to the various epistemologies on the basis of which its content may be organized scientifically."[4] In addition, according to his view the appropriateness of a particular methodology must be judged in the light of its application in the positive construction of the theological system.[5]

Thus we need to remember that Ritschl accorded prolegomena a restricted place in systematic theology, namely, that of clarifying its "principles and conditions" of procedure.[6] However, inasmuch as the application of a theological method is never automatic, a true appreciation of the scientific principles governing dogmatics obtains only as the result of actually engaging in theological work.[7] In this context, Ritschl writes: "Scientific knowledge . . . validates its general adherence to laws through the discovery of laws within the special sphere to which it turns."[8] For this reason, he contends that though certain norms guide theological reflection, the latter ceases to be scientific when subordinated to ecclesiastical doctrines or dogmas.[9]

Otto Ritschl, in evaluating his father's scientific method, recalls his predilection for the Scholastic watchword: *"Qui bene distinguit, bene docet."* The elder Ritschl was wont to supplement and complete this statement as follows: *"Qui bene distinguit et bene comprehendit, bene docet."*[10] The historian's art of distinguishing details, though important, was nonetheless not Ritschl's greatest strength. It lay, rather, in his ability to incorporate particulars within a more comprehensive perspective. This penchant for developing a synthetic picture is evident in Ritschl's historical, Biblical, and constructive writings, and Otto Ritschl is not far from the mark in regarding this talent as responsible for Ritschl's contribution to each of these fields.[11] In this regard, Albrecht Ritschl's historical, Biblical, and theological research coalesce in his great work on *Justification and Reconciliation,* and though F. C. Baur in 1838, and Martin Kähler in 1898, and others in the nineteenth century wrote on this subject, it may be said that neither Ritschl's predecessors nor his successors in the great century of modern theology surpassed his contribution. Indeed, apart from Barth's treatment, no study of this subject has appeared in the twentieth century which rivals Ritschl's work either in scope or in depth.

THE CHRISTIAN RELIGION AND THE PHENOMENON OF RELIGION

THE NATURE OF RELIGION: RELIGION AND CHRISTIANITY

In the course of modern theology, the question of the nature of religion has been much debated. The preoccupation with methodological problems in theology is due in part to the increased attention accorded the phenomena of religion and religions both in their particularity and in their connection with the Judeo-Christian tradition. Schleiermacher's creative involvement with the science of comparative religion in the prolegomena to his *Glaubenslehre* of 1830 served as a model for many of his successors, Ritschl not excepted. We cannot pursue the details of Ritschl's attempts to interpret and relate the phenomenon of religion to the Christian faith, but we must look at the rationale behind his procedure.[12]

Ritschl defines religion as a phenomenon concerned with the relationship that exists between the Deity, man, and the world. In view of this broad definition, the issue for Ritschl is whether it is possible to arrive at a "universal conception" of religion. He affirms that such a definition has only regulative and not constitutive significance in the interpretation of particular religions.[13] Contrary to rationalism, which reduces all religious phenomena to a religion of reason or to an abstract religion based upon the essential elements common to all religions, Ritschl follows Schleiermacher—and thereby rejects Kant—in evaluating positive religions in terms of some kind of historical revelation.[14] Religions are not to be understood as man's attempt to give expression to the divine spirit immanent within the human spirit as Hegel and his followers held.[15] All are in some sense rooted in revelation, and Ritschl again followed Schleiermacher in holding that all positive religions are communal in nature.[16] Although at times he seems willing to grant that all positive religions mediate between God and man insofar as they are based upon revelation, they are not of the same worth. He believes that one may speak of the common elements in positive religions and even of an ascending scale of religion in the "spiritual history of humanity," but the final attitude of the Christian toward non-Christian religions is predicated upon his conviction that Christianity is the complete and universal religion.[17]

According to some observers, Ritschl's standpoint becomes increasingly Christocentric and unapologetic in the course of his theological development.[18] "In Christianity," he writes, "revelation through God's Son is the *punctum stans* of all knowledge and religious conduct."[19] Or again in the introduction to the third edition of his *Instruction in the Christian Religion* of 1886, he affirms:

> Christianity claims to be the perfect religion, as distinguished from all other kinds and grades of religion, and to furnish man with that which in all other religions is striven after but is only dimly and imperfectly realized. That is the perfect religion in which a perfect knowledge of God is possible.[20]

The History and Goal of Religion and Christianity

Hök has shown that Ritschl wrestled over a long period with the problem of an adequate interpretation of the history of revelation and the manner in which Christianity is to be understood as its culmination. Though the idea of an ascending development of religions was quite widespread in the nineteenth century, Ritschl deserves credit for his careful historical analysis thereof.[21] He conceived of three stages in the history of religion. Within paganism, God reveals himself as absolute power and man bends his will before the divine omnipotence. God manifests himself in Judaism as absolute will requiring the transformation of man's will in relationship to himself as he realizes a particular goal and purpose within the covenant. In Christianity, however, God's revelation is coupled with a universal end, that of the Kingdom of God.[22]

This ascending progression in the history of religions in the light of God's revelation is coupled with an evolution in the understanding of the goal of blessedness or redemption. This is the more subjective pole. Ritschl reasoned that all religions seek a "solution to the contradiction in which man finds himself," and this is ordinarily envisaged in terms of some concrete goal.[23] Within paganism, man's salvation is sensual in that it is experienced in terms of his right relationship to the powers of nature. In Judaism, man's blessedness is pictured in a national context related to God's covenant purpose. In Christianity, redemption is full orbed and completely spiritual, involving the full transformation of the individual within the Kingdom of God which is universal in scope.[24]

Paralleling this movement in the history of religions is the progression from an aesthetic to a perfectly ethical religion. Ritschl combined his view of the progression of revelation and the manner of conceiving man's blessedness with the idea that successively higher developments of religion approximate the perfectly universal and ethical religion realized in Christianity.[25] Hök summarizes Ritschl's position regarding the relationship of Christianity to the history of religion as follows:

> Ritschl interpreted the development of the history of religion—of which he had a thoroughgoing knowledge—as a history of redemption grounded in God's transcendent revelation, having man's blessedness as its goal and accompanied by a movement of mankind toward that goal.[26]

Hök argues in his analysis of the evolution of Ritschl's interpretation of religion that his lectures in dogmatics in the years 1853 and 1856 give clear evidence that he accepted the idealist view that religion involves man's transformation (*Umwandlung*) or increasing dependence upon and direction by God. In this process, man's will is central. The second characteristic of religion is developed in his lectures on dogmatics in the years 1860 and 1864 under the influence of Zeller and Lotze. Religion now appears as that which has to do with man's blessedness (*Seligkeit*). Ritschl is here concerned with the tension that obtains because man as spirit is both subject to nature and superior to it.[27] "Man's self-understanding or feeling and his natural situation are, in other words, irreconcilable factors standing in tension with one another."[28] Religion, therefore, becomes the means whereby man satisfies the inner drive to realize his superiority over nature and therefore over the world. "Man is blessed when this tension is resolved and the religious drive is satisfied. In this area, the noetic moment is dominant. That is the second aspect under which Ritschl views religion."[29] It is Hök's thesis that Ritschl sought to incorporate both of these elements of religion within his interpretation of religion in *Justification and Reconciliation*—often with less than complete success.[30]

RELIGION AS *Weltanschauung*

In Ritschl's view, every religion expresses the manner in which a community sees its existence determined by the conception of deity. This is the noetic moment in religion. With the development of the understanding of God and the self-understanding of the community based thereon, we move in the direction of a *Weltanschauung*. The latter evolves from man's self-understanding precipitated by his feeling of dependence upon God and his subsequent attitude toward the world. This dual relationship to God and the world is marked by feelings of well-being or their opposite. This is the moment of feeling in religion.[31] These feelings in turn give rise to action, and in this way the volitional moment in religion comes into play. Ritschl summarizes regarding the necessary inclusion of all three elements in the interpretation of religion thus:

> Viewed subjectively, religion consists of a *Weltanschauung*, moments of feeling, and the movement of the will: it utilizes or comprehends the three elementary spiritual functions of comprehension, feeling, and willing. One cannot conceive any religion properly or fully if one regards one of these elements as more important or essential than the others. Hence it is a fruitless venture to attempt to trace back religion in principle to one of these fundamental functions of the human spirit. All three are equally represented in religion and they do not permit themselves to be reduced to one another.[32]

When Ritschl surveys the history of religion, he speaks repeatedly of the supremacy of Christianity on the basis of its more comprehensive world view enabling man to see himself in proper relationship to God, the world, and nature, and to his final destiny in the Kingdom of God. Thus he can say that the recognition of God's revelation of himself in Christ "yields this pre-eminent excellence of Christianity, namely, that its view of the world is a rounded whole, and that the goal it sets to life is this, that in Christianity man becomes a whole, a spiritual character supreme over the world."[33]

RELIGION: THE DIVINE-HUMAN RELATIONSHIP

One other development in Ritschl's interpretation of religion needs to be noted. Otto Ritschl observes that Julius Kaftan's book *Das Wesen der christlichen Religion,* which appeared in 1881, exerted considerable influence upon Albrecht Ritschl. It was primarily in the area of methodology that Kaftan's work gave impetus to revisions of Ritschl's earlier view of religion, and several letters bear this out. He writes Harnack in 1881: "In the doctrine of religion and revelation, Kaftan has provided occasion for me to express myself more clearly, and I have done so with interest."[34] Fabricius pursued this matter and shows how Kaftan criticizes Schleiermacher, Ritschl, and others who interpret religion solely in terms of man's feeling of dependence upon God.[35] Kaftan opposes them and contends that the idea of God and his power is the primary category in religion. In addition, that which moves man to dependence upon God is determined by the good or goods which man hopes to obtain from the Deity. In response to this critique, Ritschl modified his definition of religion and replaced the term "dependence upon God" with several others. Fabricius writes:

> Not only in the larger sections which were revised do we find the term "dependence upon God" avoided, but also in thirty-three other instances scattered throughout the book where it is used, we find it replaced by other expressions such as: operation of God, saving work of God, . . . relationship to, stance toward, or belonging to God. . . . in accordance with the divine disposition (*Fügung*).[36]

Fabricius suggests at least two reasons why Ritschl was desirous of dissociating himself from Schleiermacher's view of religion. First, he wished to avoid the charge that he was dependent upon Schleiermacher and his mode of quasi-mystical speculation in theology.[37] Secondly, and more important, Fabricius conjectures with good grounds that Ritschl modified his definition of religion "because [the term] was reminiscent of Schleiermacher's absolute causality and the despairing resignation of fatalism."[38] In opposition to Schleiermacher, religious pantheists, and predestinarians within Catholicism and Protestantism who stress the priority of divine grace to the extent that man's role is one of complete passivity, Ritschl accents both the priority of divine grace and man's activity evident in his faith and religious life. Fabricius finds that Ritschl's view of the relationship between God and man is always consistent at this point, even though his change in terminology might lead us to conclude otherwise.

> The situation has not changed: from the beginning Ritschl never conceived the divine-human relationship in a mechanical or hyper-mechanical manner, but rather always . . . in terms of the free activity of God and the free receptivity of man.[39]

In order to comprehend Ritschl at this point we do well to recall Otto Ritschl's reminder that a right analysis of the rationale dictating Ritschl's stance will include psychological as well as epistemological considerations.[40] For "ontology and psychology mutually presuppose each other, and their results harmonise."[41] These psychological presuppositions have a constitutive influence in interpreting the phenomena of religion and Christianity, and not merely a formal one. Among the elements Ritschl alludes to but does not develop in any systematic fashion, the following deserve mention. First, the human soul is a unity, and only as such is it self-conscious, and since it is a unity, there must be continuity between its various states.[42] As we shall see, this is important for Ritschl's understanding of the continuity between the state of man's soul as sinner and as redeemed. It also accounts, in part, for his aversion to the stress upon discontinuity between the state of man as sinner and redeemed taught by the Pietists. Second, the human soul can never be envisioned as wholly passive when acted upon. Each action upon it effects some kind of reaction. Indeed, it is in the light of this response of man that we know of the divine operation upon him. The latter would otherwise be hidden from us. This is of immense importance in Ritschl's epistemology as we shall see in a later connection. It is axiomatic for him that what is knowable concerning the divine operation upon man must be ascertained either in the light of religious states in man to which it gives rise or in terms of man's ethical activity. Therefore, he can speak both of man acting freely in response to the divine activity and in another sense of man's activity as initiated by God.

According to Otto Ritschl, the relationship between the divine will and human freedom was a decisive theological question for Albrecht Ritschl, who puts the age-old dilemma thus: ". . . how *dependence* on God, as the form of human action from love, is compatible with *freedom;* for not only is it necessary to conceive such action as free, but freedom is attested by the immediate feeling of self."[43] The solution Ritschl proposes is based upon psychological and empirical evidence derived from experience. No satisfying logical solution is possible because, in part, it always abstracts from Christian experience itself.[44] But in terms of the Christian pilgrimage, it can be said that when man adopts the Kingdom of God as his final goal, he in no way finds his freedom in conflict with dependence upon God.

> In other words, freedom is permanent self-determination by the good end, the standard of which is to be found in the law of universal love for man, or, in Christian terminology, permanent self-determination by the Kingdom of God as final end.[45]

Whenever man is determined by some end less than the universal good or the Kingdom of God, he is not free but dominated by lesser drives and motivations.[46] From this vantage point we can comprehend Ritschl's dictum that "Christianity . . . is . . . comparable . . . to an ellipse which is determined by two *foci*."[47] These two are respectively the religious moment, the redemption in Jesus Christ—in which the divine activity predominates, and the Kingdom of God—the ethical moment, which accentuates man's free activity within the Kingdom of God. This definition provides the key to Ritschl's understanding of the Christian religion and something of the focus and scope of his entire theology.

THE SCIENTIFIC CHARACTER OF SYSTEMATIC THEOLOGY

THE CHURCH AND CHRISTIAN THEOLOGY

Having looked briefly at the outer circumference that serves to illuminate the presuppositions informing Ritschl's theological method, we need to focus our attention on more immediate assumptions. As early as the opening sentences of the first volume of *Justification and Reconciliation,* he related the consequences of the redemption effected through Jesus Christ directly to the Christian community.[48] From the outset of this work, therefore, Ritschl regarded the church as the origin and focus of meaningful Christian language. The latter arises as an expression of the community's faith and therefore is not to be confused with disinterested or theoretical language.[49]

Although some of these same emphases are made in the prolegomena to Vol. III of *Justification and Reconciliation,* the accent has shifted somewhat. The stress upon the necessity of relating theology to the church is adumbrated more fully, and the book begins with a section entitled "The Standpoint of Systematic Theology in the Christian Community." It is only within the fellowship of those who have experienced the forgiveness of sins deriving from Jesus that a proper estimate of him and the whole "Christian circle of thought" can be obtained.[50] By adopting such a stance, Ritschl consciously opposes the rationalist interpretation of Jesus as a "moral legislator," "religious example," or ideal man—without reference to the community that he founded or the forgiveness of sins experienced through him. In short, the attempt to write a life of Jesus apart from any presuppositions is an impossibility—a note Martin Kähler was to sound again a quarter of a century later. Jesus is rightly known only in faith by one who as a member of the church "subordinates himself to His Person."[51]

THE CHRISTIAN RELIGION AND SYSTEMATIC THEOLOGY

Our view of Ritschl's theological method is more sharply defined as we concentrate on the next of the concentric circles that shed light on the enterprise. Earlier we alluded both to his views on the nature and history of religion and to the general manner in which he conceived of the relationship between God and man. But in order for one to have a correct "form of systematic theology," one must "first of all" have a "correct and complete *idea of the Christian Religion*."[52] Though appreciative of the creative way in which Schleiermacher related the redemption in Jesus to the Kingdom of God—thereby surpassing the "Evangelical Confessions" which stress the former to the virtual total neglect of the latter—Ritschl criticizes the author of *The Christian Faith* for his totally inadequate treatment of the teleological nature of Christianity.[53]

In an age preceding Albert Schweitzer and others, Ritschl was among the first to take new notice of the eschatological perspective of the New Testament. In all fairness this must be said no matter how we may estimate his interpretation thereof. Undoubtedly, he viewed his own correlation of redemption and the teleological direction of Christianity symbolized in the Kingdom of God as the true completion of the truncated Protestant understanding of Christianity that had existed from the Reformation to his own day. "Christianity," he writes in an often quoted statement, "resembles not a circle described from a single centre [i.e., redemption in Christ], but an ellipse which is determined by two *foci*."[54] Only as we maintain that "Jesus Himself . . . saw in the Kingdom of God the moral end of the religious fellowship He had to found" and understood it as "the organisation of humanity through action inspired by love" do we see that this teleological and ethical element is integral to a correct definition of the Christian religion.[55] Whereas for Ritschl the "spiritual redemption" effected through Jesus of Nazareth represents the religious pole of Christianity, the stress upon the Kingdom of God points us to the ethical and teleological dimension. Christianity is incomplete without both elements, and both issue directly from the "Founder of Christianity."[56]

Ritschl has Schleiermacher in mind in his definition of the Christian religion while at the same time attempting to correct his deficiencies:

> Christianity, then, is the monotheistic, completely spiritual, and ethical religion, which, based on the life of its Author as Redeemer and as Founder of the Kingdom of God, consists in the freedom of the children of God, involves the impulse to conduct from the motive of love, aims at the moral organisation of mankind, and grounds blessedness on the relation of sonship to God, as well as on the Kingdom of God.[57]

It is impossible to overestimate the significance of this formulation for the structure of Ritschl's theology: it is the essence of his entire system. He himself says that a "proper theology" is not one in which redemption relates to theology and the Kingdom of God to ethics. "On the contrary, so far as theology falls into these two sections, each must be kept under the constitutive influence of both ideas."[58]

The Scientific Characteristics of Systematic Theology

1. *The Norms and Sources of Christian Theology: The Scriptures and the Confessions.*   If we ask about the sources that guide theological statements, the introduction to Vol. II of *Justification and Reconciliation* accords Holy Scripture a central place. At this time Ritschl viewed the Scriptures as the formal principle of dogmatics in the manner of Protestant orthodoxy. He could say:

> It is precisely that formulation of theology which bears the most unmistakable imprint of the influence of Church doctrine upon it which has for its sole aim the establishment of conclusive knowledge of the Christian revelation according to the norm of Holy Scripture.[59]

This Biblical foundation of theology commends itself to the extent that a section of the prolegomena to Vol. II is entitled "The Authority of Holy Scripture for Theology."[60] Moreover, we ought not to forget that in the development of *Justification and Reconciliation,* he wrote the second volume, *The Biblical Material of the Doctrine,* before proceeding to his systematic exposition in Vol. III. Thus Holy Scripture appears as the primary norm for scientific Christian theology in the introduction to Vol. II, and the specific provision is added that a theology which seeks to develop the "authentic content of Christianity in positive scientific form must derive the same from the books of the New Testament and from no other source."[61] In addition, the confessional standards are significant for Evangelical theologians, but they are not to bind either Biblical or dogmatic theologians in their interpretation of the New Testament. Thus, for example, the presupposition that the Pauline and Reformation conceptions of justification are identical is a false surmise.[62] Accordingly, the dogmatician must sit somewhat loosely with regard to confessional standards.

In the introduction to Vol. III of *Justification and Reconciliation,* Ritschl gives evidence of a greater appreciation of both the "Pauline system" as the normative exposition of the Christian faith and the confessions of the Protestant Reformation. He writes as though his aim in analyzing the Biblical understanding of justification and reconciliation were to discover their original meaning under the guidance of the "theological principles of the Evangelical Church."[63] This is no doubt due both to his acceptance of the basic soteriological starting point of Luther and to his fear that an excessive accentuation upon the *sola scriptura* could play into the hands of both the orthodox and the Pietists.[64] At any rate, the absolute authority of Holy Scripture had been somewhat diminished by 1874, whereas the confessional standards of the Reformation, and particularly their view of salvation, play a greater role in Ritschl's theology. We find coupled with this tendency an increasing Christocentrism. Thus he essays the development of a theological program that presupposes "unconditional trust" in Jesus Christ. The Person of Christ is viewed as the origin and source of all knowledge of God and the certain ground of the redemption of the Christian community. Ritschl regards all the foregoing propositions to be "rendered imperative by the standard writings of the Reformation."[65]

2. *The Faith of the Church as the Object of Theological Investigation.* We observed earlier that Christian theology is carried on within the church and presupposes the commitment of the theologian to the understanding of the "forgiveness of sins, justification, and reconciliation" which were "called into existence by Jesus as the Founder of the Christian Church, and maintained by the apostles as its earliest representatives."[66] For Ritschl, however, theology cannot stop with the teaching of Jesus concerning the above as they are established by Biblical theology. For

> their significance becomes completely intelligible only when we see how they are reflected in the consciousness of those who believe in Him, and how the members of the Christian community trace back their consciousness of pardon to the Person and the action and passion of Jesus.[67]

Hence the

> material of the theological doctrines of forgiveness, justification, and reconciliation is to be sought not so much directly in the words of Christ, as in the correlative representations of the original consciousness of the community.[68]

Ritschl finds warrant for the elevation of the "apostolic circle of ideas" to preeminence because the "immediate object of theological cognition is the community's faith that it stands to God in a relation essentially conditioned by the forgiveness of sins."[69]

Ritschl's soteriological and Christocentric orientation involves a break with the development of Protestant orthodoxy deriving from Melanchthon in which "rational ideas of God and sin and redemption" are dominant;[70] yet he intends it to be continuous with Luther and the Reformation confessions. Such a theology can also encompass the following emphases of a Pietist such as Spener: first, that theology should have the "marks of the regenerate life" in its intimate correlation of theology with redemption experienced in the Christian community; second, that it be concerned to edify the "pulpit and pastoral work"; and finally, that theology's derivation from the Holy Spirit is validated through man's doing the will of God. Hence there is an "ethical proof of the truth of Christianity."[71]

These quotations make clear that Ritschl increasingly adopted Schleiermacher as his theological mentor at this point. The pious Christian self-

consciousness so central in Schleiermacher's theology lay under a cloud
in Vol. II of *Justification and Reconciliation* but appears to come into its
own in Vol. III. Though appreciative of the manner in which Schleiermacher relates Christian theology to the church, Ritschl opposes his thesis
that dogmatics is the exposition of the doctrine prevalent in the church at
any given time.[72] He finds the latter emphasis difficult to harmonize with
the pious Christian self-consciousness, and this is what attracts him
most.[73] Similarities in the theological method of Schleiermacher and Ritschl
are apparent from the following definitions. Schleiermacher's often cited
dictum relates Christian piety and dogmatics as follows: "Christian doctrines are accounts of the Christian religious affections set forth in
speech."[74] Ritschl writes: "For all theological propositions have for their
aim the explanation of the phenomena of the Christian life."[75] The
rationale dictating Ritschl's position here may derive from a skepticism
with respect to the possibility of attaining certainty regarding the occur-
rence of revelation in history. Thus he contends that the "gracious operations of God upon the Christian" are not directly knowable, but only
insofar as the "corresponding religious and moral acts which are called
forth by Revelation as a whole" come under the scientific scrutiny of
theology.[76] It was this pole of Schleiermacher's theology which enabled
Ritschl to say, "He is thus in terms of method my predecessor; I have
learned my method in part from him, . . . and for the other part from
Schneckenburger."[77]

a. *The mediation of revelation and religious knowledge.* It would
be misleading, however, to interpret Ritschl to be saying that the religious
experience of the theologian or the collective religious experience of the
church were per se the sources for theological construction. It is axiomatic
for him that there is no immediate relationship between the believer and
God. To affirm such would be to fall into the arms of Pietists, sectarians,
and mystics, all of whom he opposed throughout his lifetime.[78] The presence of God or Jesus Christ is always mediated through the community.
Talk about a direct relationship with God suggests sectarianism and the
fallacy of relating the Holy Spirit to the individual apart from reference to
the church.[79] In one of his mature programmatic statements Ritschl
declares:

> Hence without the medium of the Word of God which is Law and
> Gospel, and without the exact recollection of the personal revelation of
> God in Christ, there is no personal relationship between a Christian and
> God.[80]

We need to recall that in adopting this standpoint Ritschl opposes theological rationalism which rejected any idea of a supernatural revelation of
God to man in favor of a natural and universal revelation of God to man

evident in the structure of man's reason. Accordingly, in rationalism the unfolding of man's innate knowledge of God leads to a universal religion of reason. Ritschl followed in the tradition of Hegel and Schleiermacher in his attempt to conceive the relationship between God and man in terms of historical and positive religions. Hök does well to remind us that for Ritschl this is not interpreted to mean that God speaks to man today directly or in a supernatural manner.[81] Quite the opposite is the case: God revealed himself in various religions and supremely in Jesus and in the beginnings of the Christian movement. What we know of God must be mediated through acquaintance with the revelation in Jesus perceived by the early Christian community. For anyone to assert an immediate reception of revelation from God would "do away with the possibility of differentiating between hallucination and reality."[82]

Ritschl supports this agnostic stance with respect to any direct communion between God and man with the contention that an obsessive concern with individual religious experience is a sectarian, pietistic, or Methodistic perversion of the churchly orientation of the Reformers! The religious experience per se is absolutely hidden from observation and the question as to how the Holy Spirit affects man is illegitimate.[83] Instead, Ritschl never tires of stressing that it is the church, the body of Christ, which is the primary and original object of reconciliation. The Holy Spirit is not denied but affirmed when theology fulfills its task by analyzing the "spiritual processes" which are elicited by the Spirit's operation upon man instead of centering upon conversion itself. In similar fashion, all Christian doctrines are rightly interpreted when their "practical bearing" with regard to salvation is perceived as evidenced in man's religious functions.[84] Though perhaps Otto Ritschl is putting the case somewhat strongly, he is not far from the mark in maintaining that the elder Ritschl was always concerned to reject a magical or supernaturalistic explanation of Christianity.

> His whole theology is completely dominated by the presupposition that all theoretical statements of dogmatics must allow themselves to be verified by showing that their content can be made comprehensible as the real occurrence of pious experience and as suitable for fructifying Christian and ecclesiastical practical activity.[85]

b. *The subjective perspective of theology.* The fact that theology develops in the church and describes the religious and ethical response of believers to God's operation upon them does not imply that it is unscientific. Ritschl writes: "Now theology is not devotion; as a science, rather, it is 'disinterested' cognition."[86] If we ask concerning the theologian's perspective in the light of the foregoing, Ritschl finds two approaches in the history of theology. The first adopts, as it were, the divine standpoint: theology appears to view all things *sub specie aeternitatis*.[87] Such a stance is impossible even though both Catholic and Protestant Scholasticism utilized it in speaking of God as he exists in himself (*a se*). The second method that we have anticipated derives from Schleiermacher. It presupposes that all theological statements are conditioned by time and place, and consequently theology must give evidence of their empirical and historical orientation.

> If what is wanted is to write theology on the plan not merely of a narrative of the great deeds done by God, but of a system representing the salvation He has wrought out, then we must exhibit the operations of God—justification, regeneration, the communication of the Holy Spirit, the bestowal of blessedness in the *summum bonum*—in such a way as shall involve an analysis of the corresponding voluntary activities in which man appropriates the operations of God.[88]

In adopting this approach, Ritschl finds Schleiermacher to be his immediate predecessor. Such a method is opposed to orthodoxy's concern with the construction of dogmas to which intellectual assent is given without any reference to faith understood as trust on the part of the subject.[89] Such "objective delineation" is viewed by Ritschl as an inadequate manner of theologizing and contrary to the epistemological axiom set forth above that we know objects not in themselves but only as we perceive them in their relationship to us.[90] Indeed, for him there is a correlation between the degree of objectivity and the intensity of doubt regarding the veracity of Christianity.[91] In addition, the stress upon church dogmas characteristic of orthodoxy cannot be resuscitated because advances in Biblical studies and changes in the church's self-understanding and in general patterns of thought make this impossible.[92]

3. *The Movement of Theology Toward a System and a* Weltanschauung. In order to comprehend the role of theology in Ritschl's thought, certain distinctions must be kept in mind. Thus the Christian religion, ethics, and theology need to be distinguished as follows: The Christian religion has to do with the exercise of faith or worship within the cultic setting. The ethical moment in Christianity involves primarily man's activity in the world and is not to be identified with the religious moment. Finally, theology is the theoretical reflection carried on within the church that accords with its subject matter and follows a consistent epistemology. Though the discipline of systematic theology is indebted to the auxiliary disciplines of exegesis and Biblical theology, they provide no organic view of the relationship of doctrines.[93] The latter are comprehensible only within a theological system. It follows that inherent within the theological enterprise is a drive toward comprehensiveness—in short, to the development of a system.

Here we may certainly see something of the influence of Kant, Hegel, and German idealism upon Ritschl and much of Protestant theology in the nineteenth century. This must be said despite the post-Kantian preoccupation with theological prolegomena in the latter century to the neglect of dogmatics proper. Ritschl lamented this and called such theologians "fragmentarians," and consciously sought to surpass them in a comprehensive interpretation of the essentials of the Christian faith.[94] Hence the order of treatment in *Justification and Reconciliation* moves from a consideration of the historical materials (Vol. I), to the Biblical evidence (Vol. II), and finally to their fulfillment in the systematic treatment or "positive development of the doctrine" in the third volume. It therefore brings Ritschl's lifelong professional involvement in the areas of church history, New Testament, and systematic theology into fruitful interaction.

Both in his bent as a *Systematiker* and in the organization of his theology around the foci of redemption and the Kingdom of God, Ritschl reminds us of Kant and more especially of Schleiermacher. Ritschl's theology, however, has a stronger Biblical and historical orientation than Schleiermacher's, and at times he traces the latter's weakness to his inadequate grasp of the Old Testament.[95] Kant's influence accounts for Ritschl's tentativeness in matters epistemological and his antipathy toward speculative metaphysics in the grand tradition of Hegel, and for his much more practical orientation.[96] This also explains the perplexity of commentators who seek to reduce Ritschl's theological program to one overarching principle.

Both redemption and the Kingdom of God are constitutive for theological construction, but they are explicated in different ways.[97] Behind these foci lie one of Ritschl's crucial philosophical and religious presuppositions, namely, that the realm of nature must be distinguished from the realm of spirit and the spiritual life, and that the former has the latter for its end. Hence the worth of the individual soul over nature and the world mirrored in its intended *telos* in the life of blessedness in the Kingdom of God is validated as a principle of Ritschl's epistemology on both philosophical and religious grounds.[98] Armed with this presupposition, the theologian finds it incumbent upon him to show—following Kant's lead—that the

> Christian view of God and the world enables us comprehensively to unify our knowledge of nature and the spiritual life of man in a way which otherwise is impossible.[99]

It is therefore essential to remember that for Ritschl a proper interpretation of Christianity involves a complete and comprehensive *Weltanschauung* superior to all others. He writes in typical fashion:

The theological exposition of Christianity, therefore, is complete when it has been demonstrated that the Christian ideal of life, and no other, satisfies the claims of the human spirit to knowledge of things universally.[100]

His adherence to such a scientific method "gives us the certainty that theological propositions, which have been defined with logical correctness, are not mutually contradictory."[101] Such a theology has no avowed apologetic orientation: it presupposes revelation as given and does not attempt verification "by seeking to show that it agrees with some philosophical or juridical view of the world."[102] In opposition, therefore, to certain prevailing philosophical and theological currents which had grown weary of comprehensive systems of thought in the tradition of German idealism and had turned instead to methodological questions in keeping with the scientific procedures of the times, Ritschl essayed the development of a theological system.

RITSCHL'S EPISTEMOLOGY

Ritschl and the History of Philosophical Epistemology

In order to establish cogent theological propositions, Ritschl acknowledged the necessity of utilizing a proper theory of knowledge.[103] He lamented that because many of his critics had failed to read his earlier epistemological statements carefully, it became necessary to spell out his program in more detail in the pamphlet *Theologie und Metaphysik*, which appeared in 1881. There he wrote: "In the light of this [i.e., the admission of the necessity of utilizing a proper epistemology], it is quite rash and unbelievable to hold that I excise all metaphysics from theology."[104] It is crucial, however, to note how Ritschl as a theologian views the nature and role of metaphysics. He follows the Aristotelian tradition which regards metaphysics as that branch of philosophy which deals with an "elementary knowledge of things in general" enabling us to distinguish things as belonging to the realms of nature or spirit.[105] Thus metaphysics is concerned with formal knowledge, that is, with the manner in which we know. Whenever metaphysics goes beyond this and is elevated into a "final and exhaustive science of all particular ordered existence" or with a theory of knowledge that dictates what can be known in the spiritual sphere without any regard to the testimony of experience, it transgresses its bounds.[106]

We may turn from this general definition of metaphysics to particular epistemological approaches to the knowledge of God and to the establishment of valid religious language. One dominant epistemological tradition that Ritschl considers and rejects is the Platonic. Here a "thing" is known by means of its "mutable qualities" which arouse our "sensations and ideas," but in fact the thing in question "really *is at rest* behind the qualities as a permanently self-equivalent unity of attributes."[107] When applied to the Scholastic doctrine of God, both Catholic and Protestant, this epistemology gives rise to a dual knowledge of God: first, knowledge of God obtains because of his activities and their subsequent effect upon us; and second, there is knowledge of God as he exists in himself apart from his operations upon us.[108] This distinction is untenable and makes all our knowledge of God questionable, since we do not know whether the phenomena we perceive are related to the thing-in-itself.[109] Ritschl opposes the entire locus in traditional theology that speaks about a knowledge of God in himself— *a se*—as illusory because this realm is completely hidden. We have absolutely no such knowledge of God. Hence the entire metaphysical enterprise predicated upon reason's capacity to arrive at knowledge of God as he exists in himself apart from revelation is contradicted both by the basic tenets of epistemology and the truth that all we know about God is how he is perceived in his revelation.[110] Virtually the entire Western tradition in theology failed to distinguish between the religious conception of God based upon revelation and the idea of God as he is in himself arrived at through speculation.

In opposition, therefore, to a venerable tradition which taught that the Christian conception of God can be "demonstrated as a universal truth of reason," Ritschl sides with Kant and the modern philosophical and theological developments which rendered this program suspect.[111] Indeed, virtually all the questionable elements in the traditional doctrine of God can be traced to the futile attempt to coordinate a doctrine of God as he exists in himself established by means of speculative reasoning a priori with a doctrine of God derived from man's perception of God's revelation a posteriori.[112] Hence it is axiomatic for Ritschl that a general, rational, or speculative doctrine of God and the Christian knowledge of God knowable through his self-revelation are in no way identical.

This epistemological error characteristic of Catholic and Protestant Scholasticism influenced by Platonism is coupled with a deficient psychology. Basic to Ritschl, as we have intimated, is the presupposition that a thing is known only in terms of its effects upon man as this is evidenced in "the states and movements of man's spiritual life."[113] Corresponding to its assumption of a God at rest behind his operations *ad extra,* Scholastic psychology envisaged man's soul in itself at rest behind its activities. It is within this inner sanctum of the soul—removed from its activities or movement—that the mystical union of the believer with God takes place. For Ritschl, however, the soul is known only in its activities, even as God is known only in his acts.

We know nothing of a self-existence of the soul, of a self-enclosed life of the spirit above or behind those functions in which it is active, living, and present to itself as a being of special worth.[114]

This emphasis accounts, in part, for Ritschl's dissatisfaction with all mysticism. Moreover, the idea of an isolated soul in communion with God goes counter to his thesis that all knowledge of God is had in and through the community of faith. Therefore, it is illusory to speak of direct contact between God and man in the manner of mysticism.[115]

Up to this point, it would seem that Ritschl flees from Plato and the Scholastic tradition in order to embrace Kant who opposed the entire metaphysical enterprise which held that one could arrive at an a priori knowledge of God through the use of the theoretical reason. In Kant's *Prolegomena to Any Future Metaphysics,* he argues that this is untenable and maintains that no a priori knowledge of God in himself is capable of proof. The realm of the noumenal, the traditional sphere of metaphysics, lies beyond the reaches of man's theoretical reason. Hence all the traditional proofs for the existence of God are rejected by Kant and Ritschl save one, namely, the moral proof.[116] Yet Ritschl goes only part of the way with Kant. The latter was right in arguing that we know things only insofar as they are related to, and perceived by, us; the thing-in-itself both in the phenomenal and noumenal realms is removed from all direct observation. But Ritschl does not share Kant's skepticism regarding knowledge of the object external to us; our perception of the phenomena is of real objects. The object is present therefore in the phenomena; otherwise, no knowledge would be possible and "the phenomenon would have to be treated as illusion."[117] Nor was Ritschl satisfied with Kant's refusal to recognize the knowledge of God obtained through the use of the practical reason as a mode of theoretical cognition. Hence, Ritschl turns to Lotze's epistemology as a third option and adapts it to the theological enterprise. He interprets Lotze as follows:

He holds that in the phenomena which in a definite space exhibit changes to a limited extent and in a determinate order, we cognise the thing as the cause of its qualities operating upon us, as the end which these serve as means, as the law of their constant changes.[118]

Here Kant's skepticism is overcome and one is able to know things in the light of their effects and as the cause of these effects.[119]

RITSCHL AND THE USE OF EPISTEMOLOGIES IN PROTESTANT THEOLOGY

At this juncture we do well to adopt the view of Hök, Otto Ritschl, and others who argue that Ritschl's acceptance of Lotze's epistemology is not the most significant element in explaining his own theological method. The issue in question, namely, the manner in which God and man are related, or how man has knowledge of God as the "object" external to him, cannot be adjudicated primarily on epistemological grounds. For we have noted that religious knowledge claimed by positive religions purports to be based upon some revelation perceived by a religious community.[120]

Ritschl, though Schleiermacher was his mentor at this point, finds his immediate guides in certain Lutheran confessional standards and in a formula of Melanchthon's. These sources maintain that all knowledge of God derives from the manner in which God exists for us (*pro nobis* and *pro me*). This restriction of all knowledge of and discourse about God to the way in which he is perceived by man is determinative of the bent of much Lutheran theology from Luther to Bultmann, and is simultaneously the source of certain strengths and weaknesses of both Lutheranism and modern theological existentialism.[121] Ritschl praises Luther for his statement in the Larger Catechism opposing those who say that we can know the nature of God apart from Jesus Christ. "The truth rather is that we know the nature of God and Christ only in their worth for us."[122] He never tires of acknowledging Luther as his model for relating all knowledge of God to his self-revelation in Jesus Christ perceived through faith. For Luther, to know God means to be marked by "active trust in God as the highest good."[123] This is far removed from any theoretical, disinterested, or even mere historical knowledge about God. Knowledge of Christ and knowledge of God are always correlated.

In the first edition of the *Loci communes* of 1521, Melanchthon followed Luther's soteriological focus in his dictum: "*Hoc est Christum cognoscere, beneficia eius cognoscere,*" "To know Christ is to know his benefits!" True knowledge of Christ obtains with the appropriation through faith of the effects of his saving work. But this same Melanchthon—according to Ritschl—abandoned this approach in the second edition of the *Loci* in 1535 by allowing a metaphysical doctrine of God reminiscent of Scholasticism to intrude, thereby detracting from his earlier Christocentric and soteriological starting point. Ritschl finds that virtually the entire tradition of Protestant orthodoxy following Melanchthon emulated his bad example and confused a metaphysical and abstract doctrine of God with the God perceived by faith in Jesus Christ within the Christian community. Hence a rational and speculative manner of speaking about God replaced an existential and personal one. Much of modern theology—including Schleiermacher—is guilty of a similar error in allowing some kind of natural theology to be correlated with theological statements made in the light of revelation. It was Ritschl's expressed hope that his own theological program would serve to expose the fallacy of such a procedure and render repetition impossible.[124]

RELIGIOUS ASSERTIONS AS VALUE JUDGMENTS

Ritschl's attitude toward philosophical epistemologies and their theological usage has prepared us for his understanding of religious statements as value judgments. Such knowledge is to be sharply distinguished from theoretical judgments derived from scientific or philosophical investigations. On the basis of his analysis of Ritschl's unpublished lectures in dogmatics given in 1853 and subsequently, Hök affirms that in an earlier period Ritschl tended to distinguish these two spheres in terms of the divergent objects with which they dealt. Philosophy has the world and knowledge of the world for its domain and cannot become theology or religious knowledge without identifying God and the world.[125] Much the same view is adopted in the first edition of *Justification and Reconciliation* in the assertion that theoretical or philosophical knowledge always involves knowledge of particulars without coordinating these into a *Weltanschauung*. If a philosophy develops a world view, Ritschl attributes this to a religious rather than to a purely philosophical or theoretical motivation. At this stage, therefore, he held that theoretical or scientific knowledge had a subject matter different from that of religious knowledge. Its concern was with general rules governing the knowledge both of nature and spirit. The concern of religion, however, was with the manner in which man stood related to God and the world, and such an interest made a *Weltanschauung* necessary.[126]

It is apparent, however, that as early as the year 1874 his view changes and becomes similar to some of his earliest statements. It now appears that Ritschl is willing to admit the possibility that both theoretical and philosophical as well as religious cognition may aspire to a *Weltanschauung*.[127] Indeed, in the year 1883 in a section entitled "The Peculiar Character of Religious Knowledge," he affirms the following: "The possibility of both kinds of knowledge mingling, or, again, colliding, lies in this, that they deal with the same object, namely, *the world*."[128] It seems, therefore, that both spheres of knowledge utilize value judgments in that "all connected knowledge of the world" is predicated upon the supposition that what is known is of some value.[129] But here the dictum—"When two say the same thing it is not the same"—seems appropriate in helping to interpret Ritschl's position. Whereas "traditional theology" customarily grouped theological propositions according to their derivation from reason or revelation, he speaks of another method.

> In opposition thereto there has gradually come into force the contrary principle, that religion and theoretical knowledge are different functions of spirit, which, when they deal with the same objects, are not even partially coincident, but wholly diverge.[130]

Hence value judgments may indeed be involved in all three spheres, namely, the religious, philosophical, and theoretical. In order to distinguish the philosophical and theoretical modes of knowing from the religious, Ritschl has recourse to a more subtle distinction.

> We have therefore to distinguish between *concomitant* and *independent* value-judgments. The former are operative and necessary in all theoretical cognition, as in all technical observation and combination. But *independent* value-judgments are all perceptions of moral ends or moral hindrances, in so far as they excite moral pleasure or pain, or, it may be, set in motion the will to appropriate what is good or repel the opposite.[131]

In short, though theoretical and philosophical knowledge are motivated by a certain value that inheres in the object (the world) under investigation, the concern for truth is in the main disinterested and objective. The moral ramifications of the truth apprehended for the knower are not of special interest, and whenever philosophical investigation moves to a comprehensive *Weltanschauung* replete with an idea of God, we must speak about a religious rather than a purely scientific or philosophical motivation.[132]

RITSCHL'S PHILOSOPHICORELIGIOUS EPISTEMOLOGY: ANTECEDENTS AND ANTAGONISTS

By 1870, Ritschl had anticipated the final direction of his methodology. Influenced by the soteriological concentration in Luther, the early Melanchthon, and Schleiermacher, and by Kant's epistemology, he asserted that the only approach left to him was a "survey of *the moral effects of the Life, Passion, Death, and Resurrection of Christ towards the founding of the Church.*"[133] But at this juncture he is neither willing to accept Schleiermacher as the sole leader of nineteenth-century theology nor to regard his influence as beneficial at every point.[134] The latter's greatest contribution was not his recognition of the distinctiveness of religious language and knowledge, but rather the

> more general truth, that the religious moral life of the spirit cannot at all be conceived of outside of the *fellowship* that corresponds thereto, and that, in reciprocal action and reaction therewith, the individual attains his peculiar development.[135]

In this respect Schleiermacher transcends the individualistic view of religion and Christianity characteristic of both Christian Wolf and Kant.[136] And finally, on the positive side of the ledger, we have seen that Ritschl acknowledged his debt to Schleiermacher for his designation of redemption through Christ as the essence of Christianity and for the manner in which he saw "redemption, the Redeemer, and the community that is the subject of redemption" standing in "inseparable relation to one another" as the "culminating point of the religious and practical consciousness of the Reformers."[137]

On the negative side of the ledger, however, Ritschl opposes those following Schleiermacher who made the religious experience of the individual—rather than the corporate faith of the community—the organizing principle of theology. Representatives are found in Lutheran Pietism as well as in modern Lutheran orthodoxy. As early as the first volume of *Justification and Reconciliation,* he inveighed against the adoption of such a norm on the grounds that it seems to compromise "the objectivity of doctrine."[138] Pietism tends to make religious experience the final norm of Christian truth and therewith subordinates Scripture to man's subjective religious states.[139] And although he evidences some appreciation for the religious dynamic of Pietism which arose in reaction to the rigidities of Protestant orthodoxy, he finds its sectarian tendencies and its unhistorical and unscientific attitude toward Holy Scripture and the tradition of the church reprehensible.[140] It appears impossible that "a doctrine of faith so founded on individual religious experience" could arrive at a "churchly character."[141]

Ritschl maintains much the same stance in the introduction to Vol. II of *Justification and Reconciliation* in 1874. The adoption of an inspired canon of Scripture as the formal principle of dogmatics in seventeenth-century Protestant orthodoxy was coupled with the view that the Spirit of God who gave rise to the canon enabled its salvific message to be appropriated by the believing reader through the inner witness of the same Spirit. Though Ritschl cannot accept the "mystical mechanism" of this view in which the Spirit is a "mysterious postulate" because it fails to see the work of the Spirit as a "practical principle," he has little sympathy for his contemporaries who elevate religious experience into a place of preeminence in theology.[142] Their view of the latter is not to be confused with the orthodox doctrine of the Spirit illuminating Holy Scripture for the believer; rather, it is religious experience understood as an activity of the individual apart from any real doctrine of the Holy Spirit as found in Protestant orthodoxy.[143]

In the light of the foregoing, we can understand the critical stance Ritschl adopts toward the experiential and subjectivistic tradition in modern theology both in its pietistic and orthodox Lutheran representatives. Their anthropocentric starting point and procedure are described thus:

> The material of systematic theology is not derived from historical sources and validated in an objective manner, but rather in the form of the subjective religious consciousness of the individual theologian.[144]

Such a procedure could become scientific in Ritschl's view only if it compared individual with corporate religious experience. Yet even if this method were followed—as in the case of Lipsius—Ritschl contends that no exhaustive tabulation of communal religious experience is possible, and hence its scientific nature is jeopardized. Indeed, it would appear that the faith of the individual theologian would, in fact, be the final norm in the latter instance as well.[145] The only legitimate method for the theologian is to determine what Christianity is in general. Ritschl opts for the following correction of the subjectivistic and experiential epistemology.

> If, however, I utilize scientific forms in speaking about religious experience, and assuming that I therewith also bring my own experience to consciousness, I must do so solely with the intention of designating Christianity in a universal manner; and this is the specific earmark of the theological representation of Christianity.[146]

The way in which this program is to be achieved is set forth in the introduction to Vol. II of *Justification and Reconciliation*.[147] Unlike Schleiermacher and some others in the nineteenth century, Ritschl accorded the Old Testament canon a significant place in his theology. This is evident both in his programmatic statements and in the careful attention he gives to the decisive role which the religion of the Old Testament plays as the presupposition for understanding the message of the New Testament. The last volumes of *Justification and Reconciliation*, which deal with the Biblical materials and systematic development of this subject, make this abundantly clear.[148] However, Ritschl's hermeneutic requires that the New Testament writings describing the origins of Christianity be regarded as the definitive source of Christian theology.[149]

The historicocritical method must be used with the intention of uncovering both the unity and diversity of the New Testament as well as its distinctiveness in contrast to post-Biblical literature in the early church.[150] Since it is an axiom of Ritschl's hermeneutic that the governing principle of a religious fellowship is to be found at the headwater of its development, the documents of primitive Christianity have a singular importance.[151] Such a method is opposed to orthodoxy, which tends to interpret Holy Scripture in accordance with established dogmas, to rationalism, which forces Scripture into agreement with human reason, and to the pneumatic exegesis of Bengel and his school, which elevates the "individual inspiration" of the exegete to a place of preeminence.[152] To the extent that the historicocritical method enables the theologian to determine what books constitute the New Testament canon and to establish their distinctiveness in contrast to other early Christian literature, a doctrine of verbal infallibility is superfluous.[153] A further hermeneutical presupposition is Ritschl's insistence that the New Testament documents be understood, not as scientific or doctrinal statements, but as "religious speech" within the context of the community of faith.[154]

In contrast to a prevailing tradition in New Testament studies in the nineteenth century, Ritschl finds a basic continuity between Jesus and Paul, and indeed, throughout the whole New Testament—although Jesus as the founder of Christianity is always distinguished from the church that derives from him. Finally, he assumes that the "central content of the Melanchthonian-Lutheran doctrinal tradition" as it focuses in the doctrine of justification by faith is in basic agreement with the content of the New Testament when rightly understood—though it is admittedly a distinctly Pauline doctrine.[155] But the adoption of the *sola fide* as a "negative norm" governing theological investigation should neither dictate the conclusions of Biblical investigation concerning this doctrine nor hinder critical historical research into the history of its development. Indeed, the "churchly orientation" of dogmatics is evidenced for Ritschl in the manner in which the theologian actually engages in rigorous study of the history of the church and its theology. This was the focus of the first volume of *Justification and Reconciliation*. There it was apparent that the understanding of salvation in Roman Catholicism as well as in its diverse Protestant expressions transcends the New Testament level of development. Indeed, no single ecclesiastical tradition or school expresses the whole truth with respect to it. However, it was Ritschl's hope that his own positive development of the doctrine of justification and reconciliation would receive support from the diverse schools within Protestantism.[156]

CHAPTER II

The Presuppositions of the Doctrine of Justification and Reconciliation

In the preceding chapter our concern was to adumbrate the main lines of Ritschl's theological methodology. In the present chapter we need to move a step closer to the exposition of the doctrine of justification and reconciliation by surveying the context in which this doctrine is set. What are the theological presuppositions—in addition to the purely methodological ones—that provide the framework for Ritschl's undertaking? Put otherwise, we are asking what place the doctrine of justification and reconciliation occupies in the total structure of Ritschl's system. Does it alone provide his theology with its organizing principles? Or are there other presuppositions that are of equal or of even greater significance? Ritschl himself raises this question by stating that the "form of systematic theology is bound up, first of all, with the correct and complete *idea of the Christian Religion*."[1]

THE INTERPRETATION OF THE RELIGIOUS CONCEPTION OF JUSTIFICATION

We noted above the manner in which Ritschl arrives at his definition of the Christian religion. Here we need to recall certain ground rules that serve to make his position clear. First, conceptions such as justification and reconciliation are "religious conceptions" formulated by the community, which stands related to the "operation of God effected through the instrumentality of Christ."[2] Like all other religious conceptions, these terms give expression not only to man's relationship to God, but also at the same time have as their other referent the attitude of both God and the believer toward the world.[3] Thus Ritschl can say: "Three points are necessary to determine the circle by which a religion is completely represented—God, man, and the world."[4] In this connection, one of the failings of mysticism and also of

47

theologies of the religious self-consciousness in the tradition of Schleier-macher is that they fail to do justice to man's attitude toward the world. Since God creates and directs his creation, man's relationship to God should determine his stance toward the world.[5] Yet another characteristic of religion—and therewith of Christianity—is that it speaks of a highest good toward which man strives, because its value is assured by the Deity.[6] Ritschl attempts to relate these essential elements of religion to the foci determinative of Christianity, namely, the religious moment evident in the redemption effected by Christ and the ethical moment represented by the Kingdom of God. Whereas the former has to do primarily with man's relationship to God, the latter points to man's activity in the world prompted by love and directed toward the Kingdom of God. These foci determine the nature of Christianity as the perfect ethical religion.

By the year 1870 and the publication of the first volume of *Justification and Reconciliation,* Ritschl saw that an adequate exposition of Christianity necessitated showing how each of these foci was constitutive for the interpretation of the other, and the systematic exposition of the third volume of *Justification and Reconciliation* intends to show how together they provide an adequate framework for a comprehensive interpretation of the Christian faith. He writes:

> There can be no doubt that these two characteristics condition each other mutually. Christ made the universal moral Kingdom of God His end, and thus He came to know and decide for that kind of redemption which He achieved through the maintenance of fidelity in His calling and of His blessed fellowship with God through suffering unto death. On the other hand, a correct spiritual interpretation of redemption and justification through Christ tends to keep more decisively to the front the truth that the Kingdom of God is the final end.[7]

JUSTIFICATION AND RECONCILIATION AND THE KINGDOM OF GOD

Now that we have noted Ritschl's intention to give due weight to the poles of redemption and the Kingdom of God in his exposition of the Christian faith, we need to ask whether this program is carried out. Or do we find, as some interpreters of Ritschl have argued, that the Kingdom of God is the overarching, unitive principle of his total system?[8] There is no mistaking the fact that Ritschl criticized the entire history of Protestant theology from the Reformers to his own day for its failure to recognize the constitutive importance of the Kingdom of God both for the scientific exposition of the Christian faith and for understanding its practical implementation in the world. It remained for the philosopher Immanuel Kant to see for the first time the great significance of the concept of the Kingdom of God for ethics, and Schleiermacher is singled out for his acuteness in defining Christianity in terms of the twin poles of redemption in Jesus of Nazareth and the Kingdom of God. However, in Ritschl's judgment the latter failed radically both in development of the "teleological character" of Christianity and in showing how the redemption in Jesus is related to the Kingdom of God.[9] Moreover, Ritschl finds only one theologian in the tradition of Schleiermacher who makes the Kingdom of God decisive in dogmatics, and the whole history of Protestantism emulates the precedent of the Reformers in stressing redemption through Jesus to the virtual wholesale neglect of the significance of the Kingdom of God.[10] It is clear that he intended to fill this void by showing how a proper interpretation of the Christian faith accorded this concept the place of preeminence it rightfully deserved.

There is good evidence to support the thesis that in carrying out this program Ritschl finally subordinated the religious pole of theology represented by redemption to the ethical pole represented by the Kingdom of God. Commenting on Schleiermacher's failure to show the relevance of the Kingdom of God for the interpretation of the redemption effected through Jesus, he says: "For if the Divine final end is embodied in the Kingdom of God, it is to be expected that the redemption which has come through Jesus should also be related, as a means, to this final end."[11]

Though we shall develop the way in which Jesus is related to the Kingdom of God, we may anticipate by saying that Ritschl views the entire ministry of Jesus in the light of his fidelity to God's final purpose for humanity, namely, the Kingdom of God.[12] That the latter should receive priority over the pole of redemption—contrary to the usual Lutheran procedure—is stated unequivocally in a letter by Ritschl to his close friend and confidant, Ludwig Diestel, professor of Old Testament at Bonn, in July of 1871: "I am personally convinced that the idea of redemption is rightly comprehended only when it is seen as a means to the highest end of the Kingdom of God."[13] This viewpoint is underlined in one of the summary theses of the doctrine of God: "The reconciliation of sinners by God, if it is to be conceived, is conceivable without inconsistency as the means used for the establishment of the Kingdom of God by God's love."[14] However, the crucial importance of the concept of the Kingdom of God as the fulfillment of all of God's activity influences not only the doctrines of God and redemption, but also all other doctrines. No one has observed this better than Otto Ritschl, who affirms that his father regarded man's teleological perspective as that which distinguished man as spirit from the realm of nature determined by the law of causality. The fact that the teleological orientation is the correct one from which to interpret the Christian faith derives finally from the revelation in Jesus Christ. The younger Ritschl continues in this vein:

Thus the concept of the Kingdom of God as representative of God's universal and ultimate purpose is the leading idea which enables us to understand the destiny of man and also the meaning of the divine intention for the world.[15]

If anything, the pervasive influence of the concept of the Kingdom of God for the total structure of Christian theology comes to the fore more forcibly in Ritschl's handbook *Instruction in the Christian Religion* (*Unterricht*) than in *Justification and Reconciliation*. Intended as a kind of catechism for religious instruction in the secondary schools of Germany, this primer appeared in the first of several editions in 1875. In an article on "The Kingdom of God," Ritschl remarks that his purpose in the *Unterricht* was to effect a balance between the ethical and dogmatic materials in his exposition of the Christian faith.[16] Its organization discloses his aim quite clearly. Section I is entitled "The Doctrine of the Kingdom of God." The rubric of the first division of Sec. I is "The Kingdom of God as Religious Idea." Its subheadings are the following: "The Kingdom of God as the Highest Good and the Task of the Christian Community," "The Idea of God," and "Christ as the Revealer of God." In the first edition of the *Unterricht,* the second division of Sec. I bore the heading "The Kingdom of God as the Foundational Ethical Principle" ("Das Reich Gottes als sittlicher Grundgedanke"). Subheadings were: "The Extent of the Kingdom of God," "The Ethical Vocation," "Marriage and the Family," and "Law and State." In subsequent editions, the material included in this second division under the heading of the Kingdom of God was shifted to the section dealing with the "Christian Life." Although Sec. II delineates the doctrine of reconciliation or redemption, one may still argue that the concept of the Kingdom of God is determinative of the overall structure of this summary of the Christian faith.[17]

We cannot pursue the constitutive significance of the concept of the Kingdom of God in Ritschl's theological system, but we must keep in mind that it is closely related both to the doctrine of God and Christology. Ritschl analyzes these doctrines as "Presuppositions" of the doctrine of justification and reconciliation.[18]

THE DOCTRINE OF GOD AND JUSTIFICATION AND RECONCILIATION

It is no accident that Ritschl gave as much attention to the doctrine of God throughout his lifetime as to any other doctrine. His earliest purely theological writings relate to the doctrine of God and these were reworked and included within the extended discussions given to that doctrine in

Vols. II and III of *Justification and Reconciliation*. Indeed, the doctrine of justification and reconciliation is unintelligible for Ritschl apart from a correct doctrine of God. He argues that the uniqueness of every religion is apparent in its doctrine of God and that "the manner in which the Christian religion conceives of the reconciliation between God and man can become intelligible only in the light of the doctrine of God which is presupposed."[19]

THE PERSONAL GOD

We observed above that Ritschl held it to be axiomatic that all of our knowledge of God derives from his self-manifestation in history alone. The dictum so beloved of neo-orthodoxy—"Through God alone can God be known"—could well have its origins in Ritschl's viewpoint. He was among the leading nineteenth-century critics of speculative and philosophical approaches in the doctrine of God, and hence the implacable foe of natural theology within Roman Catholicism and Protestantism which allowed a knowledge of God obtained apart from his historical revelation. Moreover, the entire mystical tradition, which appeared to move beyond the revelation of God in history to a knowledge of God as he is in himself through the process of mystical contemplation, or by means of philosophical abstraction or speculation, is anathema to him.[20] God is knowable in the community of faith by those who place their trust in him because he has made himself known in his historical acts in the Old and New Covenants climaxing in Jesus Christ.

Ritschl attempts to underline the distinction between a philosophical, speculative, or abstract idea of God and that held by Christianity in maintaining that whereas the former conceives of God as impersonal, the latter views God as personal.

The explanation offered in § 29 ["The So-called Proofs of the Existence of God"] has made it clear why theology takes as its fundamental truth the full conception of God as a Person, Who establishes the Kingdom of God as the final end of the world, and in it assures to every one who trusts in Him supremacy over the world. Such a conception may be differentiated without further remark from limitless being, regarded as the substance of the universe, from the idea of a First Cause which need not be personal, and from the self-conscious but self-enclosed Final End of the world. The conception of God thus set up is of such a nature that it simply cannot be distorted into Pantheism or Deism. A theology based upon it, therefore, is not rationalistic. On the contrary, it is positive, for it starts from the Christian idea of God; and it is scientific, for the Christian idea of God must be acknowledged to be the fundamental principle which explains the coexistence of nature and morality—morality being viewed as the final end of the world—if their coexistence admits of any explanation at all.[21]

Here and elsewhere, Ritschl sees radical opposition between the Christian and speculative views of God. This accounts for his strong disapproval of Scholastic theology both Catholic and Protestant which combined speculative and Christian elements in the doctrine of God. It also enables him to adopt a critical attitude toward the entire tradition of theological idealism in which he was trained, for it, too, operated with a view of God as the Absolute and opposed conceiving God in personal terms. For Ritschl, however, the indeterminate Absolute is always an idol when seen in the light of the Christian understanding of God. The latter is known as Person—and as love and goodness—through the revelation in Jesus called the Christ.[22]

The Proofs for the Existence of God

In view of Ritschl's axiom that knowledge of God obtains only as we perceive the value of God's revelation through Christ for us, a summary statement is in order regarding the import of this for his attitude toward natural theology and the proofs for the existence of God.[23] As we have observed, the basis for his rejection of natural theology and the proofs for the existence of God are essentially one and the same: Both approaches seek a knowledge of God divorced from the historical revelation in Christ. But a theoretical standpoint removed from faith in God cannot issue in true knowledge of God. Thus the attempt to identify the God of the proofs and the God knowable through the revelation in Christ is foredoomed to failure. Such abstract, disinterested, and rational knowledge is far removed from the practical, personal, and religious knowledge of God gained through faith understood as trust. Because of these distinctions, Ritschl joined a host of thinkers following Kant who reject the traditional proofs for the existence of God. No matter how arranged, they fail to "prove the *objective existence* of God as contrasted with His existence in thought," and whatever cogency they have is in fact dependent upon a Christian view of the world.[24] Whether we speak of the "First Cause" in the manner of the cosmological argument, or of the "Final End" as in the teleological argument, or of the "Perfect Being" of the ontological argument is really immaterial, for the object in question never transcends the world or the limits of the human mind, "and therefore falls short of the Christian idea of God." They also "differ from the Christian conception of God in this, that they fail to express His worth for men, and in particular His worth for men as sinners."[25]

The fact that Ritschl applauded Kant's moral argument for the existence of God as "Moral Creator and Ruler of the World" in the successive editions of *Justification and Reconciliation* is due to the fact that the God so known is not the object ascertained through the use of the theoretical reason or by means of rational reflection, but rather by means of a "conviction of personal faith."[26] That is, Kant argues that man's innate sense of obligation to fulfill the moral law leads the practical reason to postulate the existence of God as moral governor in order to account for it.[27] Thus Kant argued for the existence of God from a quasi-religious or ethical standpoint and not on the basis of the capacity of the theoretical reason to lead to a knowledge of God as is the case in the other proofs for the existence of God.[28] It is of considerable moment that Ritschl found a precedent in Kant, the fountainhead of modern philosophy and theology, for his approach to the knowledge of God. Ritschl has Kant in mind in writing the following:

> While, therefore, the Christian religion is thereby proved to be in harmony with reason [i.e., with Kant], it is always with the reservation that knowledge of God embodies itself in judgments which differ in kind from those of theoretical science.[29]

Kant rightly saw that all knowledge of God is to be estimated as value judgments and, in addition, he recognized the supremacy of man as an ethical being over nature whose supreme good lay in obedience to the moral law in the Kingdom of God.[30]

On the basis of a detailed analysis of the variations in Ritschl's treatment of the proofs for the existence of God in the successive editions of *Justification and Reconciliation,* Fabricius contends that Ritschl moved from a more positive to a more negative evaluation of their validity. Thus the first edition allows an ethical proof for the existence of God that is in harmony with the Christian view of God; the second edition seems to regard the traditional proofs as, in fact, not the product of unaided reason, but of a covert Christian theology. In order to arrive at a comprehensive *Weltanschauung* it becomes necessary to posit the idea of an ultimate Being or God.[31] Finally, the third edition argues on psychological grounds for the sharp difference between religious and theoretical knowledge thereby rendering the proofs untenable, a position dictated not primarily by philosophy or generally acceptable religious presuppositions and considerations, but by the historical revelation in Jesus Christ.[32] This progression appears to parallel a movement in Ritschl's theological method from a more philosophical or religiophilosophical orientation to one dictated by the understanding of the uniqueness of the Christian revelation and specifically the revelation in Jesus Christ.

THE LOVE OF GOD REVEALED IN THE SON AND THE KINGDOM OF
GOD

In view of these observations, we need to show how Ritschl develops his
doctrine of God in the light of God's final goal for humanity in the Kingdom of God. The problem that he faced at this point lies in the difficulty of
speaking about God's final purpose in the world when our "individual
religious thinking" about God is historically conditioned and therefore
piecemeal.[33] If this perspective were the only one open to theology, it would
seem that God's attitude toward man is changeable. That is, temporary
human states would be regarded as due to changes in the divine attitude
toward individual men, as for example, from mercy to wrath.[34] Such a
view, however, would preclude the possibility of arriving at a satisfying
and comprehensive understanding of the intention of God's government of
all things. For this reason, Ritschl must—in the light, of course, of the
direction that revelation appears to point—speak *sub specie aeternitatis* of
all of God's revelatory acts in history in relation to his ultimate purpose in
the Kingdom of God.[35] This special kind of "theological cognition" enables
Ritschl to oppose any theology that allows for change in the "essential
relations of the Divine will," for such would be incompatible "with the
conception of the Divine knowledge and government of the whole."[36] To be
sure, such an overview of all of God's ways and works is difficult to harmonize with Ritschl's avowed empirical theological method, but he is led
to it in order to preserve an adequate doctrine of God. However, this
conclusion does not derive from a wholly speculative tour de force, but is
dictated by the community's interpretation of God's acts in history. For
therein—and particularly in Jesus Christ—God's ultimate intention for
humanity is partially unveiled to the community of faith.

The manner in which Ritschl attempts to avoid speculation in his understanding of God is evident in the consistent way in which he speaks of the
latter in the light of Jesus Christ and the Kingdom of God. Thus the love
of God predominates in his systematic development of the doctrine of
God.[37] The reader is prepared for this concentration upon the divine love
as God's primary attribute because his earlier exposition of the Biblical view
of God gave careful attention to the attributes of holiness and love.
Although conceding that the Old Testament gives priority to God's holiness
rather than his love, Ritschl rejects a fairly typical approach which interprets the activity of God in the Old Testament solely in terms of his
holiness without any mention of his mercy and love, which are the ground
for the creation and maintenance of the covenant. That he intends to show
the relationships which obtain between God's holiness and love is already
apparent from the headings that he gives to his exposition of the Biblical

materials: "The Holiness, Grace and Love of God in the Old Testament," and "The Love, Grace and Holiness of God in the New Testament."[38] Within the Old Covenant, the understanding of God as holy is not explicable in terms of Israel's adoption of a common designation of the Deity among ancient religions. It was due rather to Israel's faith in the God of the covenant whom they worshiped as the Creator and Lord of all things that they attributed holiness to him. Thus even though Ritschl frequently speaks of holiness as a comprehensive predicate for God in the Old Testament and of love in the New Testament, he avoids separating them completely. For it must be recalled that the entire covenant relationship between Yahweh and Israel is predicated upon the divine mercy, grace, and love. The fact that the divine love dominates the understanding of God in the New Testament in the light of the revelation in Jesus Christ is not interpreted by Ritschl to mean that God has ceased to be holy. The dialectic that obtains between holiness and love in the Old and New Covenants is to be understood as follows:

> By virtue of the fact that the functions of goodness, mercy and saving grace originally included in God's holiness find their new unity in the love of God expressed through Jesus Christ, it is understandable that the attribute of holiness is virtually absent in the New Testament.[39]

On the basis of this brief résumé of Ritschl's exposition of the Biblical materials pertaining to the divine attributes of holiness and love, we are prepared for the concentration upon God's love evidenced in the ministry of Jesus and his proclamation of the Kingdom of God as Ritschl develops them in the third volume of *Justification and Reconciliation.* Had Scholastic theology both Roman Catholic and Protestant derived their respective views of God more closely from the Biblical understanding of the nature of God culminating in his self-revelation in Jesus Christ, speculative and extra-Biblical notions of God as absolute justice, indeterminate will or power, and absolute and unmoved Being would have been avoided. Yet for Ritschl the affirmation of the personality of God or of him either as personal or as personal will is insufficient if this is said apart from Jesus Christ; it is only because the Son has revealed God as his Father that we know that the Fatherhood of God is goodness and love.[40]

This understanding of God derived from Jesus Christ is inextricably bound up with the apprehension of the Kingdom of God as the goal of God's activity and the clue to his relationship to the world and man. Only because God is revealed in Jesus to be a "loving will" directing all things to the Kingdom of God can man see his existence and that of the whole created order derived from and directed by God. As "loving will," God takes up the "other's personal end" by incorporating it within his own self-end.[41] We have noted that in adopting this position, Ritschl consciously opposes a long tradition in medieval theology that refuses to equate the self-end of God with that of humanity. Such a view is predicated upon the axiom that God's purpose and that of the world cannot coincide, and therefore God's relationship to the world is conceived negatively. Ritschl credits Protestant orthodoxy for having challenged this view of God by teaching that a proper understanding of human nature and the purpose of Christianity reveal that God's self-end and the destiny of man are intimately connected. Yet these same orthodox divines failed to carry through the implications of this insight for their understanding of God and his relationship to mankind; instead, they succumbed to the tradition of negative theology which defines God by distinguishing him from the world. In so doing, they did not show how God's personal end and that of humanity are necessarily related.[42]

Earlier we observed that the clue to the solution of this problem was mediated to Ritschl through the manner in which man's destiny was related to the Kingdom of God, especially in Kant and Schleiermacher. Ritschl laments that only Franz Theremin (1780–1846) among the disciples of Schleiermacher followed his lead in making the Kingdom of God constitutive for understanding the relationship between God and humanity.[43] Ritschl follows this tradition in maintaining that the "proper destiny of the human race includes spiritual and blessed fellowship with God" and that "this end cannot be unrelated to God's personal end."[44] Thus for him, the concept of the Kingdom of God encompasses both the final purpose of God and humanity.

Once the common end of God and man within the Kingdom of God is perceived in the light of God as "loving will," it becomes possible to see nature and the entire subhuman world as a means created to serve this highest end. That such a position and starting point provide Ritschl's theology with a systematic principle of great import is everywhere evident in his thought, and the following statement is typical:

> This final end of God in the world [i.e., the Kingdom of God] is the ground from which it is possible to explain the creation and government of the world in general, and the interrelations between nature and created spirits.[45]

Argument in this vein leads him into proximity to the views of Lessing, Lotze, and others in the nineteenth century who regarded the idea of the progressive development of humanity as self-evident.[46] In contrast, however, to much nineteenth-century thought that assumed an immanental teleology in the universe apart from any reference to the divine, Ritschl predicates his thesis upon an understanding of divine providence in the light of the Biblical revelation. It is in this sense that he argues for the congruence of God's knowledge and will and his direction of all things toward their final end in the Kingdom of God; we must assume, then, an evolution of the Kingdom of God in human history leading up to the *Heilsgeschichte*.

Thus all forms of "moral fellowship" among men from the family to the state—when seen in the light of the ultimate goal of the moral fellowship of humanity within the Kingdom of God—may be regarded as the "education of humanity" for the Kingdom of God.[47] Thus conceived, the Kingdom of God "both transcends and completes all the natural and particular motives which bind men together."[48] In that the Kingdom of God is the "final end" and the highest good to which man aspires, Ritschl can speak of it as supramundane.[49] Hence he must say not only that the self-end of God and humanity are therefore one but also that the Kingdom of God is the "correlate of God's love."[50] Indeed, because the Son makes the self-end of God in the Kingdom of God his own, we must affirm that the self-end of God, of Jesus Christ, and of humanity are one in the Kingdom of God. Since the self-determination of God is seen as love in the light of the revelation in Christ directed to the Kingdom of God, "He is not conceived as being anything apart from and prior to His self-determination as love. He is either conceived as love, or simply not at all."[51]

We may review the manner in which Ritschl relates the nature of God as love to the Kingdom of God in his summary statement:

> The conception of God which is given in the revelation received through Christ, and to which the trust of those who are reconciled through Christ attaches itself, is that of a loving Will which assures to believers spiritual dominion over the world and perfect moral fellowship in the Kingdom of God as the *summum bonum*.[52]

THE DOCTRINE OF THE PERSON AND LIFEWORK OF JESUS CHRIST AND JUSTIFICATION AND RECONCILIATION

In the course of the preceding section we observed that Ritschl develops his Christology within the larger context of the doctrine of the Kingdom of God. We need to examine in more detail how this is done. However, our purpose is not to develop his Christology in any complete way, but rather to point to certain elements that are relevant for his understanding of justification and reconciliation.

We observed in Chapter I that Ritschl viewed all statements about God as value judgments. This perspective requires that he adopt an agnostic stance toward many traditional Christological questions. Hence, statements about Jesus' preexistence, ascended state, or about the relationship of the divine and human natures lie beyond the pole of human and therefore theological knowledge and are of no interest to faith! Indeed, Ritschl seems often to view them as harmful because of their speculative character. Of far greater importance is the ethical and religious apprehension of Christ, that is, the recognition of Christ's special worth as Lord and Redeemer.[53] Such an acknowledgment of Jesus avoids the frequent error of separating the doctrines of the Person and Work of Christ, and Ritschl is as concerned as Schleiermacher to overcome the errors connected with this unnatural division. This is to be effected through a strongly soteriological focus: the concern is the value of Christ for salvation in view of his total ministry. He writes: "The theological solution of the problem of Christ's Divinity must therefore be based upon an analysis of what He has done for the salvation of mankind in the form of His community."[54]

THE VOCATION OF JESUS AS THE FOUNDER OF THE KINGDOM OF GOD

By approaching the interpretation of the deity of Jesus in the light of his saving work, Ritschl consciously follows the theological program established by Luther and Melanchthon. This fact, however, did not deter conservative critics from accusing him of denying Jesus' deity. In the second edition of the third volume of *Justification and Reconciliation,* he defended his approach and accused his critics of "incompetence and hasty judgment" in affirming that "I regard Christ as a mere man, and deny His Godhead."[55] Once again he appeals to Luther in contending that his opponents are guilty of attempting to establish the Godhead of Christ by means of speculation without reference to his saving work. The only legitimate approach in Christology is from the historical to the suprahistorical, from below to above. The attempt to bypass this order of knowing indicates a failure to comprehend that theological statements are value judgments based upon faith's understanding of the revelation in Jesus; as such, they are not to be confused with scientific statements established a priori. Therefore, Ritschl maintains his earlier viewpoint in saying: "We know God only by revelation, and therefore also must understand the Godhead of Christ, if it is to be understood at all, as an attribute revealed to us in His saving influence upon ourselves."[56]

He contends that the ethical evaluation of Jesus' entire ministry in terms of his vocation offers the best possibility for interpreting him correctly. In making the vocation of Jesus central, Ritschl was following the lead of Schleiermacher, J. C. K. Hofmann, and others in nineteenth-century theology.[57] It commends itself for the following reason: "In the moral world all personal authority is conditioned upon the nature of one's calling, and upon the connection between one's fitness for his special calling and his faithful exercise of it."[58] Protestant orthodoxy distinguished between the active obedience of Christ to the universal moral law and his passive obedience to the divine law; in so doing, it failed to see the life and suffering of Jesus as a unity.[59] What Jesus and all other men accomplish in their vocations is first of all for themselves and only secondarily for others. Jesus' calling was the establishment of the Kingdom of God. But in the light of the unity of God's self-end with that of humanity, Ritschl goes one step farther. "The Kingdom of God, the realisation of which forms the vocation of Christ, signifies not merely the correlate of the self-end of God, but also the goal that constitutes the highest destiny of man."[60] But the *ethical apprehension of Jesus* requires our remembering that what obtains for mankind as the result of his ministry can be evaluated properly only if it arises first of all from Jesus' pursuit of his own personal end.[61]

As early as Vol. II of *Justification and Reconciliation,* Ritschl interpreted Christ's ministry in terms of his establishment and furtherance of the Kingdom of God. Later he writes: "Accordingly, the permanent significance of Jesus Christ for His community is based, *first,* on the fact that He was the only one qualified for His special calling, the introduction of the Kingdom of God."[62] Thus, "Jesus Himself . . . saw in the Kingdom of God the moral end of the religious fellowship He had to found."[63] Indeed, both Jesus' self-understanding and the church's interpretation of him make any diminution of his role as the founder of the Christian religion illegitimate, while at the same time rationalistic interpretations that separate his teaching from his Person and his special relationship to God reveal an inaccurate historical analysis of him.[64]

THE VOCATION OF JESUS AND THE ETERNAL WILL OF GOD

The importance of Jesus as the founder of the Kingdom of God and the church is intensified by Ritschl's approach to the doctrine of election. He argues that the intimate connection between God's knowing and willing leads us to affirm that "not only in time but in the eternity of the Divine knowledge and will, Christ precedes His community."[65] Following the lead of a certain wing of Reformed theology and anticipating the outline of Barth's Christocentric doctrine of election, Ritschl reasons that Jesus Christ is the eternal object of the Father's love. The community is the object of this love secondarily and only in so far as it stands related to Christ as Lord and head of the community; individuals are objects of this love as they are related to the community which he founded and rules. Thus the "Kingdom of God as the correlate of the thought that God is love" and as the perfect moral organization of mankind in love "can be construed as the object and end of God's love only in so far as it is conformed to the type of its Founder, the Son of God."[66] The harmony with God that Jesus evidences in his life is not to be construed as a "mere abstract presentation of universal human morality."[67] Rather, on account of his vocation as the founder of the Kingdom of God, Jesus is the "prototype of that life of love and elevation above worldly motive, which forms the distinguishing characteristic of the Kingdom of God."[68]

In developing this idea, Ritschl moves to a quite irregular and speculative discussion of the eternal Godhead of the Son. Although from the human vantage point we must distinguish between the eternal divine intention concerning the Kingdom of God and its temporal realization in Jesus Christ, such a distinction cannot exist for God. Actually, then, since for God "the interval between purpose and accomplishment" does not obtain, "we get the formula that Christ exists for God eternally as that which He appears for us under the limitations of time."[69] Though Ritschl holds that knowledge of the inner trinitarian relationships is hidden from us, he utilizes it as a formal theological proof which supports and validates our "religious estimate" of Christ.[70] By interpreting the relation of the Holy Spirit to the Father along the same lines, he approximates a doctrine of the Trinity in nuce. "The Spirit of God is the knowledge God has of Himself, as of His own self-end."[71] But since the Spirit of God is the basis within the church of our knowledge of God and his purpose with regard to the Kingdom of God, one can say that the "practical knowledge of God in this community . . . is identical with the knowledge which God has of Himself."[72] It is therefore God's eternal will and purpose that "His Spirit should be the Holy Spirit in the community of the Kingdom of God."[73]

THE VOCATION OF JESUS: ITS SHAPE AND PURPOSE

In the light of our attempt to show how Ritschl—in a nontypical passage—grounds the historical work of Christ within the divine eternal will and purpose directed to the Kingdom of God, let us return to his more customary delineation of the ministry of Jesus in terms of his vocation. It is not sufficient to see the ministry of Jesus exclusively in terms of his establishment of the Kingdom of God, or of being its founder; we must go on to view his entire ministry—his vocation—in relationship to it.

The solidaric unity between Christ and God, which Jesus accordingly claims for Himself, has reference to the whole extent of His activity in His calling, and consists therefore in the reciprocal relation between the love of God and the obedience of Jesus in His calling.[74]

To realize his vocation as the "kingly prophet" called to exercise "God's ethical lordship" requires Jesus' unswerving loyalty to this supreme end, the rejection of any civil vocation in addition thereto, as well as the subordination of those conditions which normally provide security in life. The Johannine depiction of Jesus' doing the Father's will as the implementation of his mission[75] is a proper summation of his ministry; hence fulfillment for Jesus derived from doing the will of God, and not from the preservation of life and its values.[76]

The characteristics that stand out in Jesus' pursuit of his vocation in the Kingdom of God are "grace and faithfulness."[77] These attributes not only are central in the Old Testament comprehension of God but also dominate the depiction of the Godhead of Jesus in the New Testament. We are not to search for omnipotence and related attributes in Jesus Christ, since they have to do with God's government of the world and, consequently, Ritschl argues that these "could not be brought to direct manifestation in a human life, which is itself part of the world."[78] Jesus does, however, express God's loving will for mankind. And the "patience and faithfulness" that pervade his life "have their source in the desire, inspired by His vocation and sustained by His unique knowledge of God, to set up the Kingdom of God among men as their supramundane final end."[79] The distinctive marks of Christ's deity derive from what he says and does in relation to his life's purpose or vocation. There is then what Otto Ritschl terms a qualitative rather than a quantitative correspondence between the being of Jesus and the Father.[80] But since the total effect of what Jesus does is comprehensible only from the vantage point of the "community of the Kingdom of God" that issues from him, a complete interpretation of his Godhead is possible only within the fellowship of "brotherly love" that is marked by his attitude toward God, the Kingdom of God, and the world.[81]

It should be observed that Jesus' steadfast loyalty to his vocation is the basis from which his patience in the face of suffering and death is to be understood. Indeed, the latter is but the "consequence of His loyalty to His vocation" and must therefore be seen as of a piece with it.[82] As we shall observe later, this is the perspective from which Ritschl opposes Protestant orthodoxy's depiction of Jesus' death as a satisfaction of the divine justice rather than as the fulfillment of his vocation. In Jesus' fidelity unto God we have the highest example of the way in which he overcame the world, and in so doing served God's intention for him. Supremacy over the world is evidenced at every point where a man is true to his vocation even when opposing influences or experiences in the world would deflect him from this goal.[83] Jesus is the example par excellence of one whose devotion to his vocation caused him to turn away from human joys or evils, political or material considerations, or indeed anything else in his human experience that might turn him from his chosen goal.[84]

It is in this light that Jesus serves as the paradigm of what it means to be free. Undoubtedly, Ritschl wrestled with the problem of how men living in dependence upon God and acting under the impulse of love in the Kingdom of God could be regarded as free. The answer is not to be found in juxtaposing dependence upon God and human freedom, but in following that strand of Christian tradition which sees true freedom realized in dependence upon God. Since freedom is defined in a preliminary way as "the quality of self-determination by universal ideals,"[85] Jesus would not have evidenced supremacy over the world and been truly free had he made anything other than the Kingdom of God his final end. For in that case, he would have been bound by something less than the highest good. But in that he exercised complete dominion over the world in his steadfast pursuit of the highest end, namely, the Kingdom of God, he realized true freedom.[86] Moreover, it is only on account of his Lordship over the world during his earthly life that Ritschl regards it legitimate for the church to speak of his present Lordship over the world. This dominion resulted from his harmonious relationship with God, and this in turn was evidenced in his pursuit of the Kingdom of God as his goal and in fidelity to his vocation.

We shall have occasion to return to this idea later, but it was necessary to see how Jesus' relationship to the Kingdom of God has for its corollary supremacy over the world.[87] Such a view of Jesus requires that the "essential nature of Christ" be located in "His world conquering will, which marks Him as the God-man"; on this account, Ritschl broke with the "absurd idea" of his opponents who wished to speak of Christ's deity in terms of "His physical origin, which has never yet been reconciled with His historical appearance, and never can be."[88] Those who, as followers of Jesus, participate in the Kingdom of God and are therefore reconciled with God, enter into and enjoy the same relationship with God and supremacy over the world that characterized him. For Ritschl, therefore, the distinguishing mark of man as spirit—in contrast to the natural and material world—lies in his will, and therefore this category lends itself better to the interpretation of the divinity of Jesus than that of nature which has materialistic connotations.[89]

One of Ritschl's summary statements on "Christ's Person and Life-Work" draws together certain emphases which we have made in this section.

> In so far as the speech and conduct and patience under suffering, which make up the life of Christ, arise out of His vocation to exercise the moral lordship of God and realize God's Kingdom, and are the perfect fulfillment of this vocation, even to the extent of His willingly and patiently enduring the pains of death, it follows from the relation of this purpose

of Christ to the essential will of God, that Christ as the kingly Prophet is the perfect revelation of God; that, in virtue of the motive which inspired Him, namely, love, and the lordship which in His estimate of Himself and in His patience He exercised over the world, He is equal to God; and that He is the eternal object of the Divine love, and as such also the ground of the eternal election of the community of the Kingdom of God.[90]

THE DOCTRINE OF SIN AND JUSTIFICATION AND RECONCILIATION

THE METHOD OF INTERPRETING THE DOCTRINE OF SIN

The exposition of Ritschl's doctrine of sin prior to the interpretation of the meaning of justification modifies the order he adopts. The first major division of Vol. III of *Justification and Reconciliation* bears the title "The Conception of Justification and Its Relations"; the problem seeking solution is defined and the main lines of his positive exposition of this doctrine are developed. A second division entitled "The Presuppositions" treats successively the doctrines of God, sin, and the "Person and Life-Work of Christ," and in it he provides a summary of his theology. A third division, "The Proof," shows more fully how the problem of justification and reconciliation finds its resolution through Christ. The exposition of the doctrine of sin numbers less than fifty pages, and the reader may easily overlook its significance in Ritschl's system. Yet even a hasty perusal of the Table of Contents discloses that the doctrine of sin is presupposed in every section of his theology. Indeed, it is fair to say that Ritschl, like Schleiermacher, organizes his entire theology around the poles of sin and redemption. Thus, we are not surprised to find the doctrine of sin—as the negative presupposition of the doctrine of reconciliation—present as the backdrop within the first division dealing with the exposition of justification, even though its formal development is reserved for the sections on the "Presuppositions" of justification. If the doctrines of God and the "Person and Life-Work of Christ" serve as the positive presuppositions of the doctrine of justification, the doctrine of sin occupies the place of a negative presupposition.[91]

Beyond the importance that the doctrine of sin has in this connection, we must anticipate a view of Ritschl to be developed in a subsequent chapter, namely, that even the redeemed man is *simul justus et peccator*, "at one and the same time justified and sinner." Like Luther, and over against certain forms of perfectionism in Protestant and Roman Catholic theology, Ritschl reckons with the continuing fact of sin within both the church and the Christian. This is argued on the basis of Scripture and human experience. Moreover, it is an axiom of Ritschl's psychology and anthropology that there is a continuity of human existence within the spheres of sin and redemption. Indeed, so strong is his insistence upon the consciousness of sin within the justified man that some critics have accused him of holding that no transformation of man takes place in the forgiveness of his sin which actually alters his subjective consciousness.

1. *The Basis of Our Knowledge of Sin.*   We observed earlier that Ritschl makes much of the fact that valid theology takes place within the Christian community whose collective consciousness is decisively determined by the feeling of the forgiveness of sins.[92] This idea is sharpened in his interpretation of the doctrine of sin and involves a departure from both Roman Catholic and Protestant approaches. In contrast to a customary sequence in dogmatics that treats the doctrine of man's fall and sin prior to the section on Christology and soteriology, Ritschl unfolds the doctrine of sin in connection with the doctrine of reconciliation. In this he anticipates the procedure of Martin Kähler, Karl Barth, and others, but Barth indicates no indebtedness to Ritschl. He concedes that Ritschl seemed at times on the verge of transcending the limitations of a rather debilitated and unbiblical view of sin in Neo-Protestantism—especially in the manner in which he proposed to relate the understanding of sin to the knowledge of Jesus Christ. However, Barth concludes that Ritschl did not effect this correlation in any satisfactory manner, and thus failed to transcend the liberal tradition.[93] Be that as it may, Ritschl's approach necessitates his criticism of Lutheran orthodoxy, which developed the doctrine of sin in terms of the contrast between man's innocence in the state of original righteousness and his fall and sin judged in the light of the law. Even when stated in this way, the classical Protestant view of man's sin provides a more realistic assessment of man's condition than can be found outside the Hebrew-Christian tradition; yet Ritschl finds it objectionable because its view of sin remains theoretical. That is, sin is viewed in abstract and general rather than in concrete and particular terms.[94]

A more serious criticism of the traditional doctrine of sin is that the first Adam rather than the Second Adam, Jesus Christ, serves as the ideal of humanity. Such an idealization of the original state is unfounded, contradicts the Pauline perspective, and diminishes the historical significance of Jesus Christ. For Ritschl, the New Testament rather than the Old is the key to Christian anthropology; we look to Jesus Christ—not to Adam—for illumination and understanding both about the nature and extent of man's sin and his reconciliation.[95] Yet it is apparent that not all of man's awareness of sin derives strictly from Jesus Christ. Thus Ritschl can affirm that sin is known fully only in the light of the gospel of forgiveness, or in the light of the Person of Jesus Christ, or in terms of the Kingdom of God, or in contrast with the idea of the good, or of God, or of the "moral destiny of man," or of the "Christian ideal of life."[96] He uses all these norms for judging the nature and extent of sin more or less synonymously while contending that sin is knowable fully only within the Christian community, which acknowledges the moral ideal of humanity present in the man, Jesus. That Ritschl maintained this position is evident from his treatment of "Sin, Evil and Divine Punishment" under the "Doctrine of Reconciliation Through Christ" in his *Instruction in the Christian Religion*. He introduces the doctrine of sin as follows:

> The idea of the perfect common good included in the conception of the Kingdom of God, and the idea of personal goodness included in our conception of God and in our view of Jesus Christ, lay the foundation in the Christian community for a corresponding idea of evil and sin.[97]

2. *Sin as a Religious Conception.* Having clarified the vantage point within the church from which sin can be rightly assessed, Ritschl needed to distinguish the Christian doctrine of sin from all other philosophical, religious, or civil conceptions. We are dealing here with a religious concept of an "indirect kind." Only those conceptions, such as justification and reconciliation, which describe God's "operation" upon man are "religious conceptions" in the strict sense. Since sin cannot be attributed to an operation of God upon man or deduced necessarily from the nature of man, it is a religious conception or "value notion" of an "indirect kind." That is to say, the designation of certain actions as sinful and the depiction of man as sinner give expression to a "judgment upon the unworthiness of such actions when contrasted with God's precepts and honour."[98] Or put more concretely, sin can be known only in the light of its opposite, namely, the good or the Kingdom of God, or in the light of the "Person and Life-Work of Jesus Christ"—the man who did not sin. At this juncture we need to be careful not to overlook Ritschl's acknowledgment that the awareness of sin antedates the rise of Christianity; the point is rather that the understanding of God, the "supreme good," the "moral destiny of man," and of the redemption peculiar to Christianity lead to a specifically Christian understanding of the nature of sin.[99]

3. *Ritschl and the History of the Doctrine of Sin.* Ritschl is appreciative of certain insights of the traditional doctrine of original sin relative to the nature of sin and man as sinner—such as the stress upon the primacy of the will in sin, the collective involvement of all men in sin, the gravity of sin and the impossibility of self-redemption; yet he rejects it as incapable of

giving expression to the "highest possible sense of sin."[100] Though Augustine was right in arguing against Pelagius for the universality of sin over against a totally atomistic understanding of man as sinner, neither his exegesis nor that of his successors—nor the subsequent development of the doctrine—is convincing to Ritschl. He therefore opts for the excision of this doctrine on exegetical, historical, and theological grounds; Augustine and all his successors are guilty of speculation in constructing a doctrine that lies beyond the boundaries of human experience and therefore of empirical verification. Their conclusions lie in the realm of theological opinion and are therefore in no way binding.[101]

a. *Ritschl versus the doctrine of original sin.*   If we ask concerning the further deficiencies of the doctrine of original sin, Ritschl is armed with a reply. First, the concepts of "inherited sin and personal guilt cannot be combined in thought without inaccuracy or a *sacrificium intellectus.*"[102] If one agrees with Augustine that all men preexisted in Adam, there is no inherited sin; if, on the other hand, men inherit their guilt from Adam, there is no personal responsibility. Ritschl finds no basis for attributing to the apostle Paul a theory of the transmission of sin or guilt via natural generation. At this point his sympathies lie more with Pelagius, who argued for the possibility of the human will to choose the good, for only in this way can personal responsibility for sin be maintained. Indeed, the stress upon man's passivity and helplessness in the traditional doctrine of original sin goes counter to Ritschl's anthropology and his insistence that man— like God—is known essentially by what he wills and does.[103] Second, the construction of the doctrine of original sin contradicts his hermeneutical axiom that sin must be understood in the light of the good or of reconciliation through the Second Adam, and not in terms of a view of original righteousness and the sin of the first Adam. Third, the doctrine of original sin gives no place to actual sins as over against inherited sin or guilt. That is, it speaks of humanity as a "natural species" and does not allow for the uniqueness of each man. Fourth, although proponents of the doctrine of original sin teach that sin perverts the will, it is wrong to deny man all semblance of freedom of the will to choose the good and to counteract evil. Fifth, the ecclesiastical doctrine of original sin contradicts man's experience in affirming that each infant as Adam's descendant is deserving of "eternal condemnation." Sixth, the traditional doctrine allows for no gradations in sinfulness, yet man's ethical consciousness regards this as self-evident. In practical judgments, the doctrine of original sin tends to conceive of the original relationship between man and God in legal terms, that is, in terms of the moral law and subsequently in the light of the Mosaic law.[104]

b. *Ritschl versus Pelagius, Socinus, and the Enlightenment.*   Ritschl's positive analysis of the doctrine of sin attempts to steer a course between the errors of Augustine and his successors in Protestant orthodoxy on the one hand and Pelagius, Socinus, and the rationalists on the other. Subsequently we shall show that Ritschl attempted to preserve certain valid insights of the Reformers not preserved by Protestant orthodoxy. We have seen that the doctrine of original sin stemming from Augustine and adopted somewhat uncritically by the Reformation was perpetuated in Protestant orthodoxy as an adequate basis for understanding the nature of sin and man as sinner; moreover, the reasons for Ritschl's dissatisfaction with this tradition have been delineated. However, Ritschl does not flee Augustine only to embrace Pelagius. The latter is guilty of overlooking the corporate dimension of sin in his desire to ground sin in the individual will. Socinianism errs in similar fashion by failing to see the collective aspects of sin and the forgiveness of sins in relation to the church. Moreover, Socinianism tends to make forgiveness contingent upon ethical action, delaying it until a later stage in the Christian life—thereby giving rise to the possibility of a kind of "works righteousness."[105]

Theologians of the Enlightenment—though they learned from Socinians and Arminians how to criticize traditional doctrines of original sin, justification, and reconciliation—were much farther removed than their predecessors from historic Christianity in their excessively optimistic view of man and in their redaction of the universal moral law in the direction of an individual morality. Be that as it may, Ritschl attributes much of the blame for the Enlightenment's failure to recognize the gravity of man's sin and guilt to orthodoxy's preoccupation with the establishment of objective guilt by means of the doctrine of original sin to the total neglect of the questions of personal liability, responsibility, and subsequent guilt.[106] He therefore speaks of the "Complete Disintegration of the Doctrines of Reconciliation and Justification by the German Theologians of the Illumination," and of the "New Formulation of the Problem of Reconciliation by Kant."[107]

c. *Ritschl and Kant: new possibilities.* Kant more than Schleiermacher deserves plaudits in the modern period for the "scientific strictness" with which he "established critically. . . those general presuppositions of the idea of Reconciliation which lie in the consciousness of moral freedom and of moral guilt."[108] Especially in the area of the presuppositions of the doctrine of reconciliation—rather than in his positive reconstruction—Kant provides Ritschl with an acute criticism of orthodoxy and the Enlightenment; and at the same time, he developed a positive and viable alternative which transcended both of these traditions. The Enlightenment had relativized sin almost to a point beyond recognition by reducing "man's obligation towards God's law to the relative criterion of their internal and external situation, and on the other hand by denying all internal conviction of guilt."[109]

Over against Protestant orthodoxy, Kant finds a secure basis for the establishment of man's guilt—something that the doctrine of original sin never achieved. He does this by correlating man's freedom with his obligation to obey the absolute moral law to which he knows himself responsible. Ritschl interprets the intention of the "great philosopher" at this point as follows:

> That conception of the absolute obligation of the moral law which Kant developed in accordance with the notion of freedom, provides him with the means of establishing, on a surer basis than was afforded by the Old Protestant doctrine of original sin, the corresponding subjective consciousness that we are in effect guilty in the eye of the law. For the old doctrine, though put forward with a thoroughly practical design, had never been able to produce a corresponding practical consciousness; since the attribute of guilt in original sin was never adequately proved, and indeed could not be proved.[110]

This reestablishment of the absolute moral law and the experience of guilt which is aroused by the conscience accusing man of the misuse of his freedom vis-à-vis the moral law represents an incalculable gain over the efforts of orthodoxy and the Enlightenment to describe the human situation. One crucial reason for the demise of the Protestant orthodox view of reconciliation was that the "purely forensic view of law and punishment is not adequate to the ethico-religious problem of the removal of guilt and the consciousness thereof."[111] Ritschl continues in this vein:

> Accordingly, both parties alike lost the sense of the absolute validity of the law, based on the essential nature of God. And so when Kant furnished a fresh proof of this thesis from the nature of man—from his legislative freedom—a step was taken which marks not only the defeat of the principles of the Illumination, but also the renewal of the *moral* view of the universe due to the Reformation. For only a superficial criticism will hold it for an irreconcilable contradiction that the Reformers deduce this law from God, Kant from human freedom.[112]

Thus for Ritschl one of Kant's great contributions is seen in the way in which he interpreted human freedom, bringing back into meaningful focus once again the volitional dimension of human existence so necessary both for Christian anthropology and an adequate doctrine of sin. The consciousness of guilt "without which the whole Christian idea of reconciliation is unintelligible, becomes methodically possible only when we judge ourselves after the idea of transcendental freedom."[113] Man will not acknowledge "objective guilt" hanging above him as a fate apart from the "subjective consciousness of guilt" that is "generated by the idea of freedom." Unless he sees his guilt in this way, man "regards his sin either as his right or as a weakness which it does not fall to him to answer for."[114] It is noteworthy that when Ritschl pursues Kant's reasoning regarding man's disobedience of the moral law through the misuse of his freedom, he finds that it "secures that a man shall pass upon himself the very same moral judgment as is presupposed as the normal estimate of self by Christianity in its Protestant form."[115]

The fact that Kant's ethic provided a basis both for interpreting man's actions in terms of his response to the moral law and for understanding the concomitant development of man's feeling of guilt arising from his failure to obey the same would be sufficient to show Ritschl's indebtedness to the sage of Königsberg. But there is still another important teaching of Kant's that he adopted, namely, the idea of a corporate kingdom of sin which stands opposed to the Kingdom of God.[116] For Ritschl, this conception serves as a replacement for the doctrine of original sin while at the same time preserving the important elements that the latter intended but could not secure.[117] If we ask now where Ritschl disagrees with his philosophical mentor, we must reply that he does so—contrary to what one might anticipate—at the point of Kant's failure to regard sin with adequate seriousness. Though Kant develops a theory of radical evil approximating the Christian view at many points, he is unwilling to admit man's inability to fulfill the moral law. Moreover, though Kant at times moves in the direction of regarding Jesus as the paradigm of one who fulfills the moral law perfectly, he cannot admit that Jesus is necessary for the forgiveness of sins. The feeling of obligation to obey the moral law carries with it the ability to fulfill its demands in one's own power; at least man strives toward the moral ideal in his own strength regardless of whether there is consciousness of sin or not.[118] Hence, for Kant, in the last analysis, Jesus as reconciler and the forgiveness of sins are unnecessary. Man requires no Savior.[119]

d. *Ritschl and Schleiermacher.*   Ritschl's more immediate predecessor is Schleiermacher, and the latter influenced his construction of the doctrine of sin at decisive points. Not only did Schleiermacher surpass Kant in interpreting Christianity communally rather than individualistically, but he also brought the consciousness of sin and redemption into close correlation with one another; expressed differently, for Schleiermacher, the consciousness of sin and blessedness are corollaries. Prior to Ritschl, Schleiermacher saw human nature coming to completion in Jesus Christ, the perfect man, in whom the God-consciousness is always dominant over the sensible self-consciousness; in Jesus, therefore, we have a standard by which to measure the defections of man as sinner. However, Schleiermacher is less successful than Kant in relating man's God-consciousness to the Kingdom of God, thereby forfeiting the basis from which sin could be judged in the light of his own definition of Christianity. He also fails in his attempt to relate all actual sin to the traditional doctrine of original sin and is guilty of so stressing the corporate consciousness of sin that he overlooks the necessary stress upon individual awareness of sin. It would seem, therefore, that Ritschl's doctrine of sin is more indebted to Kant than to Schleiermacher, but this requires further refinement. These two thinkers complement each other and provide the context in which later theological reflection on this problem and many others was carried on.[120]

RITSCHL'S DOCTRINE OF SIN

1. *Sin—A Breach in Man's Relationship to God.* We noted that Ritschl regards sin as a "value notion" (*Werthbegriff*) or as a religious concept knowable in its fullness only within the Christian community and in the light of its opposites, namely, the Kingdom of God, the good, forgiveness, or the Christian ideal of life manifested supremely in Jesus Christ. Such a position allows for an extra-Biblical awareness of sin when measured in the light of the good or the moral law, and a still deeper knowledge thereof in the light of the law of the Old Testament. Yet attempts to comprehend the meaning of sin along avenues that bypass the knowledge of sin that derives from the Christian apprehension of the norms just enumerated are—like the doctrine of original sin—unable to establish a true apprehension of the essence of sin. Finally, the designation of certain actions as crimes or wrongs by society is on yet another level of judgment.[121] All the above approaches share a somewhat theoretical view of sin which, along with other deficiencies, fails to see clearly the personal dimension of sin.

Ritschl finds support in the Reformers for the close correlation that he posits between the true knowledge of sin and the experience of grace. He writes: "As far as individual experience is concerned, Luther first, and after him Calvin, maintained . . . the explicit maxim that hatred of sin proceeds from love of the good, a love which entirely coincides with faith in Jesus Christ."[122] Although the following statement has partial reference to what constitutes true repentance for the Reformers, it provides a summary of the manner in which Ritschl finds Reformation precedent for his own view.

> While the Reformers made justification in the course of conversion to proceed from the successive influence of law and of gospel upon the consciousness of the sinner, they were originally agreed on this point, that the Holy Ghost and faith are to be presupposed before the law can become effectual in producing repentance.[123]

Ritschl follows the Reformers, and Luther in particular, in viewing sin primarily in religious and secondarily in moral categories. That is to say, sin is first a breach in man's relationship with God—a defect—which subsequently manifests itself in sinful actions. Following Luther, Ritschl argues against the tradition of Augustine and Protestant orthodoxy which conceives the original relationship of our "first parents" toward God in legal rather than religious terms. Luther is closer to the truth in teaching that prior to the Fall man lived in a state of trust and confidence in the "kind providence of God."[124] This harmonious relationship with God is evidenced preeminently in Jesus who, in turn, intends this relationship toward God for his followers. The latter state is what Ritschl describes as the ideal Christian life-style (*das christliche Lebensideal*). Sin, therefore, is the opposite of this Christian mode of existence marked by reverence toward and "trust in God, by which we rise superior to the world."[125] This religious understanding of sin is intended to break with the Augustinianism which defines the essence of sin as "*concupiscientia,* selfish desire."[126] Although the latter description of sin could have been developed so as to show man's "anti-religious attitude towards God," this was never done. This is due, in part, to Augustine's assumption that the "moral law" was the "original dispensation between God and men," whereas Ritschl, following Luther, assumed a relationship predicated upon grace.[127]

2. *Sin—Evident in Man's Individual and Corporate Moral Perversity.* The preceding statements are sufficient to rebut the criticism that Ritschl viewed all sin as ignorance. The latter charge is already dubious in the light of his rejection of Schleiermacher's contention that sin be regarded as but an imperfect stage in man's movement toward moral perfection and not as active opposition to the good.[128] Ritschl has no difficulty in speaking of sin in terms of man's opposition to and contradiction of the divine will. "Sin is not an end in itself, not a good, for it is the opposite of the universal good. It is not an original law of the human will, for it is the striving, desiring, and acting against God."[129] Or again, he writes of sin as the "perverted attitude which the sinner adopts towards God."[130] Everything that he says concerning sin's manifestations in the moral sphere arises out of this perverted religious relationship toward God as the "Benefactor and Governor" of human life.

In turning to the "antimoral" aspect of sin, we must recall that this, too, must be determined in relation to its opposite, variously described as the "Christian ideal of life," the "common good," and the *summum bonum* evident in the Kingdom of God. The following is a typical description of the norm by which man's moral perversity is measured: "Action prompted by love towards our neighbor and tending to produce that fellowship which, as the *summum bonum* represents at the same time the perfected good."[131] Sin in its ethical manifestation is seen as the contradiction of this ideal.

Now sin is the opposite of the good, so far as it is selfishness springing from indifference or mistrust of God, and directs itself to goods of subordinate rank without keeping in view their subordination to the highest good. It does not negate the good as such; but, in traversing the proper relation of goods to the good, it issues in practical contradiction of the good.[132]

Although Ritschl seems more concerned to point to the individual relationship to God when discussing the religious aspect of sin as mistrust and irreverence toward God in order to make man's personal responsibility apparent, and though he argues that one moves from a consciousness of personal sin to that of corporate sin—the collective and corporate aspects of sin are never absent from view. This derives in part from his axiom that man is a social being and that religion is always social. It follows from this that there is something like a corporate kingdom of sin and evil paralleling the Kingdom of God and the good. Hence "sin cannot be completely represented either within the framework of the individual life, or in that of humanity as a natural species."[133] This assertion requires a rejection both of Pelagius, and therewith of all atomistic and overly individualistic doctrines of sin, and of Augustine, for whom sin inheres in human nature as such. Ritschl continues:

The subject of sin, rather, is *humanity as the sum of all individuals,* in so far as the selfish action of each person, involving him as it does in illimitable interaction with all others, is directed in any degree whatsoever towards the opposite of the good, and leads to the association of individuals in common evil.[134]

As we have seen, Kant was right in juxtaposing the Kingdom of God and the kingdom of sin (*Reich Gottes und Reich der Sünde*). This concept more nearly accords with human experience than the doctrine of original sin in that it can account both for the influence which the kingdom of sin exerts upon the individual and the individual's active participation in the kingdom of sin.

Man's choice of sinful action is not attributable to an innate or inherited depravity of the will; the latter is acquired through evil actions through which the "will acquires . . . an evil character."[135] Hence it must be assumed that even though the radical evil of which both the doctrine of original sin and Kant speak is evident within the individual, his own actions are predicated upon the will's self-determination, and the possibility exists, at least ideally, for man to choose either good or sinful actions. Indeed, all education presupposes a "general, though still indeterminate, impulse towards the good" within each child, although there is no "complete insight into the good," nor has this impulse been put to the test in

actual situations in life.[136] Such an approach preserves individual responsibility for sin. Nevertheless, Ritschl holds out little hope for man's realization of the good in conformity with this impulse. On the contrary, he also
recognizes the universality of sin. But how is this to be understood?

We have seen that the development of the sinful will is neither attributable to man's natural endowment nor to God's intention; nor is it "adapted
to further his moral development." It is acquired in response to the satisfaction of certain appetites and desires. Moreover, the kingdom of sin is a
destructive and negative influence, leading man to sin or choose the lesser
good. Ritschl writes:

> The *fact* of universal sin on the part of man is established, in accordance
> with experience, by the fact that the impulse to the unrestrained exer-
> cise of freedom, with which everyone comes into the world, meets the
> manifold attractions to self-seeking, which arise out of the sin of
> society.[137]

The end result of man's repeated sinful action arising out of "selfish
resolves" is "an ungodly and selfish bias."[138] There is a gradual "blunting of
our moral vigilance and our moral judgment" as men are influenced by the
kingdom of sin and in turn contribute to its pervasive influence through
sinning themselves and causing others to sin.[139]

Some four decades after Ritschl wrote these words Walter Rauschenbusch and later Reinhold Niebuhr in the United States spoke of the corporate kingdom of evil which corrupts men and institutions. So did the Christian Socialists Leonhard Ragaz and Hermann Kutter in Europe before them
at the beginning of the twentieth century. But all of them surely learned
much from Ritschl, who spoke with prophetic power at this point. He
could write with insight of this "sinful federation" which envelops men so
that they do not choose the supreme good, the Kingdom of God, which
God intends, but the lesser goods which run "counter to that final end."[140]
Man's selfish proclivity can infect his loyalty to "particular goods" such as
family, state, social class, and church confession. When this state of affairs
obtains, man is acting counter to the good and the goal intended for all
men in the Kingdom of God. "This whole web of sinful action and reaction,
which presupposes and yet again increases the selfish bias in every man, is
entitled 'the world,' which in this aspect of it is not of God, but opposed to
Him."[141]

The first of Ritschl's summary theses appended to the doctrine of sin
provides a résumé of his position thus far:

> Sin, which alike as a mode of action and as a habitual propensity extends
> over the whole human race, is, in the Christian view of the world,

estimated as the opposite of reverence and trust towards God, as also the opposite of the Kingdom of God—in the latter respect forming the kingdom of sin, which possesses no necessary ground either in the Divine world-order or in man's natural endowment of freedom, but unites all men with one another by means of the countless interrelations of sinful conduct.[142]

These are the lines along which Ritschl develops his understanding of sin, attempting in the process to be fair both to the Biblical view of man as God's creature and yet sinner and to the historical development of the doctrine. Along the way the voices of Augustine and Pelagius are both weighed, and something is learned from each. Above all, the Reformers, and particularly Luther, provided Ritschl with a vantage point that encouraged further reflection and development. That Kant influenced Ritschl at many points is clear from our analysis, but the fact that he did so is not to be understood as due to his philosophical acumen alone. For in Kant philosophical insight came into creative interplay with the Christian tradition of the West and more especially with Protestantism in its Lutheran form.

3. *Sin—The Consciousness of Guilt and Divine Punishment.*   In the section bearing the title "Evil and Divine Punishment," Ritschl dissociates himself from a major segment of Christian tradition, which views evil as the punishment for sin. Unlike the term "sin" which Ritschl has defined by contrasting it with the attitude of trust toward God and a "religious estimate of the universal moral law," the "notion of evil [is determined] by the relative standard of the freedom of the individual."[143] By this, Ritschl means that "since we have experience of our freedom in the conception and execution of our ends, evil signifies the whole compass of possible restrictions of our purposive activity."[144] Thus the notion of evil is not a religious concept, but points to a "natural event" that is differently interpreted because of divergent ways in which men react to its effect upon them. Thus what some regard as evil may be viewed as good or conducive of a moral good by others, and this could never be said of sin.[145]

The traditional correlation of evil with divine punishment for sin is due, in part, to the juristic context in which the relationship between God and man was conceived.[146] This is misleading as is the failure of the traditional doctrine of reconciliation to make clear that beyond deliverance from sin and guilt, reconciliation effects a different attitude toward the world and nature. With this new perspective "unmerited evils" either of the natural or social type are explicable on the grounds of man's involvement within "the organized system of nature" and society. In this regard, Ritschl finds Jesus transcending a pre-Christian and more primitive *Weltanschauung* which connected evils with sin by seeing them as a sign of divine punishment.

The fact that sickness, natural catastrophes, and social evils occur and restrict our freedom does not mean that they represent divine judgment. In most instances these occur on account of the warp and woof of the created order and human existence within it. However, Ritschl is willing to admit that in a more restricted sense certain evils that befall man may be interpreted as divine punishments. For this situation to obtain, however, there must be a feeling of guilt indicating a breach in man's relationship to God or in his experience of divine sonship.[147] The basis, then, for regarding evils as divinely ordained is to be located in man's subjective feeling of guilt. The following is typical of Ritschl's position on this point: "The sense of having forfeited one's right of Divine sonship, which forces one to regard an experience of external evils as a Divine penalty, is the feeling of guilt that separates from God."[148] As we have observed earlier, it was Kant more than anyone else who taught Ritschl that the misuse of one's freedom in response to the absolute moral law gave rise to a sense of guilt or a troubled conscience.[149]

It should now be evident that man's consciousness of guilt is the clue to his attitude toward that which is generally regarded as an evil. Indeed, the feeling of guilt is the most heinous consequence of sin and that which keeps a theological doctrine of sin from wandering in vague abstractions. Ritschl writes: "It follows that the unrelieved feeling of guilt is not so much one penal state among others, but is itself actually that of which all external penal evils are but the concomitant circumstances."[150] Hence we are not surprised to find that the section entitled "Forgiveness of Sins as the Removal of the Separation of the Sinner from God Acknowledged in the Feeling of Guilt" is followed by "Forgiveness of Sins as Removal of Guilt."[151] For the feeling of guilt does not involve for Ritschl an actual and objective separation of man from God when seen from God's viewpoint. "We ought therefore rather to transpose 'the removal of the separation of sinners from God' into 'the removal of the consciousness of guilt.' "[152]

Against this backdrop, another of Ritschl's summary theses becomes intelligible:

Of the evils which make themselves perceptible as hindrances to human freedom, those have the significance of Divine punishments—presupposing the Divine government of the world—which each individual, through his unrelieved consciousness of guilt, imputes to himself as such—that consciousness of guilt, as expressive of the lack of religious fellowship with God, being itself already the initial manifestation of punishment as the forfeiture of the privilege of Divine sonship.[153]

In order at this point to determine the extent and gravity of sin, we must keep before us its debilitating effects upon both the individual and society symbolized in the kingdom of sin. We observed that man's sin leads to a feeling of guilt and a breach in his experience of divine sonship. The fact that man's consciousness of guilt points to a subjective state in no way makes it less real for Ritschl; indeed, only when sin is understood thus do we move from the realm of theorizing about sin to that of actual experience. Against Duns Scotus, who argued that neither the state of guilt nor that of forgiveness were real but were merely the "colourless presupposition of our being made righteous through grace," Ritschl counters as follows: "The *contradiction of God* and our own moral destiny which is expressed in the conception of guilt, and is felt with pain in the consciousness of guilt, is by this concomitant circumstance marked as a real disturbance of human nature."[154] The accusing conscience testifies to the sickness of man's will and to the reality of guilt. "Thus in the domain of the will, sin, as the disturbance of the ideal relation of the will to its final end, or to God as representing that end in the world-order, is a real contradiction."[155] Beyond these and other effects of sin upon man's religious relationship with God and his moral activities, we have considered the cumulative influence and power of sin in the kingdom of sin which poisons men and institutions. Along these lines Ritschl speaks of the universality of sin and the gravity of man's situation as sinner.

4. *Sin and the Possibility of Forgiveness.*   Given this dilemma, we must ask about the possibility of forgiveness. Ritschl finds much of the traditional discussion about the origin of sin, its extent and purpose, to be pure speculation. In particular, the idea of the "infinity of sin" leads either to a dualistic world view or represents a "subjective impression." If the latter is true, then we have no possible way of estimating "the extent of sin in space and time, and its power to disturb the orderly course of human history."[156] In a manner that anticipates a position of Karl Barth's, Ritschl warns against absolutizing the power of sin. "Sin, as a product of the limited powers of all men, is yet limited, finite, and quite transparent for God's judgment."[157]

Against this backdrop, and more specifically in the light of his entire doctrine of God as a loving will, Ritschl speaks of gradations of sin and God's proportional response. Such distinctions need to be made, in part, to counter the Augustinian tradition which makes guilt attaching to original sin deserving of eternal damnation—a position Ritschl rejects as unbiblical. Moreover, he contends that throughout the New Testament one finds the "idea of the *graduated value of sin*" which allows for a distinction between sins which are forgiven and that final opposition to God and salvation which is of quite a different order.[158] At this point in his argument, Ritschl makes no mention of Kant, though in an earlier treatment he alluded to Kant's recognition of various levels of evil.[159] More important is Ritschl's claim of New Testament precedent for grouping all sin that does not represent final hardening and rejection of God, the good, and salvation as ignorance (*Unwissenheit*). This state of "not knowing" is not restricted solely to those whose opposition to God and the moral law is undeveloped or sporadic; indeed, Ritschl argues that we must leave it to the divine prerogative to judge whether or not those whom man regards as confirmed in their opposition to God are yet capable of conversion, and thus to have God view their sin as ignorance.

Here it should be stated emphatically that the designation of sin as ignorance "has the significance only of a standard for God . . . because its specific application does not belong to us."[160] The context in which Ritschl developed this category is clarified by his summary statement: "In so far as men, regarded as sinners both in their individual capacity and as a whole, are objects of the redemption and reconciliation made possible by the love of God, sin is estimated by God, not as the final purpose of opposition to the known will of God, but as ignorance."[161] This leads us to that sin which is represented invariably as final and thoroughgoing opposition to God, sin against the Holy Ghost, or a "self-determination . . . which has deliberately chosen evil as its end."[162] Having said this, however, Ritschl reminds his readers again that such divisions are knowable only to God, and it is not man's lot to divide men into groups or to speculate whether there are those who are beyond the pale of the divine love. It would appear that for him it is enough to know that God's intention for man is life and not death; as loving will, he intends even those who are his enemies in their sin to become his friends, and to find their fulfillment in his forgiveness and in their appointed end in the Kingdom of God. The manner in which this transformation comes to pass is the subject of our next chapter.

CHAPTER III

The Nature of
Justification and Reconciliation

INTRODUCTION

Up to this point our concern has been to develop in broad compass something of the rationale governing Ritschl's approach to the interpretation of justification and reconciliation. Accordingly, we turned first to his theological methodology (Chapter I), then to a consideration of the relationship of the doctrine of justification and reconciliation to the major doctrines of his theology, namely, God, Christology, the Kingdom of God, and the doctrine of sin (Chapter II). In all of this our intention was to prepare the way for a proper assessment of Ritschl's conception of the restored relationship between God and man which results from his justification and reconciliation. We do well to recall the scope of this doctrine as Ritschl portrays it in the opening paragraph of his work on *Justification and Reconciliation*:

> The Christian doctrine of Justification and Reconciliation, which I purpose to unfold in a scientific manner, constitutes the real centre of the theological system. In it is developed the determinate and direct result of the historical revelation of God's purpose of grace through Christ—the result, namely, that the Church founded by Christ has freedom of religious intercourse with God, notwithstanding the fact of sin, and at the same time, in the exercise of that freedom, directs the workings of its own will in conformity with God's expressed design. To the religious discernment this implies in itself the moral restoration of man, and all religious blessedness.[1]

Although the focus of our study is on Ritschl's positive exposition of the doctrine of justification and reconciliation, we should remind ourselves that he regarded his systematic conclusions to be the fruit of his historical and Biblical investigations pertaining to this doctrine.[2] Philip Hefner argues with some warrant that the bulk of secondary literature on Ritschl is dominated by analyses of his doctrinal conclusions seen against the back-drop of his philosophical, ethical, and psychological presuppositions to the virtual total neglect of his foundational historical research which provides the key to his dogmatic conclusions. Although Hefner has rectified a weak-ness of some interpreters of Ritschl, he fails to give adequate attention to certain influential philosophical presuppositions and Biblical investigations informing Ritschl's thought.[3] In our study to this point, we have tried to show in rather broad terms what Biblical, historical, and philosophical investigations and presuppositions contribute to Ritschl's theological con-clusions.

In the face of divergent ways of viewing justification in mid-nineteenth-century Protestant theology—not to mention the disagreement between the Evangelical and Roman communions that had obtained since the Reforma-tion—Ritschl expresses the hope that his own unbiased interpretation of the apostolic viewpoints set forth in the Bible might lead at least to some resolution of intra-Protestant divisions.[4] During the period of his early studies of Reformation views of justification in 1857, Ritschl wrote his father, lamenting the prevailing confusion within Protestantism over the meaning of justification.[5] Later in his career, he was less optimistic about the reunion of opposing factions even within his own Lutheran com-munion, having himself borne the brunt of numerous attacks inflicted by devotees of orthodox Lutheran confessionalism and Lutheran Pietism.[6] Nevertheless, he undertook his study of this doctrine with the purpose of testing the various post-Reformation Protestant views of justification—in addition to major types developed within medieval Roman Catholicism—in the light of the witness of the Scriptures and the teaching of the Re-formers, recognizing in the process that no single Protestant communion could lay claim to being the complete expression of the truth inherent even within its own tradition.

THE NECESSITY OF JUSTIFICATION AND RECONCILIATION: DIVER-GENT INTERPRETATIONS

Our analysis of the nature of sin has made it clear that Ritschl stands in the Reformation tradition in his conception of man as sinner to the extent that all possibilities of man effecting his own redemption—by whatever means—are rejected. Man's broken relationship with God evidenced pri-marily in his mistrust of God, divine providence, and in his concomitant subjection to the world seen in his moral disabilities is neither resoluble by man himself nor by the means available to the church understood as the dispenser of grace. Man's forgiveness and restoration to fellowship with God is effected by God through Jesus Christ. The way this occurs will be developed later in this chapter. Here it must suffice to say that Ritschl's conception of "justification through faith alone" in the tradition of the Reformation provides the norm by which aberrant interpretations of justification both Roman Catholic and Protestant are judged.

Ritschl regards most Roman Catholic–Protestant discussions of justification as wide of the mark because of a common failure to recognize their mutually divergent perspectives. He states the difference thus:

> The Roman doctrine of justification professes to state the causes and the means through which a sinner becomes actively righteous; that is, it professes to explain how one who believes in Christ is made capable of his *moral* vocation.[7]

Accordingly, cooperation between man's freedom and God's grace is affirmed. Hence, although Ritschl repeatedly expresses appreciation for the Roman Catholic accent upon the overarching grace of God both in the initiation and fulfillment of man's justification, a certain ambiguity is present in its formulations which qualifies the freedom of God's grace. This is attributable, in the main, to a common tendency of both Roman Catholicism and Protestant orthodoxy to conceive of Christianity as a religion of law rather than of redemption; this legalistic perspective leads to a perversion of the doctrine of justification. In contrast, a true Reformation understanding of justification "is intended to explain the *religious* character of the individual's life."[8] This involves man's new relationship with God and attitude toward the world in virtue of the divine judgment of pardon appropriated through faith—a state that in its inception and continuation obtains apart from any moral activity or meritorious actions.

This view of God's free grace as the sole ground of man's justification necessitates Ritschl's rejection of certain aberrant Protestant formulations of justification. In his eyes, Socinianism is the Protestant counterpart of Roman Catholicism because it views Christianity as a religion of law rather than of redemption; it transforms Christianity from a religion into a "system of scholastic ethics or a legal mode of life."[9] Accordingly, Socinians argue that forgiveness of sins and salvation result only after man obeys the law in faith; thus the quest for moral perfection becomes the ground for God's forgiveness. This is a kind of works righteousness opposed to the Reformation *sola fide, sola gratia.* Moreover, such a stance denies another essential tenet of Ritschl's theology noted above, namely, that Christianity is basically a religion and only secondarily an ethical system or way of life. Socinianism fails to see this and thereby overlooks an essential thrust of the Reformers. Instead of acknowledging that man's sin must be forgiven and therewith his relationship to God restored before there can be good works, it tended to see the latter as prerequisite to the former. To be sure, Ritschl insists on the close correlation between faith and ethical action; they must be held together, but not confused, interchanged, or mixed with one another. "For, in the first place, Christianity as a whole is a religion; in particular, it is the specifically moral religion."[10] Moral action grows out of the life of faith and its "religious functions"; the former does not give rise to the latter.[11] Ritschl's clarity on this point necessitates careful scrutiny of frequent charges that his theology represents nothing but a disguised Kantianism or moralism.

Ritschl's dissatisfaction with Socinianism and later related Enlightenment interpretations of Christianity also derives, in part, from his rejection of their excessive individualism and deficient ecclesiology as they relate to man's justification. Following the Socinian lead, the Enlightenment spoke of man's ethical self-development apart from his involvement with the church or mankind as a whole. This led Enlightenment theologians to dispense entirely with the idea of the church in the discussion of man's development, since a beneficent God rewarded the man who acted insofar as possible in accordance with the law of his own being. Ritschl believed that here man is "thrown upon his own resources and condemned to seek a merely relative morality."[12] In this respect, he sees Kant as a true child of the Enlightenment—despite all his virtues—for we have seen that in the last analysis Kant sees no need for a Redeemer or the forgiveness of sin.[13]

Ritschl's rejection of rationalistic and Enlightenment reinterpretations of the doctrine of justification and reconciliation restricted the possibilities of affirming any post-Reformation interpretation as adequate. We observed above and shall detail below his critique of the understanding of justification and reconciliation in Protestant orthodoxy. Though appreciative of certain Reformation emphases in the latter, orthodoxy departs from the Reformer's characteristic stress upon the practical effects of justification within the Christian's life toward assent to it as a doctrine. This view, coupled with orthodoxy's proclivity for interpreting the whole divine-human relationship in legal categories, transformed Christianity from a religion of redemption into one of law. Ritschl acknowledges that Pietism —with its emphasis upon subjective religious experience and the Christian life—represents a legitimate criticism of the static nature of a doctrinaire orthodoxy. Yet we shall have occasion to observe his lifelong criticism of Pietism on the grounds that it represented a renaissance of sectarian, medieval piety incompatible with the Reformer's view of justification by faith. If orthodoxy was guilty of stressing the objective work of Christ to the neglect of its subjective appropriation through faith, Pietism reversed the emphasis. But in the process, Pietism often developed a kind of religious individualism that undermined the necessary priority of the church to the individual believers, and tended in the direction of making faith meritorious.[14]

Finally, Ritschl could not accept F. C. Baur's contention that speculative idealism climaxing in Hegel provided a satisfying interpretation of the doctrine of reconciliation in effecting a balance between the objective or speculative and subjective or experiential poles of this doctrine. Their protests notwithstanding, Ritschl saw speculative idealism guilty of failing to take seriously either the historical revelation marking the origin of Christianity or the historicity of man.[15] On the basis of his survey of post-Reformation views of justification, therefore, he held that he could affirm no prevalent school of thought as the legitimate extension of the perspective of the New Testament and the Reformation.

Ritschl's attitude toward earlier formulations of the doctrine of justification and reconciliation is, however, by no means wholly negative. Though he laments that it is difficult to chart its development after Schleiermacher, certain common features stand out. (1) There is "thorough unanimity" that reconciliation is to be understood in the light of the love of God and not in terms of his justice, and (2) the love of God is seen extending "throughout the whole life and passion of Christ." (3) Christ is man's vicarious representative before God in his humiliation as the head of the new humanity or as the head of the church. (4) Increasingly, the action and suffering of Christ are integrally connected by means of the concept of vocation thereby making it possible to comprehend his saving work in terms of his response to duty. (5) Even those who utilize the orthodox idea of penal satisfaction transcend the juristic framework through a more ethical interpretation of the same. (6) Finally, on the basis of the New Testament exegesis of J. C. Hofmann and J. T. Beck, the possibility arises of affirming the identity of reconciliation and justification.[16] Ritschl's stance vis-à-vis these elements is reflected in the following statement:

> These are, as I have said, elements which open up, to any attempt at a theoretical reconstruction of the doctrine that shall proceed upon them, the prospect of meeting with sympathy from the present tendencies in theology.[17]

It was this "theoretical reconstruction" which Ritschl himself was attempting to fashion between 1870 and the publication of his positive and systematic statement in 1874.

JUSTIFICATION, THE CHURCH AND THE INDIVIDUAL

It is important to recall that Ritschl regards theology as a function of the church whose relationship to God is determined by the consciousness of the forgiveness of sins. Whereas in the first edition of Vol. III of *Justifi-*

cation and Reconciliation he spoke in a Schleiermacherian vein of "Justification as the Religious Expression of a Specific Dependence Upon God," beginning with the second edition this heading was omitted and he was concerned to speak of justification and reconciliation as "religious conceptions." The latter means that "they are always the possession of a community" and express not only a "relation between God and man," but also an attitude of God and Christians toward the world.[18] This shift in emphasis is indicative of Ritschl's increasing recognition both of the social character of religion and of the close connection he found between the doctrine of justification by faith and ecclesiology in the Reformers. This accounts for a further significant transposition of sections in his analysis of the context in which justification takes place. With the passing years, he reacted more negatively toward an individualistic and subjectivistic interpretation of the Reformation *sola fide* which did not reckon with the priority of the church as the matrix out of which the individual's faith arises. Whereas in the first edition of Vol. III Ritschl seemed at points to accentuate the Christian's faith without reference to his relationship to the church, in later editions he elevated the section entitled "Justification Referred to the Community of Believers and to the Individual in It" to a place of preeminence.[19]

In order, therefore, to place the doctrine of justification or forgiveness in proper context, Ritschl points us to the following progression for comprehending its origins and the manner of its appropriation: first, the ground of forgiveness as the gracious and merciful will of God; secondly, the mediation of the gospel of forgiveness through Jesus Christ; thirdly, the transmission and proclamation of forgiveness of sins through Christ—in the church founded by Jesus Christ—through Word and Sacraments; and finally, the individual's appropriation of the forgiveness of sins by means of faith in the gospel proclaimed by the church.[20] Ritschl credits Luther for having held the doctrines of the church and justification by faith together; the church is constituted by Jesus as the community marked by the forgiveness of sins, and it proclaims the forgiveness of sins. This correlation was overlooked by Melanchthon, who failed to include a locus on the church in the first edition of the *Loci communes,* and thereafter the individualistic interpretation of justification apart from any mention of the priority of the community of faith became normative in Lutheran theology.

The latter emphasis accounts in part for Ritschl's hostility toward all forms of mysticism. As a rule, mystics seek to transcend the manifestation of God's revelation in the preached Word and Sacraments in their quest for the mystic union. Moreover, though lip service may be given to justification by faith, it is no longer central, but is "so depreciated as to become a mere formal precondition of the immediate union with God . . . which Mysticism strives to attain."[21] However, Calvin and the Reformed tradition

avoided the Lutheran tendency toward individualism by maintaining the
close correlation between the doctrines of the church and justification by
faith.[22] Ritschl's concern is to recover and develop the teaching of the
Reformation on this point. This means that faith cannot arise or be maintained "in isolation from the already existing community of faith, and that
the community is coextensive with the spread of the Gospel, that is, the
public preaching of the forgiveness of sins."[23]

While occupied during the years 1860–1865 with his research on
Socinianism and various Reformation schools of thought, Ritschl first
became aware of the importance of the correlation of the doctrines of
justification and the church in the Reformers. On December 5, 1867, he
wrote his friend Diestel concerning this unanticipated result of his study
of the sources.

> I maintain that the doctrine of reconciliation through Christ, under-
> stood in terms of its general effect, is completely reciprocal with the
> doctrine of the community of faith as the whole which logically precedes
> the individual who becomes a believer and is reborn; thus the concept
> of the community must be seen as the telos or purpose of reconciliation
> and included within that doctrine, and reconciliation must be under-
> stood as giving rise to the community. For one departs from the doctrine
> of the universal satisfaction effected by Christ whenever the [Ana-
> baptist] sectarian or the [Socinian] scholastic interest in the individual
> as such in his relationship to God comes on the scene. To be sure, even
> in Lutheran doctrine the aforementioned correlation has become oc-
> cluded whenever one views reconciliation as the reconciliation of God
> and ties the justification of the individual as a distant consequence
> thereof to it. The justification of the individual, or better his conscious-
> ness of justification, is certainly preceded by the justification or founding
> of the community, even as the covenant sacrifice presupposes the corre-
> sponding community; and in like manner, this corresponds to Jesus'
> desire to give his life as a covenant sacrifice.[24]

Ritschl's increasingly clear delineation of the priority of the church to
the believing individual involved him in a sharper polemic against divergent Protestant views and led to accusations concerning his Catholic lean-
ings. This provided the occasion for him to criticize Schleiermacher's well-
known distinction between Protestantism and Roman Catholicism to the
effect that the devotee of the former makes his relation to the church
dependent upon his relationship to Christ while the latter makes his fellowship with Christ dependent upon his relationship to the church. Ritschl
finds this definition in contradiction to Schleiermacher's opening statement
on the doctrine of redemption, namely, that the "consciousness of redemption through Christ is referred to the mediation of His religious fellowship."[25] Thus he finds it necessary to reject Schleiermacher's distinction.
He continues:

For even the Evangelical Christian's right relation to Christ is both historically and logically conditioned by the fellowship of believers; historically, because a man always finds the community already existing when he arrives at faith, nor does he attain this end without the action of the community upon him; logically, because no action of Christ upon men can be conceived except in accordance with the standard of Christ's antecedent purpose to found a community.[26]

JUSTIFICATION AND THE KINGDOM OF GOD

A further serious deficiency in traditional interpretations of justification and reconciliation is their failure to relate justification and the Kingdom of God. We noted earlier how he intends to structure his entire theology around these two poles. We need not review that discussion here; suffice it to say that Ritschl's positive exposition of the doctrine of justification and reconciliation begins with the reminder that these two foci must always be seen in their interrelationships. At first glance, it might appear that these conceptions are not homogeneous: justification would seem to refer to the preeminence of the divine grace redeeming the sinner; the Kingdom of God, to the moral activity of man in realizing God's rule in the world. Such a distinction would be false. Each term points to both the overarching activity of God and the necessary and correlative activity of man, and we have noted that theology must take due cognizance of each of these poles.

Ritschl accentuates the teleological aspect of justification evident in man's realization of the divine will in the Kingdom of God, the *summum bonum*. Hence divine action and human response are integral to both conceptions, and justification "encompasses the whole life of man" and therefore cannot be understood apart from the notion of the Kingdom of God.[27] By relating these conceptions, he holds the religious and ethical poles together, and his system is thereby afforded great cohesiveness. He writes: "Justification, reconciliation, the promise and the task of the Kingdom of God, dominate any view of Christianity that is complete."[28] We shall have occasion later to turn to the teleological dimension of the doctrine of justification.

THE DOCTRINE OF JUSTIFICATION AND RECONCILIATION

JUSTIFICATION AS THE ACT OF GOD: THE OBJECTIVE POLE OF THE DOCTRINE OF JUSTIFICATION

Ritschl's doctrine of justification and reconciliation has been criticized by many as a reversal of the Reformers' procedure. It is argued that whereas the latter gave priority to the foundation of man's justification and salvation in the historical work of Christ and thereby accentuated the objective pole of the doctrine, Ritschl reacts against theological objectivism and puts the entire stress upon the subjective appropriation of justification.[29] Although informed students of Ritschl acknowledge his overriding interest in the practical ramifications of justification in the life of the believer in the church and the world and his opposition to orthodoxy's static view of justification which robbed the doctrine of its religious significance, the charge of subjectivism requires careful scrutiny.

In our analysis of his theological method we noted that he opposed Pietists, who regarded all theology as an expression of the theologian's piety.[30] Moreover, Ritschl's lifelong critique of Protestant Pietism as a subjectivistic distortion of the Reformers ought to have made him particularly sensitive toward succumbing to subjectivism in theology. In this connection, it is not incidental that his positive exposition of the doctrine of justification and reconciliation is arranged so that the objective pole of the doctrine, as depicted in the judgment and act of God effected through Jesus Christ, appears prior to any discussion of the subjective appropriation thereof by the believer.[31] This is in harmony with the priority Ritschl always accords the religious over the ethical moment. In so doing, he expressed his intention of reaffirming the priority of the objective ground of man's justification in the judgment and act of God as taught by the Reformers and Protestant orthodoxy in opposition to pietistic and other subjectivistic theologies which tended to undercut this approach in their zeal to speak about religious experience. This polemic against Pietism follows quite logically from his earlier comparison of the views of Osiander (1498–1552) and Luther in an article published in 1857. The former prostitutes Luther by arguing that man's justification follows as a consequence of his regeneration, thereby moving in the direction of making man's subjective experience meritorious.

In countering this tendency, Ritschl asserted the following program as the only viable one for a sound doctrine of justification as early as 1857:

The temporal unity of objective justification and the subjective consciousness of the same which has its rightful place in religious experience must be dissolved in the theological treatment of the matter. Thereby it becomes possible to conceive justification as an attribute of the historical work of Christ, and this is still the tendency of Lutheran theologians in opposition to Osiander and [it is] also the direction of Paul's conceptuality. In that form which justification has as the judgment of God with respect to humanity both the synthetic character as well as the priority of the same over regeneration is secured—which as such affects the individual. Finally, with these presuppositions it becomes possible to conceive the consciousness of justification through Christ as the necessary attribute of the state of regeneration, which viewpoint protects piety both from the false path of works righteousness and from doubt concerning salvation. It is only with this approach that one has the right norm for opposing and overcoming the theory of Osiander. The latter is analogous to the Pietistic and modern conceptions of justification as is evident not only in terms of the sympathetic hearing which Osiander has received since Gottfried Arnold, but which also can be proven from opposing viewpoints.[32]

This conception of the shape of a valid doctrine of justification expressed by Ritschl as a young professor of thirty-five years of age is in harmony with the systematic exposition of that doctrine by the mature Ritschl. In the year 1874 he projected the exposition of the doctrine of justification and reconciliation in four sections. "*First*, we ascertain what is meant by justification and reconciliation; through what attribute of God we are to conceive justification, in what relation to men, and how far extending [cf. *J. R.* III, § 5–22]; finally, in what subjective functions this Divinely-originated relationship expresses itself actively" [cf. § 23–26].[33] That some such order would obtain was also anticipated in his analysis of the "Reformation Principle of Justification by Faith in Christ" in the first volume of *Justification and Reconciliation*. Both here and subsequently, he rejects a typical reading of Luther, Zwingli, and Calvin which locates their major contribution in the significance they attached to religious experience. Exponents of the latter view are criticized for overlooking the way in which the Reformers related justification to their view of the church. The failure to observe and follow their procedure is to subjectivize and individualize man's justification in such a way that one cannot claim Reformation precedent.

Ritschl goes even farther in breaking with the customary interpretation of Luther and the Reformation in terms of what had come to be known as the formal and material principles. He writes: "Luther's theological first principle is rather the thought of the abiding revelation of love as the essence of God in Christ."[34] Since this is the case, it is quite misleading to regard the "religious disposition" as the "leading principle of the Reformation" above "every outward expression of it, and above every outward means of producing it. For justifying faith, as the Reformers understood it, is a frame of mind that is essentially determined by regard to the historical (and thus objective) appearance of Christ."[35] In his essay of 1876, "Concerning the Two Principles of Protestantism," Ritschl asserts that the so-called material and formal principles of the Reformation stem from neither Luther nor orthodoxy, but were first coined by Twesten in 1826! Since the formula is neither hallowed by tradition nor illuminating, he suggests it be laid to rest! He concludes:

Parenthetically, one may reflect whether a formula descriptive of the essence of Protestantism can be useful which is not oriented with respect to the concept of the church and the Christian ideal of life.[36]

Thus the conception of justification by faith must be seen in "its close reciprocal connexion with that objective conception of the Church which regards it as being before everything, and before all legal ordinances, the divinely-founded community of believers."[37] Ritschl cites Luther's exposition of the third article in the Small Catechism in support of his point here and on numerous other occasions. It reads:

> I believe that it is not of my own reason or by my own strength that I believe in Jesus Christ my Lord: it is the Holy Ghost that by the Gospel has called me, with His gifts has enlightened me, though genuine faith has sanctified and sustained me, just as He calls, gathers together, enlightens, sanctifies, and sustains by Jesus Christ, in true, proper faith, all Christendom. *Within which Christendom He daily gives to me and to all believers abundant forgiveness of all our sins.*[38]

Ritschl intends to effect some such balance between justification and ecclesiology in his own view. In this way, the error of sectarianism is avoided and the church is built upon the "Ground of the Universal Church." In opposition to Anabaptists and sectarians who seek to constitute the church solely from "actively holy persons," and Socinians, who tend to see the church composed of "those acquainted with the saving doctrine of Christ," he adopts what he held to be the true Reformation position in affirming the priority of the church and its message of *sola gratia* as the basis of man's acceptance with God prior to any individual response.[39] Let us now turn to the way in which Ritschl depicts God's grace.

1. *Justification or Forgiveness as the Acceptance of Sinners Back Into Fellowship with God.* We do well in this section to follow the progression of Ritschl's thought. The manner in which he uses the terms "justification" and "forgiveness of sins" interchangeably and the meaning he attaches to them is seen in the following thesis:

> Justification or the forgiveness of sins, as the religious expression of that operation of God upon men which is fundamental in Christianity, is the acceptance of sinners into that fellowship with God in which their salvation is to be realised and carried out into eternal life.[40]

He supports his use of the terms "justification" and "forgiveness of sins" synonymously on historical and lexical grounds. Although the term "forgiveness of sins" is used in the Old Testament and by Jesus to refer to the manner in which the broken relationship between man and God within the covenant is restored, it appears to have a somewhat negative connotation when contrasted with the Pauline term "justification." Paul does "oppose the Pharisaic perversion of the idea of active righteousness" with his understanding of justification; but ordinarily he relates justification to the sin of humanity as a whole and its primary referent is not the covenant people.[41] Like forgiveness, however, justification points to the manner in which the divine grace restores the sinner to communion with God. Although the Reformers used forgiveness and justification interchangeably, their attachment to Paul and the possibility of contrasting justification with the universality of sin commended the latter. We have seen that the attempt to distinguish these terms by regarding forgiveness of sins as a preliminary first step in salvation and justification as a positive consequence occurred first in Protestant orthodoxy, a precedent influenced by their conception of the original relationship between God and man in legal categories rather than in terms of grace. Ritschl rejects this distinction and claims Scriptural and Reformation precedent for using justification and the forgiveness of sins synonymously.[42]

Although we cannot detail the Biblical evidence that Ritschl marshals for the positive content he gives the terms "justification" and the "forgiveness of sins," especially in the teaching of Jesus and Paul, the entire second volume of *Justification and Reconciliation* has this for its concern. He regarded his "exposition of Biblical theology" to be for the purpose of ascertaining "what idea of the forgiveness of sins, justification, and reconciliation—together with their relations—had been called into existence by Jesus as the Founder of the Christian church, and maintained by the apostles as its earliest representatives."[43]

The first chapter of Vol. II of *Justification and Reconciliation* bears the caption "The Relationships of the Idea of Forgiveness of Sins in the Thought-World of Jesus."[44] Both rationalists and supranaturalists follow a fallacious procedure in separating Jesus' teaching from his acts, thereby transforming him into a teacher of doctrine. Jesus himself makes no use of the terms "justification" or "reconciliation"—not to mention the lack of any formulated doctrine thereof.[45] Nevertheless, he appears as the kingly Prophet proclaiming the advent of the Kingdom of God in his Person in the midst of the covenant people. He conceives of the fulfillment of the Kingdom in a community of disciples who acknowledge his Lordship and Messiahship. For Ritschl, it is significant that Jesus had authority to forgive the sins of those who attached themselves to him during his ministry, and that this occurred through Jesus' initiative—apart from any merit on man's part. The ensuing transformation of individuals within the community of Jesus' followers is tied up with their obedience to the Kingdom of God as the highest good.[46] Forgiveness, therefore, is always correlated with the

Person and Work of Jesus as it relates to the Kingdom of God and the community that he established.

The preceding discussion has led us to a consideration of the relationship of Jesus to the Kingdom of God. Since the essentials of Ritschl's position have been reviewed above, we need not pursue this matter again.[47] However, we must inquire somewhat further about the manner in which the forgiveness of sins is related to the "Person and Life-Work of Christ." We have noted Ritschl's insistence that a properly scientific understanding of Jesus must begin with an "ethical apprehension" of his Person. That is to say, we must view the life and work of Jesus first in terms of what he purposed and did for himself; we must see that "we have grasped the historical manifestation of Christ under the form of the human Ego, that is, have viewed it *in the light of its inherent unity as judged by ethical laws.*"[48] This means that any legitimate depiction of the life of Jesus must reckon with his personal independence before injecting categories into the picture which either overlook or diminish its significance. In some respects Ritschl mirrors the procedure of many theologians of the mid-nineteenth century influenced by the development of a rigorous historical mode of thinking in contending that the interpretation of Jesus must begin with the Jesus of history rather than with the Christ of Christological dogma. This was the approach common to the entire "quest for the historical Jesus." However, Ritschl dissociates himself from those purporting to write "lives" of Jesus apart from any presuppositions in maintaining that no full understanding of him is possible apart from faith in him as a member of the community he established.[49] Ritschl proposes an "ethical apprehension" of Jesus that concentrates upon Christ as "Himself the subject of religion." Efforts in traditional Christology to interpret Jesus in terms of his two natures or three offices fail to view him in this perspective; yet "this aspect of His person is easily seen to be at once the centre and the circumference of all that was purposely accomplished by Him, with a bearing on others."[50] This attempt to understand Jesus as the subject of religion remained of interest to followers of Ritschl such as Wilhelm Herrmann. However, whereas Ritschl uses ethical categories to interpret Jesus, Herrmann's attempt to uncover the "inner life" of Jesus is more psychological in orientation.[51]

The model that commends itself to Ritschl as a means of arriving at an ethical interpretation of the total ministry of Jesus is that of vocation. It enables us to see how Jesus understood himself, for he viewed his entire ministry as the pursuit of his vocation or self-end, namely, the establishment of an ethical fellowship of love among men in the Kingdom of God. The fact that the self-end of Jesus in the Kingdom of God is at one and the same time the fulfillment of God's purpose and the highest destiny of mankind enables Ritschl to say that in fulfilling his vocation Christ "has ministered to the salvation of mankind as a whole."[52] The important thing is that the latter follows as a consequence of Jesus' fidelity to his vocation. Hence the ethical self-estimate of Jesus is supplemented by his own religious self-estimate, namely, that he stood in a special relationship to God by virtue of being the revealer of God, the "Bearer of the Divine self-end" and the "revelation of the love of God."[53]

Ritschl can use traditional Christological categories by relating them to the overarching idea of vocation in order to show how the lifework of Jesus effects man's salvation. Jesus is first of all the kingly Prophet who represents God to men; he does this by demonstrating to men "His Father's love, grace, and truth" in the exercise of his vocation.[54] Consequently, Ritschl can agree with the Socinian claim that God's forgiveness is not contingent upon the death of Jesus. Indeed, the heart of Jesus' ministry lies in his manifestation of the divine love for sinners, and herein lies one of the major errors of traditional satisfaction theories of the atonement. Jesus did not have to satisfy the divine righteousness before God could reveal his forgiving love to sinners. To hold the latter view violates a fundamental thesis of Ritschl's theology, namely, that the Bible subsumes all of God's attributes beneath that of his love. Ritschl presumes that his earlier investigation of the divine attributes has established that no essential opposition or tension exists between the divine love and righteousness.[55] For Ritschl the traditional Protestant orthodox view of satisfaction tears the unity of the Godhead asunder and leaves faith forever insecure.[56] He opposes this view as unbiblical and suggests instead that the entire life of Jesus be seen in terms of his kingly Prophethood which has for its aim the manifestation and proclamation of the divine intention to forgive which is grounded in the very nature and purpose of God himself. Thus the forgiveness that Jesus grants is the historical expression of the loving intention of God to draw men through his Son unto himself, and because of the special communion that Jesus enjoys with the Father, and by virtue of his special vocation, he is able to grant forgiveness during his earthly ministry.

It is not necessary to detail the development of Jesus' ministry as the kingly Prophet inasmuch as an earlier section gave attention to the way in which Ritschl's Christology determined his doctrine of God.[57] We need only note that the accent falls on Jesus Christ, the kingly Prophet, rather than on the kingly Priest as the following quotation makes clear:

> In so far as the speech and conduct and patience under suffering, which make up the life of Christ, arise out of His vocation to exercise the moral lordship of God and realise God's Kingdom, and are the perfect fulfilment of this vocation, even to the extent of His willingly and patiently enduring the pains of death, it follows from the relation of this purpose of Christ to the essential will of God, that Christ as the kingly Prophet

is the perfect revelation of God; that, in virtue of the motive which inspired Him, namely, love, and the lordship which in His estimate of Himself and in His patience He exercised over the world, He is equal to God; and that He is the eternal object of the Divine love, and as such also the ground of the eternal election of the community of the Kingdom of God.[58]

The interpretation of Jesus in terms of his Priesthood provides much greater difficulty for Ritschl because of its associations with an illegitimate satisfaction theory of the atonement. According to the latter view, the obedient death of Jesus Christ as Priest assuages the divine justice, righteousness, or even wrath. Ritschl regards his Biblical investigations to have shown conclusively that it is unbiblical to assume opposition between God's righteousness and mercy and to interpret righteousness in the direction of "inexorable retribution." This conclusion is of crucial import for him as the following makes evident:

> God's righteousness is His self-consistent and undeviating action in behalf of the salvation of the members of His community; in essence it is identical with His grace.[59]

Ritschl argues in much the same manner in maintaining that the wrath of God in the Old Testament is related to God's holiness and must be seen as his punishment of apostates who break the covenant and of foreign nations who attempt to thwart his covenant purpose. Nowhere is the wrath of God connected with Adam's fall. But even in the Old Testament, the stress is upon God's gracious will as the ground of his action and the basis of his election of Israel.[60] In the New Testament, the divine love predominates even more and Ritschl finds that the wrath of God is reserved for those who oppose finally the means of salvation and the "ethical world order" that he has ordained. This reaction of God has its origins in the Old Testament idea of the violation of his being as the Holy One. It is illegitimate to view the wrath of God in relationship to God's jealous or spurned love. Indeed, he concludes that since we cannot relate any actions in the world to God's wrath, the conception of the wrath of God for the Christian "possesses no religious value; it is rather both a homeless and formless theologumenon."[61]

In harmony with the foregoing, his study of the sacrificial system in the Old Testament leads him to reject all atonement theories that claim Old Testament precedent for interpreting Christ's death as a sacrifice that moves God's disposition from wrath to mercy. The contrary is the case because the sacrificial system is predicated upon the divine grace toward the covenant people. The priest who offers the sacrificial gift unto God acts as the people's representative, and they are brought into relationship to God through him. The satisfaction atonement theories err in assuming that "the sacrificial offering includes in itself a penal act, executed not upon the guilty person, but upon the victim who takes his place."[62] Thus it is evident that Ritschl cannot accept atonement theories based upon the idea of satisfaction which claim Old Testament support for relating the sacrifice of Christ primarily and directly to God and only indirectly and subsequently —and under certain conditions—to men. These important deviations from the understanding of the priestly work of Christ and the death of Jesus in traditional atonement theories based upon the idea of satisfaction must be kept in mind as we look at Ritschl's "complete remodeling" of the kingly Priesthood of Jesus.[63]

In keeping with the aforementioned axiom in analyzing the life of Jesus, Ritschl distinguishes his view from that common in Protestant orthodoxy by affirming that "Christ is first of all a Priest in His own behalf before He is a priest for others." From this perspective, Jesus is "the subject of that true and perfect religion" which consists in his perfect fellowship with, and knowledge of, God.[64] Such statements are reminiscent of Schleiermacher who interpreted the uniqueness of Jesus in terms of the dominance of his God-consciousness over the sensible self-consciousness in every moment of his life.[65] Through obedience in his vocation, steadfastness in prayer, and the constant ordering of his life in keeping with God's providential leading, Jesus maintained that perfect fellowship with God "which was the aim of every religion" and experiences "in Himself in its fulness the reciprocal and saving influence of God."[66] Jesus' unique fellowship with God transcends both in "constancy" and "spirituality" anything analogous in the Old Testament, and differs from all Old Testament examples of piety in its power to give rise to a religious community. Thus by virtue of his perfect priestly relationship to his Father during his ministry, Jesus was qualified to usher others into that same fellowship.[67]

The preceding is sufficient to indicate how Ritschl conceives of Jesus as being first a Priest for himself. In what sense is it legitimate for him to speak of Jesus as a Priest for others? Are those critics correct who say that the sacrificial death of Jesus is not integral to Ritschl's understanding of justification and reconciliation? To be sure, we have seen that Ritschl cannot utilize many elements characteristic of the traditional interpretation of Jesus' Priesthood which require his death to be viewed in the category of satisfaction or substitution. In addition to the weaknesses listed above, Ritschl finds the theory of satisfaction deficient at yet other points: first, Jesus' death in itself is not redemptive, but the manner in which he met it is important; second, to interpret the death of Jesus in terms of substitutionary punishment contradicts the Biblical understanding of God and does not provide a basis for viewing his life and death as a unity; third, it is

erroneous to hold that the relationship between God and man can be understood in legal terms; fourth, in order for the sufferings of Jesus to be equivalent in worth to the enormity of man's sin, Jesus would have to evidence
a corresponding consciousness of guilt and a recognition that his sufferings
were a punishment.[68] With respect to the latter, Ritschl is unequivocal:
"For Christ had no sense of guilt in His sufferings; consequently He cannot
have regarded them as punishment, nor even as punishment accepted in
the place of the guilty, or in order to deter men from sin."[69] In what sense
are we then to interpret the death of Jesus? The only option for Ritschl
is to regard the obedience of Jesus in the face of death as the consistent
outcome of his fidelity to his vocation and therewith to the will of God; by
acting in this fashion, Jesus triumphs over the drive for self-preservation
and therewith over the world.[70]

In the light of Jesus' life and sacrificial death, we can say that as the
kingly Priest he represents *man before God*. At this juncture we must underline Ritschl's insistence that Jesus be seen in the context of the community of which he is the founder. During his lifetime, he exercises his
priestly ministry by leading men through the forgiveness of sins into the
same communion with God that he enjoyed. Therefore, the Socinian and
Enlightenment viewpoint that speaks of an overarching love of God that
effects the forgiveness of sin apart from any necessary reference to Christ
is incomplete.[71] Of course, Ritschl can also speak in this manner when
referring to the ultimate ground of forgiveness in the merciful and loving
will of God. But one must go on—if one is not to end in abstraction—by
relating this forgiveness to the historical Jesus. Hence he entitles an important chapter "The Necessity of Basing the Forgiveness of Sins on the
Work and Passion of Christ."[72] The forgiveness of sins so viewed is tied
to the total ministry of Jesus, both to his life and death, and to the community of the new covenant which he thereby established.[73] There is no
need to recapitulate the forceful manner in which he relates the forgiveness
of sins or justification to one's inclusion in the community of believers.[74]
To belong to the community of which Christ is the head is equivalent to
experiencing the forgiveness of sins, which in turn is equivalent to the
sinner's reception into fellowship with God. Ritschl puts it succinctly:

> The forgiveness of sins or reconciliation with God, as the common and
> permanent determination of the relation of men towards God, is not
> recognisable and operative outside the community founded by Jesus
> Christ, and dependent upon His specific action.[75]

It is in this manner, therefore, that we can speak of Christ's exercising
a priestly ministry even prior to his death, since he leads his disciples into
fellowship and communion with the Father. Thus whereas the kingly

Prophethood of Jesus as the proclamation of the divine intention to forgive sinners has humanity as its referent, his kingly Priesthood points to the way in which the divine intention for man is realized in a specific community through the instrumentality of the one who represents them before God.[76]

Jesus' fidelity exercised in his vocation and in his sacrificial death "constitutes the highest proof of His personal communion with God as His Father, . . . and it is but logical to connect with Christ's death the forgiveness provided for later generations."[77] At this point Ritschl acknowledges that the traditional idea of the "meritorious obedience" of Jesus has its place if properly conceived.[78] It is not that his obedience served as a satisfaction of the divine wrath, but rather that his maintenance of obedience even in his suffering and death provided the means whereby the community of which he is the head and representative could be taken up into the fellowship with God which he enjoyed. There is a kind of imputation of Christ's righteousness for Ritschl in that the "position of Christ relative to God is imputed to His disciples when God, for Christ's sake, takes them also up into His effective love."[79] In view of the high-priestly discourse in the Fourth Gospel, the parables of the flock and shepherd and the vine and branches, and the words of institution spoken at the Last Supper, Ritschl affirms that "Christ as a Priest is the representative of the community which He brings to God through the perfect fulfillment of His personal life."[80] These are the lines along which Ritschl finds it possible to view Jesus as the kingly Priest who represents men before God.

Our concern in this section to show how he grounds man's justification or forgiveness in the will and purpose of God mediated through the historical "Work and Passion" of Jesus is summed up in the following thesis:

If forgiveness or reconciliation is understood as the right of this community to place itself, in spite of sin and a lively sense of guilt, in the relation towards God of children to their father, it is indispensable to trace forgiveness to Christ in the sense that He, as the Revealer of God, through His whole conduct inspired by love to men, manifested God's grace and truth [*Treue* = faithfulness] for their reception into God's fellowship, and, with the intention of creating a community of the children of God, proved His religious fidelity to God by the faultless discharge of the task of His vocation; and that God vouchsafes to sinners who are or shall be Christ's disciples, that position relatively to Himself which Christ thus maintained.[81]

2. *Justification or Forgiveness as the Removal of Guilt, the Feeling of Guilt, and Man's Sinful Will Toward God.* In the preceding section we observed that the most comprehensive definition of justification or forgive-

ness was the restoration of the sinner to fellowship with God. In maintaining this position, Ritschl opposed Protestant orthodoxy's view that the forgiveness of sins is but the first stage in man's restoration to fellowship with God to be completed by his being declared righteous or justified. Orthodoxy's rationale must be noted. Consistent with its underlying presupposition that the basic relationship between God and man was legal in nature, it held that the first stage in man's salvation involved being freed from the law's demands to which he was bound as the means for obtaining blessedness. This occurs first of all because Christ renders satisfaction to God through "active obedience" to the law in man's behalf and in his place; thus Christ's righteousness satisfies God's demand for man's obedience to the law and therewith frees man from its requirements. Christ's "passive obedience" in his suffering and death serves as the payment to God for the penalties that man as sinner had incurred. In these two ways, Christ's righteousness has the "value of satisfaction for God." Thus in the orthodox scheme, forgiveness of sins is but the first step in salvation. The second and positive stage obtains when the righteousness of Christ viewed as meritorious is imputed to man so as to effect his justification.[82] It would appear that the only thing right about orthodoxy's approach in Ritschl's estimate is the recognition that sin effects a separation between man and God. The main weakness is the refusal to allow God's mercy to come into play before the requirements of his justice have been met. Moreover, it contradicts Ritschl's view that forgiveness of sin is equivalent to justification and not just a stage that is antecedent to it.

Beyond these deficiencies he finds orthodoxy's manner of dealing with the reality of man's guilt deficient. If guilt is a primary consequence of man's sin, theology must be able to account both for its presence in the sinner and its removal. Orthodoxy fails at both points. It holds first that the objective judgment of God rests upon the sinner apart from any attention to his consciousness of guilt. Ritschl replies that in order not to "bifurcate the human consciousness" there must be an awareness of guilt in the state of sin; otherwise, man could neither regard himself as deserving of judgment nor long for redemption. Orthodoxy overlooks the fact that apart from the sinner's consciousness of guilt, the whole legal framework between God and man is jeopardized. Both here and at other points orthodoxy does not provide an adequate explanation of the sinner's consciousness of guilt.[83] Thus orthodoxy gave little attention to man's subjective states.

In the second place, the orthodox doctrine of the imputation of Christ's righteousness mirrors the same deficiency in its failure to observe the change effected in man's consciousness by the forgiveness of his sins. This does not mean that Ritschl regards guilt as wholly subjective. Guilt results from man's rejection of, and opposition toward, God and is therefore a "real disturbance of human nature."[84] Hence the objective fact of guilt and the subjective consciousness thereof are coordinate and both characterize man's plight as sinner. The consciousness of guilt arises out of the "opposition of the sinful will to God" and to the fulfillment of man's destiny in the Kingdom of God.[85] But these disabilities are resolved with man's forgiveness or justification. Ritschl summarizes the progression of our argument to this point as follows:

> Justification is conceivable as the removal of guilt and the consciousness of guilt, in so far as in the latter that contradiction to God which is realised in sin and expressed in guilt, works on as mistrust, and brings about moral separation from God.[86]

This statement accentuates an important aspect of Ritschl's conception of forgiveness as it bears upon the removal of man's guilt and his consciousness thereof. It would be contrary to God's immutability and the law of truth were God's forgiveness to mean that he forgets man's sin completely; with reference to man, it would be false to claim that forgiveness involves the complete eradication of the feeling of guilt. The latter remains—though weakened—due to the continuity of man's selfhood within the states of sin and redemption. Ritschl's variation on the Lutheran theme *simul justus et peccator* is based upon the ordinary meaning of human pardon. When such occurs, the memory of one's offense is not entirely removed. It remains in the consciousness even though the barrier blocking one's relationship to the offended party has been removed. Ritschl applies this to God's pardon of man as follows:

> If, therefore, the forgiveness of sins is interpreted after the analogy of human pardon, it is as far as possible from signifying such a removal of the guilt of sin and of man's consciousness of guilt as might come to be incompatible with truth. The forgiveness of sins as pardon, rather, merely renders inoperative that result of guilt and the consciousness of guilt which would manifest itself in the abolition of moral fellowship between God and man, in their separation or mutual alienation. God, in forgiving or pardoning sins, exercises His will in the direction of not permitting the contradiction—expressed in guilt—in which sinners stand to Him, to hinder that fellowship of men with Him which He intends on higher grounds. And so far as this intention works determinatively upon sinners, it does not, indeed, free them altogether from the consciousness of guilt, but from that mistrust which, as an affection of the consciousness of guilt, naturally separates the injured man from the offender.[87]

3. *Justification or Forgiveness in Relationship to Reconciliation, Eternal Life, and Adoption.*   Part of our difficulty in analyzing the precise nature

of justification in Ritschl's thought stems from the bewildering number of theological terms referring to aspects of man's salvation that he relates to it. In this procedure, however, Ritschl intends to restore and reformulate the true understanding of justification found in the Reformers. This necessitates criticism of Protestant orthodoxy for its failure to comprehend the dynamic nature of justification in the theology of the Reformers, especially as it relates to the practical consequences of the latter in the Christian life. Even Gerhard (1582–1637) is taken to task for listing the effects of justification in such fashion that it appears "as though we were dealing with a rubbish heap."[88] Later developments in Protestantism are worse rather than better. Socinianism, for example, tends to conceive of faith as a work, and Pietism's obsessive preoccupation with regeneration and subjective religious experience as the ground of man's justification undermines the priority of God's grace. In opposition to these aberrant interpretations of justification Ritschl tries to restore the doctrine of justification to the place of preeminence it held among the Reformers. Since for them justification was the heart of the gospel and the church's confession, Ritschl reasoned that communions within that tradition should be of like persuasion. We need to see how he pursues this goal in this concluding section relating to the objective pole of the doctrine of justification.

The manner in which Ritschl relates justification and reconciliation can be seen best if we recall the major emphasis of this entire section, namely, that justification has its final ground in the gracious will of God. This is the consistent Reformation position espoused by Ritschl against his ever present foes on one side represented in the main by Socinians, Pietists, and mystics. Pietism, as well as an earlier tradition in Lutheranism, tends to detach justification from the judgment of God effected through Jesus Christ by making it contingent upon faith. Of course, we shall observe in the following section that Ritschl wants to correlate the work of God effected through Jesus Christ as the ground of man's justification with man's faith. His primary concern, however, is to view man's faith as subordinate to, and derivative from, the judgment of God effecting his salvation. This accounts for his opposition to the Socinian position as early as 1857 when he wrote that "justification must be comprehended as an attribute of the historical work of Christ; this is in fact the tendency of Lutheran theology in contrast to Osiander, and also the direction in which Paul points us."[89]

The dilemma that the Reformers and their successors faced here was how to relate man's justification to the historical and redemptive work of God in Christ while at the same time giving room to man's response. The Reformers saw justification secured in and with the redemptive work of Jesus Christ. Yet Ritschl's analysis of justification in the Reformers leads him to conclude that they went awry at this juncture "since they never allowed theoretical reflection to work independently of their religious experience."[90] They reasoned that since their religious experience pointed to a coalescence in time of the redemptive activity of Christ and their appropriation of it through faith, the formulation of the doctrine of justification should reflect this fact. This led to the view that "justification takes place then first of all when the individual fulfils the condition of it in the possession of faith."[91] This view was further encouraged when Lutheran theology distinguished the effects which the work of Christ had upon God and man respectively. In the case of the former, the effects were immediate; with respect to the latter, they were viewed as the "mediate result" of Christ's pacification of the divine wrath. "But the formula that Christ at that time reconciled God with the sinful human race, and that God in consequence thereof imputes the righteousness of Christ at all times to those who perform the act of faith, is *no* doctrine of the Reformers."[92]

With this point in mind, we can appreciate the thrust in Ritschl's discussion entitled "The Synthetic Form of the Justifying Judgment of God." Utilizing Kantian terminology, he writes: "This conception of justification, which has been developed in essential agreement with the intention actuating the Lutheran and Reformed theologians, *is, in form, a synthetic judgment.*"[93] That is, justification must be conceived of in terms of the divine resolve or as derivative of his will. "But such an act is conceived when God through the revelation in Christ receives those who are separated from Him by sin into fellowship with Himself, to the establishment of their salvation."[94] The derivation of justification from the synthetic judgment of God distinguishes the Reformation view from that of Roman Catholicism, Socinianism, Arminianism, certain expressions of Protestant orthodoxy, and Pietism. All of these traditions—in one way or another—make God's judgment concerning man's justification dependent upon his faith, fulfillment of the law, assurance of salvation, or some combination of these. In short, the judgment concerning justification becomes analytic; that is, it is determined by God's evaluation of something man does rather than upon his free resolve alone. In this respect Ritschl is more sympathetic with Protestant orthodoxy, which derived justification from the "Judicial Act of God" as Lawgiver, than he is with Pietism.

Although Ritschl prefers to see the judgment of God concerning justification comprehended in the light of his being the "Founder and Ruler of the Kingdom of God," or under the attribute of his Fatherhood, rather than in terms of being a Lawgiver, orthodoxy nonetheless did intend to derive justification from the judgment of God.[95] Pietism and its predecessors and successors, however, transformed the decree of justification into an analytic judgment of God based "upon the moral worth of faith, in so far as faith, as a result of conversion, includes the power of moral action."[96]

This obsessive preoccupation with man's subjective experience of conversion and assurance of salvation within Pietism reversed the procedure of the Reformers whose concern in interpreting justification was to direct attention toward, and to magnify, God's free grace revealed in Jesus Christ for man's salvation.[97]

From the point we have reached we can see why justification plays a decisive role in Ritschl's exposition of the Christian faith. In a sense, everything essential in Christianity relates at some point to justification or the forgiveness of sins. On the objective side, justification must be seen in relationship to the ultimate will of God, the person and lifework of Jesus Christ, and to God's final purpose in the Kingdom of God. With respect to man and on the subjective side, justification involves the understanding of his life as sinner, his new life as a child of God within the church, and his Christian pilgrimage in the Kingdom of God both present and future. For Ritschl, an adequate doctrine of justification must include all of these elements.

In attempting to build upon the Reformers and Luther, in particular, Ritschl finds precedent for maintaining the virtual identity of justification, reconciliation, forgiveness of sins, and adoption.[98] This is due to the fact that all these terms intend in varying ways to describe the new fellowship between believers and God. His argument deserves citation at this point.

> If justification places sinners in a positive relationship of congruence towards God, and if the declaration that they are righteous is not to make their destination to active righteousness wear a semblance of superfluity, it must find its limit in that fellowship with God which is expressed, to begin with and in an indeterminate way, by nearness to God, and then, further, by the right of communion with God. Not only, however, does this open a prospect that all that is still attainable for the salvation of believers and in opposition to their sin will result from this new and peculiar relation to God; but these results, up to the goal of eternal life, are included by intention in justification (*sind in der Rechtfertigung mit beabsichtigt*), as surely as justification determines the lasting and unvarying character of believers.[99]

Here it is evident that Ritschl can refer everything relating to man's restoration to fellowship with God to the idea of justification. Though occasionally he claims Pauline precedent for using the terms "justification" and "reconciliation" synonymously, we must keep in mind the following distinction. In essence, reconciliation is the realization of justification. Whereas the decree of justification envisages man acted upon by God, the term "reconciliation" connotes that "the person who is pardoned actually enters upon the relationship which is to be established."[100] Hence, the successful outcome of God's decree of justification is evidenced in man's reconciliation, that is, in the removal of "man's enmity with God" and his "harmonious direction towards God."[101] Thus although "both ideas expressed the divinely-initiated fellowship of men with God which is no longer obstructed by sin," distinctions can be made. It would seem, therefore, that insofar as man's guilt and consciousness thereof are barriers to fellowship with God, we must see them rendered inoperative by his justification or forgiveness. On the other hand, to the extent that the esence of man's sin evidenced in the "active contradiction" of his will toward God is removed, one must attribute this to reconciliation. The latter has a wider range than justification in that it expresses the new harmony between man and God intended in justification. The close correlation between these two conceptions remains, however. "Justification or forgiveness, conceived as effective, thus is identical with reconciliation as expressive of mutual fellowship between God and man."[102]

One of the ways in which Ritschl restores the dynamic that justification had among the Reformers is to recapture what is variously called its practical or teleological dimension. Reformation confessions that relate justification to eternal life and blessedness are cited.[103] These consequences are viewed as present by way of intention within justification. Special credit is due seventeenth-century Reformed theology for keeping this teleological dimension of justification in view. It recognized that since man's original destiny—forfeited through sin—was eternal life, restoration to fellowship with God through justification marked at least the new beginning of eternal life and therewith of blessedness.[104] Eternal life and therewith blessedness are present possessions.

Adoption is related to justification in much the same manner as reconciliation. Since sonship marks the new relationship between those justified and God, these two concepts are closely related. Hence if justification or forgiveness "refers generally to the admission of sinners to fellowship with God in spite of sin," adoption points to the "confidential relation to God which is thereby established"—a relationship described "in terms of the normal relation of children to a father."[105] Ritschl reasons that had orthodoxy recognized the obvious fact that the New Testament always traces man's forgiveness to God as Father rather than as Judge, many problems that plagued their attempts to coordinate the preceding conceptions could have been resolved.

The following thesis summarizes the argument:

In so far as justification is viewed as effective, it must be conceived as reconciliation, of such a nature that while memory, indeed, preserves the pain felt at the sin which has been committed, yet at the same time the place of mistrust towards God is taken by the positive assent of the will to God and His saving purpose.[106]

JUSTIFICATION AS THE ACT OF MAN: THE SUBJECTIVE POLE
OF THE DOCTRINE OF JUSTIFICATION

The preceding section focused attention upon the foundation of justification or forgiveness in God's will and revelation. Or to use Ritschl's image,
we envisaged justification, as it were, "from above"—from the divine
vantage point—or in terms of the priority of the divine grace. To do so,
however, required assuming the involvement of the believer, even though
his activity was not under review, and we recall that Ritschl attaches crucial
significance to the thesis that all statements about God presuppose man's
response to his revelation.[107] Although theology must emphasize God's gracious action more than man's response, the failure to develop the latter leads
to the rigidities of objectivism and orthodoxy. This danger on the right explains his repeated approbation of Melanchthon's dictum that "to know
Christ is to know his benefits," and also accounts for his appreciation of
Schleiermacher's methodology according to which all theological statements
express the perception of the divine activity by the believing subject.[108]
Hence theology cannot be satisfied with a description of God's role in man's
justification and reconciliation while neglecting man's subjective response.

The task of dogmatics in portraying the salvation effected by God is to
depict "the operations of God—justification, regeneration, the communica-
tion of the Holy Spirit, the bestowal of blessedness in the *summum bonum*
—in such a way as shall involve an analysis of the corresponding voluntary
activities in which man appropriates the operations of God."[109] Ritschl gives
expression to this point in a letter written in 1875. "Religion always has to
do with conviction, and 'where conviction is involved'. . . 'objective content
is not decisive in and for itself, but rather always in a subjective form' "[110]
In the face of alternative viewpoints either excessively objectivistic or subjectivistic he sought an effective balance between the divine and human
poles in theology and in this doctrine. This required steering a difficult
course between the dangers of orthodoxy and the theology of speculative
idealism on the one side and the perils of subjectivism found in some
successors of Schleiermacher on the other. Ritschl no doubt felt he had
recovered the healthy balance characteristic of the Reformers, and especially
of Luther. The extent to which he succeeded in this endeavor may be
described in our conclusion.

1. *Faith as the Condition of Justification: The Nature of Faith.*   If
to this point our exposition of Ritschl's understanding of man's justification
at the hands of God and therewith in the light of what God does in man's
behalf in Jesus Christ has appeared to minimize man's activity, our purpose
has been achieved. This is in keeping with the progression of Ritschl's

thought and provides the best possibility of interpreting him correctly. But now it is necessary to bring man's response into focus. Man's justification involves both passivity and activity. Hence, Ritschl speaks of man as the "subject of faith."[111] We must note the contours of the human activity involved in faith in order to avoid a mechanical view of justification and to do justice to man as a responsible being under God invested with human freedom.[112] Although the history of the church is replete with controversies between those magnifying the divine initiative and grace on the one hand and human response on the other, both poles have their rightful places. Let us turn then to Ritschl's view of man as the subject of faith.

The reader approaching him assuming that his entire theology may be reduced to value judgments and is therefore wholly subjective is unprepared for Ritschl's strictures against a theology based solely upon an analysis of man's religious experience and subjectivity. If one leaves out of account the sections dealing with the consequences of justification, the far larger portion of Vol. III of *Justification and Reconciliation* deals with the objective basis and foundation of justification rather than with the subjective appropriation thereof.[113] This is due, no doubt, in part, to Ritschl's lifelong controversy with Protestant mystics and Pietists and to his desire to expose those successors of the Reformation as illegitimate. At the same time, he was anxious to avoid any moralistic understanding of faith similar to Roman Catholic or Protestant precedents. These factors coupled with his reluctance to attempt a detailed account of the transition from the state of sin to that of reconciliation—a realm that "eludes all observation" and "remains a mystery"—must be kept in mind as we deal with this area in his thought.[114]

Faith may be seen as a "condition of justification" in that justification and faith are always correlates. His problem at this point is not to make it appear that justification ensues only upon faith or upon the life of faith. This error is avoided by the close connection he posits between justification and reconciliation so that in one sense the result is included in the prior cause. But more important, we must observe that faith cannot be understood apart from the prevenient grace of God. He puts it thus:

> Where the faith which is related to justification comes into exercise, it is related also to God. And as it is called forth by reconciliation on God's part, it must be considered, in its relation to justification, not as a work of man possessed of independent value, but rather as the act through which the new relation of men to God, realised in justification, is religiously recognised and actually established.[115]

Such a conception of justifying faith is distinguished from much Roman Catholic theology which holds that the faith involved in man's justification must be completed by love of neighbor; Ritschl opposes this teaching with his often reiterated thesis that the religious moment marked by faith in God is distinct from the ethical moment involving man's action in the world. To be sure, we shall observe that the ethical dimension of faith must be brought into proximity to the religious moment, but they are not to be confused, nor does the latter of necessity flow from the former.[116] We noted earlier that Ritschl's idea of justifying faith also necessitates his break with Pietism. Although Pietism does not make love of neighbor the condition of justification, its "wresting of the idea of justification to mean an analytic judgment on the value of faith . . . is an approach to the Catholic view."[117]

Although Ritschl initiates his discussion of the subjective pole of justification with a section on "Faith as a Condition of Justification" apart from any mention of the priority of the church, the argument makes its role pivotal. Since we have already seen how the individual's faith comes to birth and is nurtured by the believing community, we may be brief here.[118] Ritschl usually begins with a consideration of the church and views individuals within it; this order obtains, in part, because of the general truth that "every spiritual acquisition is brought about by the incalculable interaction between the freedom of the individual and the stimulating and guiding impressions which he receives from the fellowship with others."[119] More specifically, this subordination of the individual believer to the church as the "Mother of the Faithful" derives first from Christ's establishment of the church as the fellowship of forgiveness, and secondly, from the church's commission to proclaim the message of reconciliation through Word and Sacraments.[120] Thus the individual's faith in God means that "he is reconciled by God through Christ in the community founded by Christ."[121] He never tires of stressing the connection between faith and the church in order to avoid the perils of subjectivism and individualism in matters religious which developed because of an illicit interpretation of the Reformers and the influence of the Enlightenment.

Ritschl's favorite term to describe the nature of faith is "trust." This attitude indicates a direction of the will toward God which is the opposite of the mistrust and withdrawal from God characteristic of man's status as sinner. Here Ritschl follows Luther and Melanchthon rather than Calvin, who derives trust from faith. The term "trust" is most desirable because it involves a movement of the will and avoids the objectivism characteristic of both Catholic and Protestant Scholastic definitions of faith. "For faith," Ritschl writes, "regarded as trust, is no other than the direction of the will towards God as the highest end and the highest good."[122]

In another connection we observed Ritschl's increasing dissatisfaction with Schleiermacher's definition of faith as the feeling of "absolute dependence" upon God; the latter could be construed to allow a mystical understanding of the divine-human relationship and also failed to account properly for the priority of the will and its direction of subjective feelings.[123] Ritschl's attempt to preserve the best in the Lutheran conception of faith while bypassing orthodoxy is clear from the following: "From various passages in Melanchthon we ascertain that faith means neither the acknowledgment of the correctness of traditional facts, nor the acceptance of orthodox propositions, but trust in God's grace."[124] This idea so crucial for comprehending Ritschl's conception of faith became a kind of watchword of later Ritschlianism, and passed from it into the stream of theological thought in the late nineteenth and early twentieth centuries.[125]

The notion of trust is more suitable as a description of faith than the term "knowledge," which may be construed too abstractly and impersonally. This is in keeping with our analysis of Ritschl's epistemology and his concern to distinguish faith statements as value judgments from disinterested or theoretical knowledge about God. We do not intend to say that he denies altogether a noetic moment in faith; our purpose is rather to emphasize that the knowledge and acknowledgment which are part and parcel of faith are not to be construed in a theoretical or impersonal manner. The following lengthy statement encompasses the major elements that recur in all of Ritschl's descriptions of faith:

Christ comes to act upon the individual believer on the one hand through the historical remembrance of Him which is possible in the Church, on the other hand as the permanent Author of all the influences and impulses which are due to other men, and like in nature to Himself; and this necessarily takes place in a personal, and not in a material form. Accordingly, the result of reconciliation appears in its normal completeness in subjective *faith in Christ*. Here it is only necessary to repeat and to bring in what has already . . . been set forth as the view of the Reformers and as the inevitable result of observation. To believe in Christ implies that we accept the value of the Divine love, which is manifest in His work, for our reconciliation with God, with that trust which, directed to Him, subordinates itself to God as His and our Father; whereby we are assured of eternal life and blessedness. Faith in Christ is neither belief in the truth of His history nor assent to a scientific judgment of knowledge such as that presented by the Chalcedonian formula. It is not a recognition of His Divine nature of such a kind that, in affirming it, we disregard His life-work and His action for the salvation of those who have to reckon themselves as belonging to His community. In so far as trust in Him includes a knowledge of Him, this knowledge will determine the value of His work for our salvation. This value is to be decided by the fact that Christ, as the Bearer of the perfect revelation of God, through His solidarity with the Father, in the right exercise of His love and patience over the world, demonstrated his Godhead as man for the salvation of those whom, as His community, He at the same time represented before the Father by His obedience, and still represents. In this way He awakens the trust in Himself which, as passionate personal conviction, overcomes and subordinates to itself all the other motives of life, using as it does the tradition of Christ propagated in the Church, and thus putting itself into connection with all those who believe in Christ.[126]

2. *Justification by Faith and Assurance of Salvation.*[127]   Although the preceding quotation regarding the nature of faith is comprehensive, Ritschl allowed for latitude in the individual's experience of faith so long as it did not become determinative of scientific and ecclesiastical definitions. The latter must always show that true faith is related to Jesus Christ as its object. Thus he says that "faith in Christ is the full and clear expression of our subjective conviction of the truth of His religion."[128] That this "subjective conviction" which derives from, and is nurtured by, the church proclaiming Christ through Word and Sacraments must be presupposed in a dogmatic definition of faith has been noted, but Ritschl does not thereby rule out completely the realm of "immediate personal relation to Christ" in which the mediation of the community does not appear to be primary.[129]

However, Ritschl's attempt to revivify the Reformation understanding of faith involved him not only in debate with prevalent Roman Catholic views, but also with divergent Protestant and especially Lutheran views. One facet of this controversy focused on the problem of the assurance of salvation (*Heilsgewissheit*). We need to see both how Ritschl differed from others on this point and something of the problematic surrounding discussions of faith in his time.

a. *In the Reformers, Protestant orthodoxy and Lutheran confessionalism.*   Ritschl's disagreement with Protestant orthodoxy and nineteenth-century Lutheran confessionalism on the grounds for the assurance of salvation are similar and we may consider them together. Though Melanchthon deserves credit for speaking of faith as trust, he is the initiator of Protestant Scholasticism. Whereas Ritschl applauds Luther's conception of "pure doctrine" as a mark of the true church the "bare way . . . in which Melanchthon now proclaimed the *pura doctrina evangelii* as the characteristic of the Church betokens the scholastic style which distinguished the *praeceptor Germaniae* from the *reformator ecclesiae.*"[130] This pedantic perspective affected the whole tenor of orthodox theology, and particularly its analysis of justification and its consequences. Luther makes the *sola fide* central and "means by justification through faith in Christ a subjective religious experience of the believer within the Church, and not an objective theological *dictum* in the Church's system of doctrinal beliefs."[131] Moreover, he accents the practical import of justification for the entire Christian life, and we have seen that Ritschl develops this emphasis in showing the significance of justification for a total style of life.[132]

Whereas Ritschl sees a coalescence of the work of Christ and man's justification in Luther or the tendency to see the work of Christ as a means to man's salvation, orthodoxy, like medieval Catholicism, moves in more Scholastic fashion in placing the "doctrine *de officio Christi* or *de Christi mediatore* over against the doctrine *de justificatione* as its general historical prerequisite."[133] Faced with this alternative, Ritschl sides with the Reformers' religious understanding of justification which aligns it closely with the historical work of Christ on man's behalf, thereby avoiding orthodoxy's tendency toward distinguishing between the satisfaction rendered to God by Christ on the one hand and the appropriation of the merits of Christ by believers at a later date on the other.[134] Calvinism held the work of Christ and man's justification together because of its view that Christ always acted as the head of the church or in behalf of the elect. The proclivity of Lutheran orthodoxy, however, was to move in the direction of making man's justification contingent upon his regeneration.[135]

In yet other ways the Reformers' teaching on justification as it relates to assurance is markedly different from that of orthodoxy. Melanchthon, Calvin, and Protestant confessions teach that faith, which relies upon the work of Christ and the promise of forgiveness, issues in "peace of mind, inward satisfaction, and comfort."[136] In place of the sinner's feeling of guilt and uncertainty regarding salvation, the "certainty which accompanies trust in the justification assured by Christ can therefore only be interpreted as a feeling of pleasure."[137]

This correlation between God's act in Christ and man's trust brings us to the essential element in the Reformers' view of assurance, namely, that the "subjective *certainty of justification* springs only from a vision of the object of faith."[138] However, both Melanchthon and Calvin make allowance for a fluctuation in man's subjective certainty of salvation. Both also speak of the believer's good works as a possible confirmation of his faith, and point toward that ideal state of faith when feelings of doubt disappear. Like Luther, they also assert that this "stage . . . of faith [i.e., when certainty of salvation does not exist] can only be overcome by deepened attention to God's gracious promise."[139]

Orthodoxy departs from the Reformers by attempting to effect assurance of salvation through encouraging assent to the doctrine of justification. In Lutheranism this involved the individual's "practical experiment" of subsuming himself beneath the "universal promise of grace in the Divine word." Since it was held that the Holy Spirit moves within the orbit of God's promise, assurance obtained through the subjection of the individual to the universal. In Calvinism, it is axiomatic that God's promise of salvation is effective for the elect. This leads to concern about the marks of true faith which authenticate one's certainty of salvation. Once again it is believed that the Holy Spirit operates in this progression to effect full assurance of salvation. The Reformed approach argues for the assurance of salvation in terms of deductive or syllogistic reasoning.[140]

Since Ritschl sees no prospect of the subjective desire for certainty of salvation being satisfactorily answered in orthodoxy, it is understandable that he opposed its revival in nineteenth-century confessional Lutheranism. He sees their common error thus: "They come to this, that we should derive our individual assurance of salvation inferentially from the general article of faith of the forgiveness of sins through the merits of Christ, instead of ascertaining it directly from the subjective effects of reconciliation."[141] Ritschl's theological method and his view of justification preclude sympathy with this approach. These factors, coupled with their failure to recognize that human nature cannot be comprehended in terms of knowing and willing alone, but must include the realm of feeling and subjectivity, account for his rejection of the solution proposed by orthodoxy and Lutheran confessionalism on the manner in which assurance of salvation obtains. Had they comprehended the teleological or practical aspects of justification anticipated in the Reformers, suggestions for a creative solution to this problem would have been at hand.

b. *In Roman Catholicism.*   Ritschl appears more sympathetic toward Roman Catholic views on assurance of salvation than toward Protestant orthodoxy. We noted that the Roman Catholic tradition differs from the Evangelical in that it seeks to show how a sinner is transformed into an actively righteous person; this leads one tradition in medieval Catholicism to maintain that justification and the assurance of salvation are dependent upon both faith and works. According to this view, however, absolute assurance of salvation may not or need not be attained.[142] However, Ritschl finds that the tradition of Bernard of Clairvaux approximates the Evangelical position in affirming that complete trust in the divine grace carries with it "certainty of its object and satisfaction in it."[143] He sees both of these traditions represented in Trent and concludes—contrary to the usual Protestant interpretation of the Sixth Session of Trent, which opposes the Evangelical view of assurance—that the Tridentine dogma "by no means betrays an intention altogether to deny the assurance of faith."[144] Obviously, the Roman Catholic polemic against the Evangelical affirmation that assurance is bound up with man's justification is predicated upon the assumption that the faith of schismatics outside the Roman Church is subjective delusion. That is, since it does not have the true God for its object, it cannot lead to certainty.[145]

In post-Tridentine Catholicism, both of the preceding positions regarding the assurance of salvation are maintained. The monastic tradition of Bernard allows for a kind of perfection deriving from man's obedience to the divine laws prescribed by the church. But even here, the childlike fear of God (*timor filialis*) which is enjoined accords neither with the Biblical nor the Evangelical understanding of the same. In place of a relationship of trust in God as one's Father which is the essence of the Evangelical view, Aquinas and others see fear engendered by man's repeated breach of the divine law and authority.

Obviously, this view of the fear of God leads to uncertainty about man's salvation.[146] That Roman Catholicism allows for a state of perfection which goes beyond childlike fear to one in which there is "freedom of familiar intercourse with God" does not seem to Ritschl to be the pathway to the attainment of the assurance of salvation and the true fulfillment of one's justification. The mystical union breaks down the necessary distinction between the Creator and the creature; it is also deficient because it is predicated upon a "deliberate straining of feeling" which is "only too quickly dispelled by the sense of desolation, desertion, and dryness of soul."[147] Hence even the monastic tradition of Bernard in Catholicism— which allows for the possibility of the assurance of salvation—is marred by flaws. But these are not so serious as those afflicting the church's more normative teaching on assurance about which Ritschl speaks in a polemical vein: "On the other hand, for the sake of the discipline of the great mass, it is expedient to foster the feeling of uncertainty about one's salvation, in order to intensify the people's zeal for the works which the Church prescribes."[148] Thus Roman Catholicism makes no final resolution regarding the Christian's assurance of salvation. It is able to embrace these divergent approaches with regard to assurance in the same manner in which Augustine and Pelagius are included within the fold. Ritschl concludes that "this Church fares best by using a double measure and a double weight."[149]

c. *In Pietism.* Pietism's solution to the question of the certainty of salvation is, in a sense, an answer to unresolved problems within Roman Catholicism and Protestantism.[150] Ritschl was so involved in a running controversy with Pietists holding influential ecclesiastical and theological posts in mid-nineteenth-century Germany that his theology cannot be understood fully apart from his opposition to them. His encounter with Pietism appears to place him in a dilemma. On the one hand, we noted his dissatisfaction with orthodoxy's inadequate grasp of the subjective appropriation of salvation; this derived from their Scholastic bent and a seeming incapacity to appreciate the significant role that man's feeling plays in life in general and in the experience of salvation in particular.[151] On the other hand, Pietism seems to fill this vacuum by giving primary attention to the realm of feeling in matters religious. Ritschl applauds their intention. However, the manner in which the sphere of religious feeling and experience finds expression in Pietism, and the theological deficiencies connected therewith, led Ritschl to become a most vigorous opponent of Pietism.[152]

According to Ritschl, Pietism fell heir to the problem that orthodoxy failed to solve, namely, how the general truth concerning the forgiveness of sins becomes real for the individual.[153] He agrees with Pietists that the "problem of personal assurance is insoluble if it be conceived in a form which represents the subject as passive."[154] However, whereas Ritschl always ties justification and the assurance of salvation to one's participation in the believing community, Pietism isolates the individual from the church in its obsessive quest for personal certainty of salvation. On the basis of his research, Ritschl traces Protestant mysticism and Pietism to medieval antecedents by way of Luther's positive evaluation of the sermons of Tauler and the *Theologia Germanica,* a popular handbook on mysticism and medieval piety published twenty-six times in the sixteenth century in the edition Luther utilized!

Lutheranism in particular provided fertile ground for elements of medieval piety to take root because both traditions were concerned with the problem of individual certainty of salvation.[155] In Pietism, the individual's quest for certainty of salvation leads to the creation of conventicles apart from the church, that is, the gathering of those giving themselves to the *praxis pietatis.*[156] Thus a separatist Pietism, which counseled withdrawal from the world as necessary for obtaining personal sanctity and the assurance of salvation, replaced the ordinary means of grace as the pathway to assurance with an emphasis upon an acute conversion experience, certain penitential exercises, and the quest for personal holiness.

A major source of Ritschl's displeasure with Pietism stems from its concentration upon an acute conversion experience as the basis for arriving at assurance of salvation. To require this presupposes a radical state of sin which has not had the benefit of the regenerative influence of the church and its nurture.[157] Moreover, the kind of conversion encouraged is suspect because it leads to an isolation from the larger body of Christ and minimizes the ordinary means of grace in preaching and Sacraments. A more serious error is the pietistic tendency to regard regeneration or the "new birth" effected through the Holy Spirit as the basis for justification, thereby making God's decision contingent upon man's.[158] Repeated claims concerning the Holy Spirit appear to Ritschl as typical of sectarian attempts to find support for "passionate zeal, or pathological experiences, or forced, vague, aimless efforts to reach passive assurance of salvation."[159] The portrayal of the Holy Spirit as a "hyperphysical natural force" or as a substance is a clear departure from the New Testament.[160] For Ritschl, the Spirit works in the church and is attested when trust in God and moral activity in his

Kingdom are present; esoteric experiences of individuals isolated from the church in which the Spirit dwells are therefore suspect.[161] This does not mean that regeneration fails to occur; however, this fact is knowable only within the community that proclaims forgiveness of sins and in which the Word is heard in faith. Further description of the precise manner in which regeneration takes place is hidden from theological analysis. Hence, Ritschl rests his case as follows: "How this state is brought about eludes all observations, like the development of the individual spiritual life in general."[162]

A passage from the second edition of *Justification and Reconciliation*—subsequently deleted—reveals both Ritschl's polemic against Pietism and something of his own position:

> I am again and again deluged with recurring assertions that I must adopt and acknowledge an immediate, personal relationship to Christ, a direct relationship to God; otherwise all discussion concerning ethical and religious functions supposedly lack the necessary context and inter-relationships. According to my viewpoint, theology has for its concern communal knowledge. The manner in which the religious functions of the community are modified by individuals is not the subject matter of theology, and the way in which normal religious experiences are re-stricted or falsified either through lack of reason or sin falls under the aegis of pastoral care (*Seelsorge*). . . . If it were supposed that I accepted their position [i.e., Pietists, mystics, and others], I could say nothing about it as a theologian. But I do not countenance it at all because I see in their demand for, or claim to, an immediate, personal relationship to Christ what the Reformers saw in certain Anabaptist manifestations—what they called enthusiasm (*Schwärmerei*). One has a personal rela-tionship to Christ, namely reverent faith in him only through the media-tion of the Gospel with which he clothes himself—as Calvin teaches. . . . In this light it is understandable that my opponents will not consent to a discussion of the grounds of their assertions, but retreat repeatedly to a repetition of their slogan; but they ought not in so doing to com-mend themselves as Lutheran or churchly.[163]

Another spiritual exercise inculcated by Pietists as the means of effecting certainty of salvation was the "conflict of penitence" (*Busskampf*), a per-version of an earlier Protestant doctrine and practice.[164] The fact that the *Confessio Augustana* and other Lutheran confessions relate the believer's repentance both to the law and the gospel—in keeping with certain state-ments of Luther and Melanchthon—represents a serious misunderstanding in Ritschl's estimate. It makes it possible that the repentant believer will not recognize that the Lawgiver who judges him is the "God of his salva-tion," with the result that he ends in uncertainty concerning the forgiveness of his sins as he undergoes terrors of conscience.[165] Ritschl's positive alter-native always refers us back to the understanding of faith in terms of trust evident in Luther and Melanchthon. "The real change in the sinner is proved by the fact that he is impelled, by the forgiveness of his sins, by the Divine decision that for Christ's sake he is *deo acceptus* . . . to exercise that reverent trust in God which is the characteristic activity of the new life."[166] This does not mean that Ritschl proposes a perfectionism which denies the presence and consciousness of sin in the Christian's life; on the contrary, these are real, but are seen in the light of the forgiveness promised by Christ to his followers and not in terms of the law apart from him.

In concluding Ritschl's analysis of Pietism's methods for attaining assurance of salvation, we need to mention one other characteristic. His historical studies led him to conclude that medieval patterns of devotion which stressed the love of the believer to Christ got a foothold within Lutheranism soon after the completion of the *Book of Concord* and somewhat later in the Reformed tradition.[167] We noted that Ritschl was under constant attack from Pietists and others who held that "an immediate personal relation to Christ and to God is the kernel of the Christian life"; they interpreted his view as dated because of its agreement with Reformation confessions.[168] To this charge, Ritschl replies: "I affirm, on the contrary, that the Reformation antiquated that 'love to Christ' which is here in question. For love very distinctly implies the equality of the person loving with the beloved."[169] The kind of intercourse between believers and Christ in Bernard is patterned upon the love between bride and bridegroom in the Song of Solomon. Ritschl finds this imagery reprehensible and out of keeping with the New Testament and the Reformation because it does away with the reverence due God, lowers God to man's level, and overlooks the Godhead of Christ in its desire for a sensuous relationship with Jesus in his humanity alone.

In addition to these objections, Ritschl adds the following: First, the assumption that Christ is present without mediation in the act of religious intuition or imagination is naïve. His epistemology requires him to say that the thing-in-itself is never directly perceived as it is, for it is always modified by an entire cluster of phenomena. Applied to the apprehension of, and devotion to, Christ this means that he comes to us through the community and the means of grace he has ordained.[170] Secondly, the religious experience involved in this kind of piety lies beyond the aegis of a scientific theology and is something less than edifying for the church. Third, the mode of devotion in question not only pulls Christ down to man's level in a manner out of keeping with Evangelical piety, but also goes awry in seeking feelings of pleasure and happiness as the goal of contemplative love. This represents what Otto Ritschl somewhere refers to as a "feminine type of piety" for which his father had little or no sympathy! Ritschl interprets the goal of Evangelical piety to be that "religious strength" which enables the believer to realize his reconciliation by living victoriously in the world. This represents the *Lebensführung*, or mode of life, which results if reconciliation is truly appropriated. Fourth, and most important, the encouragement of "strainings of fancy" in order to effect this sensuous relationship with Christ does not lead to blessedness and assurance, but rather to "unhappiness," the feeling of desertion, and "dullness of feeling."[171]

We may summarize the main reasons for Ritschl's dissatisfaction with the interpretation of justification, the assurance of salvation, and the Christian life in Protestant Pietism and mysticism by reviewing the characteristics of this type of individualistic and sectarian piety. They are: the requirement of a radical experience of repentance and conversion; the practice of self-abasement through penitential exercises; the love of Christ which leads to immediate union with him as the beloved; the inculcation of an attitude of withdrawal from the world; and the attainment of the assurance of salvation through adherence to these steps. Whether taken individually or as a whole, these pietistic procedures represent a radical reversal of the Reformation view of justification. The fact that Pietists and mystics made such significant inroads within Protestantism is clear evidence that the "teleological relation of the idea of justification to eternal life as consisting in freedom over the world had been forgotten."[172] By this, Ritschl intends to point up the thesis—yet to be developed—that justification properly understood is determinative of the believer's attitude toward, and action in, the world.

In terms of our model, the Reformation stressed the objective pole and therewith the divine ground of man's justification; Pietists accented the subjective pole and thus the manner of its appropriation. The Reformation spoke of the community under God; Pietists, of the individual under God. The Reformers and orthodoxy saw God's judgment concerning justification as synthetic, since it was grounded solely in God's will; Pietists made the judgment of justification analytic and based it upon the character of man's faith and moral perfection. Both Pietism and orthodoxy held that the righteousness accruing to the believer by virtue of the divine judgment must be understood in terms of moral perfection. But whereas orthodoxy taught that Christ's moral perfection was imputed to believers by God in spite of their imperfection, Pietists regarded this as a bit of divine duplicity. They argued that such a judgment would not pacify the anxious conscience and held "that God imputes to the believer the moral perfection which is contained in faith as the principal of the new life that is beginning."[173]

Thus in different variations, Pietism in the nineteenth century regarded the "life of God in the believer" as the basis of his gradual moral transformation and perfection, and therewith of his full justification. In the process, the priority of the religious pole over the ethical pole of Christianity is rejected. Though Ritschl contends that concentration upon man's moral transformation roots in mysticism and can be traced through Kant and Schleiermacher up to his own time, it is not in keeping with the New Testament, Paul, or the Reformation.[174] Normative Evangelical Christianity exalts "the common religious transformation above the moral renewal of the individual."[175] Ritschl finds Pietism to be reminiscent of Socinianism, which makes justification dependent upon the individual's "practical obedience of faith," even though God judges man's imperfect obedience as though it were perfect. He opposes this whole tendency not only because it is predicated upon the false assumption that man's justification is dependent upon "moral renewal" but also because the basis for arriving at assurance by this means is dubious. Ritschl questions whether the individual's acknowledgment of God's judgment concerning his perfection upon the grounds of the germ of perfection present within him—which does not correspond with his own self-knowledge—can lead to inner peace and the "joy of sanctification."[176] The latter viewpoint appears less tenable than the orthodox doctrine that it sought to replace.

Our concluding statement must provide a glimpse into Ritschl's alternative with respect to the subjective appropriation of justification and the assurance of salvation in contrast to the preceding approaches—Roman Catholic, orthodox Protestant and confessional Lutheran, Pietist and mystical. We are now able to see what forces played upon him as he developed his view of the "consequences" of justification or reconciliation.[177] We now know the road Ritschl has traveled and the direction he is going. Certainly one of the keys to interpreting his theology as a whole, and the doctrine of justification and reconciliation in particular, is to be found in his first systematic treatment of the subjective aspects of justification. The section entitled "Justification as Ground of the Positive Freedom Given by Faith in Providence" and the following one tracing the history of this idea in Protestantism are crucial for interpreting Ritschl. Here for the first time we see the full import of the practical thrust of his doctrine of justification and reconciliation, and he returns repeatedly to this theme at decisive points in this volume and in other writings.[178]

Ritschl's concern is to accentuate the practical effects of man's justification and reconciliation. We saw above that he could express this idea by speaking of man's dominion over the world. Hence even as Ritschl's definition of religion requires that man's attitude toward God have as its correlate his attitude toward the world, so man's justification through God's verdict carries with it—if properly understood—man's changed attitude toward the world. The initial programmatic statement of his thesis reads as follows: "If justification by faith is the basal conception of Evangelical

Christianity, it is impossible that it can express the relation of men to God and Christ without at the same time including a peculiar *attitude of the believer to the world* founded upon that relation."[179]

At last we have found the point at which assurance of salvation obtains for Ritschl. He writes:

> The sinner who, by his former mistrust of God, shows himself to be dependent on the world, can be proved to have undergone a change through his trust in God's forgiveness, only if with that trust there is combined a new lordship over the world due to confidence in God's all-embracing care. Thus, too, this exercise of faith in providence and of patience under divinely-ordained sufferings is the form in which the believer attains assurance of the salvation guaranteed to him through Christ alone. For since the dominion over the world, exercised through faith in the Reconciler, brings with it its corresponding feeling of pleasure, the *laetitia spiritualis* contains in itself the conditions of its continuity and inward equipoise. Apart from these functions of trust and patience, we can find no place for assurance of our justification by faith. Auditory hallucinations conveying anything of the kind have nothing to do with the case.[180]

This résumé of Ritschl's analysis of the practical ramifications of justification provides preliminary confirmation of his adherence to the theological method set forth in the introductory paragraphs of the final volume of *Justification and Reconciliation.* We noted his insistence that the object of the theologian's investigations was the measurable effect that Christian faith had upon the *Lebensführung,* or mode of life, characterizing the Christian community. Neither traditional theological formulas nor esoteric individual experience are acceptable norms for verifying the consequences of man's new relationship to God.[181] Ritschl's program and its lineage became clear to him in the course of his Biblical and historical research. He writes:

> We must give up the question—derived from Scholastic psychology, but insoluble—how man is laid hold of, or pervaded, or filled by the Holy Spirit. What we have to do is rather to verify life in the Holy Spirit by showing that believers know God's gracious gifts (1 Cor. ii. 12), that they call on God as their Father (Rom. viii. 15), that they act with love and joy, with meekness and self-control (Gal. v. 22), that they are on their guard above all against party spirit, and cherish rather a spirit of union (1 Cor. iii. 1–4). In these statements the Holy Spirit is not denied, but recognised and understood. Nor is this method of procedure anything new. On the contrary, it has been employed by Schleiermacher, and the explanation of justification by faith to be found in the *Apology of the Augsburg Confession* follows the same plan. If Christianity is to

be made practically intelligible, no method but this can be adopted. For Christianity is made unintelligible by those formulas about the order of individual salvation, which are arrived at on the opposite view and prescribed to faith without a directly appended explanation of their practical relations and their verification.[182]

We are ready to look in more detail at Ritschl's development of the practical implications of man's justification in terms of what he regards to have been the true intention of the Reformers. Though acknowledging that his own position has required him to modify certain aspects of the Reformers' teaching and the Lutheran Symbols, he stresses the similarities between them. He concludes his treatment of the objective and subjective poles of the doctrine of justification and reconciliation by maintaining that "on the whole" his development of the doctrine of justification "stands in the line of direct continuity with the intention of the Reformers and the standards of the Lutheran Church. Especially is this the case as regards the practical aspect of justification, its significance as explaining the peculiar character of that view of the world and of life which we owe to the Reformation."[183]

CHAPTER IV

The Consequences of Reconciliation: The Christian Life and the Kingdom of God

INTRODUCTION

Our interpretation of Ritschl's understanding of justification and reconciliation has followed in the main the sequence of his argument. Thus we have placed the discussion of the consequences of reconciliation at the conclusion of our exposition—a pattern he established by making this subject the concern of the final, brief chapter of *Justification and Reconciliation*. This brevity may be welcomed by the reader somewhat wearied by the scope and complexity of Ritschl's position, but it would lead to a disastrous misunderstanding of his entire system and of the doctrine in question were we to measure its significance by its length.

At several points we called attention to Ritschl's insistence that a proper correlation of the doctrines of justification and reconciliation and the Kingdom of God encompass everything essential in Christianity. The discussion of the consequences of reconciliation with God brings these two foci of his theology into closer interaction than at any other point. For the teleological thrust of God's reconciling activity, which pertains both to the individual and to humanity, is correlated throughout with the concept of the Kingdom of God. Only in this way can the full import of reconciliation be clarified. To omit dealing with its effects upon the corporate consciousness of the church, the subjective consciousness of the individual, and the destiny of humanity would be indicative of theological objectivism. The grandeur of reconciliation is evidenced in the way man's religious functions are altered and further how these in turn lead to changed moral attitudes and actions.

Ritschl relates justification and reconciliation to certain religious and ethical virtues so often that Wendland can speak of this as a "pet theme."[1]

Fabricius adopts a similar view in suggesting that the development of the consequences of reconciliation may well be regarded as a third focal point of his theology in addition to the foci represented by redemption and the Kingdom of God.[2] This proposal has some merit, for one can argue, as we have just suggested, that the religious and ethical poles in Ritschl's theology interact more fruitfully in this section than anywhere else. The end result of man's reconciliation with God is a changed relationship between man and God which finds expression in a new *Lebensideal,* or ideal style of life, marked by different religious attitudes and functions and a new kind of moral activity determined by man's relationship to the Kingdom of God. We may hold in abeyance the question whether the pole of redemption represented by reconciliation or the ethical pole represented by the Kingdom of God actually dominates this area of Ritschl's theology. Now we must look at the picture of the redeemed man: this is what man is intended to be in relationship to God, his neighbor, and the world. What is more, here we see Ritschl's vision of humanity fulfilling God's purpose in his Kingdom.

Various excerpts from Ritschl's correspondence attest his own conviction that the religious and ethical ramifications of justification and reconciliation occupied a central role in his thought. At the time of the completion of the manuscript of the second volume of *Justification and Reconciliation* in 1872, he wrote his friend, Diestel, that his Biblical investigations of the problem of "Righteousness as the Attribute of Believers" had led to significant findings. This research confirmed Ritschl's hunch that justification by faith was closely correlated with the religious attitudes of trust in divine providence and humility.[3] In January of 1874, Ritschl, on the verge of completing the final volume of his magnum opus, was invited to deliver a lecture to the "Göttingen Women's Auxiliary." He chose a theme that had engaged him in the closing pages of that work, namely, "Christian Perfection." Fabricius is no doubt correct in viewing this brief monograph— which received a wide circulation with the title *Die christliche Vollkommenheit*—not simply as a repetition of what Ritschl had just written in his larger volume; rather, it is a distillation of the essential ethical and practical ideas in his theology.[4] In March, 1874, the month in which the second volume of *Justification and Reconciliation* was published, he wrote his publisher the following:

> I have had the opportunity at this critical juncture to make considerable improvements in the manuscript [*J. R.* III, published in August, 1874] which is to appear shortly. In this respect, the construction of the lecture [*Die christliche Vollkommenheit*] which I sent you exerted a very salutary influence. In that I conceived this lecture out of the overflow, as it were, of long years of labor, certain ideas—which were threads running through the larger work—became completely clear to me for the first

time. Thereafter it was possible to recast certain pivotal sections of the latter [J. R. III] which I had originally written with some difficulty—despite the fact that they had been re-written three or four times—in the light of the whole which this lecture afforded. In this way the book [J. R. III] has benefited appreciably.[5]

Seen in this light, Ritschl's essay on *Christian Perfection* occupies an important place in his writings and provides one of the best points at which to grasp the bent of his whole system. He himself often called attention to the fact that the Reformers' characteristic view of salvation found its fulfillment in their conception of Christian perfection—a point he attempts to establish in the historical and Biblical investigations in the first two volumes of *Justification and Reconciliation*. On June 13, 1872, he wrote his brother in this vein:

> Melanchthon and Calvin make it abundantly clear that belief in providence and patience in the face of evil, that humility and the feeling of freedom, represent the manner in which we experience peace with God; thus they should be seen as the immediate reflex of justification.[6]

Indeed, at times Ritschl can maintain that a correct understanding of Christian perfection provides the only true norm of Evangelical Christianity, and that it should replace the confession of dogmas. "Membership in the Evangelical Church is rather to be determined by what constitutes Christian perfection according to Evangelical teaching."[7]

CHRISTIAN PERFECTION, OR THE PROTESTANT *LEBENSIDEAL*[8]

Although Ritschl did not organize all the materials relating to the religious and ethical consequences of man's reconciliation in the final chapter of *Justification and Reconciliation* in terms of the Evangelical idea of perfection, it certainly does no violence to his thought for us to do so. The latter is synonymous with what is elsewhere designated the Protestant *Lebensideal*, or ideal life-style, and is referred to often in the later writings after 1874. Thus in *The History of Pietism*, one of Ritschl's aims was to show the basic differences between Roman Catholic and Protestant *Lebensidealen*. In no small measure these were due to divergent conceptions of perfection: whereas Roman Catholicism correlates perfection with monasticism—the ideal of the few—which negates and depreciates life in the world, Protestantism—following the lead of the Augsburg Confession—correlates perfection with justification by faith, regards perfection as the mark of every believer, and sees it coming to expression in the Christian's life in the world. Ritschl summarizes this as follows:

According to the ideal life-style of our Reformation, faith in God's providence stands side by side with prayer and the high estimation of one's vocation as the place for the practice of love towards men. . . . This interpretation of one's vocation is thus also a basic principle of Protestantism: it is the practical expression of the truth that Christianity is not to be understood as negating the world, but rather as permeating and transforming it. This reading of the significance of the Reformation principle concerning vocation and its influence is integral to it, even though it is neither efficiently grounded nor systematically developed by them.[9]

At various points, he is at pains to show that his conception of the Evangelical *Lebensideal* and Christian perfection represent the legitimate completion of the Reformers' correlation of justification and reconciliation with perfection. They rightly interpreted certain emphases of the apostle Paul in this regard, but they and even more their successors failed to realize the full import of this correlation.

The disregard of the practical implications of justification for the Christian's life in the world in orthodox Lutheranism provided one basis for the rationalistic critique and subsequent dissolution of Evangelical Christianity. Yet Ritschl credits the Enlightenment and rationalism for preserving a belief in providence, although they erroneously saw this belief as a tenet of natural religion. Since Pietists held it to be axiomatic that everything taught by rationalists was false, they allowed belief in providence as a mark of Christian perfection to go by the board. To be sure, Pietism developed a view of perfection, but Ritschl rejected its ascetic, individualistic tendencies for being more reminiscent of medieval monastic piety than of the Reformation. Nineteenth-century Lutheran confessionalism saw no connection between justification by faith and Christian perfection and its doctrinaire interpretation of the Christian faith served only to contribute, in Ritschl's estimate, to the increasing disenchantment of the laity with a version of Christianity unrelated to human existence. Ritschl's version of the Protestant ideal style of life is set forth in order to show that Protestantism has something relevant to say about man's life in the world. It is noteworthy that in the process Ritschl affirms in modified form elements of the Enlightenment and Immanuel Kant relating to the ethical sphere of Christian existence.[10]

THE RELIGIOUS VIRTUES CHARACTERISTIC OF CHRISTIAN PERFECTION

For Ritschl, there are two dimensions of Christian perfection, the religious and the ethical, corresponding to the two poles constituting Christianity, and though we shall observe the reciprocal effects that each has upon the other, he does not want to equate them. A statement from *Instruction in the Christian Religion,* which first appeared in 1875, expresses this distinction more precisely than some earlier statements:

> The Christian perfection which corresponds to the personal example of Christ Himself separates itself into the religious functions of sonship with God and dominion over the world, i.e., trust in the fatherly providence of God, humility, patience, prayer, and into the ethical functions of dutiful action in one's calling and the development of the ethical virtues. In this coherence of the spiritual life the individual attains to the value of the whole which is superior to the worth of all the world as the order of a partial and naturally conditioned existence. In this is included independence toward all special authority. This attainment of the Christian religion is the end actually aimed at in all religions [§ 8], namely, the assuring of the value of our spiritual life, in spite of its limiting complication with nature or the world, by means of the appropriation of the divine life or of the evident divine purpose.[11]

This quotation indicates that he intends both to distinguish and to relate the religious and ethical virtues evident in the Protestant *Lebensideal.* Although we cannot pursue the question here, Fabricius may be correct in suggesting that Ritschl gave increasing priority to the religious rather than the ethical pole in his thought in his later years.[12] At any rate, by the time he wrote Ch. 9 of Vol. III of *Justification and Reconciliation* in the years 1873–1874, it is evident that he wants to show that the religious virtues precede the ethical. The three editions of this volume reveal no change in the title affixed to the division dealing with "the Consequences" of reconciliation. The title reads: "The Religious Functions Which Spring from Reconciliation with God, and the Religious Form of Moral Action."[13] Moreover, no substantive changes are made in these pages after the first edition. He chooses to analyze the religious virtues prior to the ethical in order to avoid a Catholicizing view which makes man's salvation dependent upon good works. Both the religious and ethical activities lead to blessedness, but the former is not contingent upon the latter.[14]

Let us turn first to a consideration of the religious virtues. One statement from the Augsburg Confession—cited frequently as a guide—and another from Luther indicate how Ritschl relates virtues and perfection:

> Christian perfection consists in reverence towards God and this trust, grounded in Christ, that God is gracious to us; in the sure expectation of His aid in all things which are undertaken in our vocation, and at the same time diligence in the doing of good deeds in the service of our vocation. True perfection and true service to God entails these activities and does not involve refraining from marriage, or in begging, or in filthy clothes. . . . The state of perfection is evidenced in the fact that with confident faith one despises death and life, fame and the whole

world, and that one is of service to all in radiant love. But one hardly finds men who place more store in life and fame and who are more impoverished in faith and fear death more than the monks.[15]

Although both religious and ethical virtues are included in these quotations, they serve to introduce our entire discussion. Commenting on these statements from the Augsburg Confession and Luther, Ritschl writes:

> I take the liberty of grouping these statements so that I draw together reverence and trust in God in *humility;* in place of the expectation of the help of God and the despising of death and the world I put *faith and commitment* to the divine providence; thereto is added *calling upon and giving thanks to God in prayer;* and finally, *faithfulness (Treue) in one's ethical calling for the common good.* Christian perfection consists in these activities which represent the task of every person.[16]

The religious virtues characteristic of the Protestant *Lebensideal* evident in the above quotations and typical in Ritschl's discussions of this topic are faith in the divine providence and its corollary, dominion over the world, patience, humility, and prayer. Of the religious virtues singled out, a dominant position is accorded faith in divine providence and its corollary, namely, man's dominion over the world. We must recall that religion for Ritschl always has to do with the triad composed of God, man, and the world. We are further prepared for this coupling if we recall that an earlier discussion of the subjective side of justification included an important section entitled "Justification as Ground of the Positive Freedom Given by Faith in Providence."[17] Belief in divine providence appears again and again as the chief validation of man's reconciliation with God. *"Faith in the providence of God,* namely [the belief] that all evil as well as good is ordered for our development is not at all due to observation of the world, or to scientific investigation, or to natural religion; it is rather the most characteristic test of the religion of reconciliation."[18] This leads Ritschl to designate one of the two pivotal sections dealing with the religious perfections resulting from man's reconciliation with God as "Faith in the Fatherly Providence of God."[19]

To believe in God's providential leading in all of life is to move from the state of sin characterized by mistrust, or perhaps fear of God, to one of trust and confidence in him. This is the divine-human relationship God intends. This change in man's subjective consciousness is what Ritschl refers to as a different *Selbstgefühl.* Thus he can write: "It [i.e., justification by faith] creates in man a peculiar feeling of self (*eigenthümliches Selbstgefühl*) which evidences itself in his hope of permanent acknowledgment by God and in patience under suffering, and which is charged with a power superior to all the forces and dispensations of this world."[20] This new *Selbstgefühl*—manifesting itself in trust toward God and related religious virtues—is the experiential and empirical verification of reconciliation with God. Especially, Luther recognized that the freedom of the Christian man is seen in "that those who are righteous by faith are made kings and priests—priests, through the opening of the *accessus ad patrem* and the right of prayer to God; kings, through their trust in God Who governs all things for the best, and will help the believer to surmount all obstacles."[21] This new relationship between man and God which derives from Christ, the Reconciler, assures man of his blessedness (*Seligkeit*) and eternal life.

Apart from the exercise of the virtues of patience, humility, and prayer, which attest man's belief in divine providence, it is difficult to say anything further as to what this means about God's activity. That is to say, Ritschl is always more concerned to point to the effects which God's action and revelation have upon man than to that activity in itself. To be sure, he does develop the "Doctrine of the Person and Life-Work of Christ" so as to show the bearing of the same upon believers in their relationship to God. In a manner clearly reminiscent of Schleiermacher, Ritschl at several points interprets one aspect of the uniqueness of Jesus in terms of his perfect and complete communion with God. Religion, which concerns, in part, fellowship between man and God, comes to perfect expression in Jesus, and "no other has been able to bring men to the desired goal of nearness to God."[22] Thus in responding to the impulse deriving from Christ, we, too, may enjoy communion with God similar to his. Though generally it would seem that Ritschl is more reserved and agnostic than Schleiermacher in speaking about the God-consciousness of Jesus and therewith of his relationship to God—preferring the ethical estimate of his Person—it is clear that Jesus' complete exercise of the religious virtues reveals that humanity comes to fulfillment in him. He writes:

> If, then, Christ is to be thought of as Priest, the fundamental form for this priestly activity is contained in each moment of His unique consciousness, that as the Son of God He stands to God as Father in a relation of incomparable fellowship, which is realised in His knowledge of God, in the surrender of His will to God's providential guiding, and in the security of feeling [*Gefühlsstimmung*] which accompanies the same.[23]

Despite the fact that Ritschl could speak in this vein about the God-consciousness of Jesus, his penchant is always to accentuate the way it affects the religious and ethical attitudes of other men toward the world. In a letter to Hermann Scholz, a pastor and teacher in the Moravian tradition in which Schleiermacher was schooled, Ritschl advised against adopting a kind of emulation of Jesus characteristic of Pietism but out of keeping with either the New Testament or Lutheran Symbols. "Reconciliation with God through Christ is experienced in one's belief in providence etc." and not in the kind of piety involved in imitating Christ which is more medieval and sectarian in provenance.[24] Even though here and elsewhere Ritschl relates man's confidence in God's fatherly providence to the attitude adopted by Jesus, his orientation is not always as Christocentric as one might antici- pate. To be sure, he affirms that it is by virtue of God's saving revelation that we know of his "general saving purpose" in the world. In the discus- sion of "Civil Society a Pre-condition of the Kingdom of God," Ritschl follows the Reformers in teaching that God is effecting his purpose in the state as well as in the whole course of human history. But he reminds us even more of Schleiermacher in developing a strong doctrine of the divine government of the world, while remaining reticent about speaking of any "antecedent knowledge" concerning the "special designs" in which God realizes his salvific purpose either with respect to individuals or nations.[25]

The remaining religious virtues of patience, humility, and prayer will come into focus in our consideration of the corollary of belief in divine providence, namely, man's dominion over the world. It is already apparent that man's new relationship to God must find expression in a changed atti- tude toward the world. The human dilemma that cries for solution at this point is one which agitates the idealistic tradition both ancient and modern, namely, how man, who belongs both to the natural world and yet as spirit transcends it, is to realize his superiority over it. In Ritschl's view, all religions seek to show how man, who is in some sense akin to deity, is assisted by divine powers to realize his superiority over the natural and material world. The fact that man raises this question is itself a sign of his kinship with God, and Christianity is neither the first nor only religion that promises some resolution of man's dilemma. However, though other religions and even philosophies inculcate a self-awareness which assures man that as a spiritual personality he is superior in worth to the natural order, none of them approximates the purity of the Christian answer to man's query. Let us listen to the way Ritschl describes man's problematic situation due to his being constituted of both nature and spirit.

The destiny of each to become a whole in his own order (*zu einem Ganzen in seiner Art*) is grounded necessarily in the peculiarity of Christianity so that the latter is not comprehended or transmitted fully if one keeps the doctrine of perfection hidden under a bushel. For it [the doctrine of perfection] provides the answer to the question which is put in all preceding religions and the satisfaction of the quest which is at work in all religions; moreover, it rescues man from the contradiction in which the natural man finds himself in that he is an infinitesimal fragment of the world and yet as spirit is in God's image, and that as such, he has a different value from all the rest of nature with which he nonetheless shares the fate of belonging to the world. For what does man seek in all the heathen religions but the fulfillment of himself through fellowship with the divine life which he makes efficacious for himself through the activities involved in the service of the deity. This quest for fulfillment through God's help is the ordinary expression of the need to have the value of a whole, a need which man desires to have satisfied in order to ameliorate the feeling that, by nature, he occupies a miserable position as part of the world. The guarantee of this fulfillment is sought by the human spirit in the conception of God, in his dependence upon God, in the service of God and in the feeling of nearness to God. Religion in this sense is a law of the human spirit. But religion in all of its heathen forms does not reach the desired goal. For within heathenism the idea of God is not marked off securely from the world and its parts; faith in the gods is enmeshed with a veneration of nature. Therefore, the heathen idea of God is itself too lacking in the character of wholeness to provide a resolution of the human quest for a transcendent fulfillment. This goal, however, is assured in Christianity which therefore represents not only the most complete form of religion as over against the incomplete types, but also the true religion itself.[26]

From this perspective we may cast a backward glance at the way in which Jesus once again serves Ritschl as the model for revealing what constitutes man's dominion over the world. The special fellowship Jesus enjoyed with the Father and the manner in which he adopted the Kingdom of God as his goal had as its corollary his "supremacy over the world." The latter expression refers to the way in which Jesus' dedication to God and his Kingdom freed him from any and all subservience to the world and its lesser powers and goals.[27] Jesus' constancy and patience in pursuit of this end is evidenced in his freedom over the world even in the face of death. In this way, he attested the supremacy of life over death, even as in his ministry he taught that each human life was of greater worth than the whole world. This truth is underlined for Ritschl in the words of Jesus in Mark 8:35–36: "For whosoever would save his life shall lose it; and whosoever shall lose his life for my sake and the gospel's shall save it. For what doth it profit a man, to gain the whole world, and forfeit his life?" (ASV) Concerning the latter, he comments: "This statement reveals the *supramundane* worth, that is, the worth as against the whole world, of the spiritual life of each individual man, and shows the way in which this entirely new perception attains objective reality."[28] In this connection, the apostle Paul is the true interpreter of Jesus in his "triumphant conviction" that the religious consciousness of the believer rightly related to God through Christ is able to provide equilibrium even in the face of the worst calamities that may befall him in life. This is asserted in the Pauline passage which serves Ritschl repeatedly as the true summation of belief in providence and therewith of the meaning of supremacy over the world. "I am persuaded, that neither death, nor life, nor angels, nor principalities, nor things present, nor things to come, nor powers, nor height, nor depth, nor any other creature, shall be able to separate us from the love of God, which is in Christ Jesus our Lord." (Rom. 8:38–39, ASV.)[29]

There is, then, a new self-consciousness characteristic of the Christian which expresses itself in his supremacy over the world. We would misconstrue Ritschl's meaning were we to interpret this to mean that man either has complete control of nature or is exempt from the operation of natural law. That is obviously not the case. "Lordship over the world, accordingly, though it is not technical and empirical, but ideal, is not therefore unreal. For the will which exercises religious dominion over the world is the real; and it is at the same time as much ideal as real."[30]

Faith in divine providence assures no exemption from all the difficulties and anxieties that mark human existence in the world. Rather, man's new self-understanding enables him to interpret all events in the light of his new relationship to God and his destiny in the Kingdom of God. Hence, Ritschl writes:

> So long as the view is held that certain restrictions of our freedom are evils unconditionally, our dependence on natural and partial causes, that is, our dependence on the world, is admitted. But when we change our feeling as to the value of evils, not merely do we attain freedom from the particular things in which these evils take their rise, but freedom from the world as such. For not only do particular evils represent just those aspects in which the whole world is a restriction on our freedom, but the counterbalancing thought, that we are the objects of Divine care, implies that each of us, as a spiritual whole, has in God's sight a higher value than the whole world of nature. This is the reason why a man, when by patient endurance of suffering he rules himself, likewise rules the whole world, which is the correlative of the suffering and unhappy Ego (unglücklichen Selbst).[31]

The three religious virtues that reflect man's new self-understanding as it is determined by his consciousness of reconciliation with God are humility, patience and prayer. This trilogy mirrors how man's changed self-consciousness effects a difference in his relationship both to God and to the world. The first pair, humility and patience, reflects the correlation that exists between faith in the divine providence and dominion over the world. Humility describes the proper attitude of the Christian toward God; patience refers to the manner in which the believer, who has humbly submitted himself to God, responds to difficulties that encounter him in the world.

Humility, the first of these virtues, is interpreted by Ritschl in the light of its Old and New Testament usage to mean man's willing submission to God. Whereas in the Old Testament this virtue often relates to man's attitude in the face of undeserved suffering, the example of Jesus' fidelity to his vocation and the New Testament evidence lead Ritschl to interpret it to mean "the resolve to submit ourselves to God."[32] Again, we are dealing with an inner attitude or "tone of feeling" that informs and guides our existence in the face of both joy and sorrow. In one sense, the feeling of humility is the most comprehensive description of the proper attitude of man in relationship to God. It is quite apparent in the following definition of religion how closely Ritschl follows Schleiermacher's famous formulation:

> Humility is properly the whole of religion as found in man. For in so far as religion, in all its species and stages, is the acknowledgment—concentrated in feeling—of our subjection (Abhängigkeit, Unterordnung) to God, humility—granted the omnipotence of God and our reconciliation with Him—will be subjective religion itself. Now this is correct, in the sense that humility is the Christian religion in the form of religious virtue.[33]

That Schleiermacher's definition serves as a guide is even more clear from Ritschl's succinct statement in *Christian Perfection*: "For this religious virtue [i.e., humility] may well be designated as the feeling (Stimmung) of dependence (Abhängigkeit) upon God."[34]

If humility is the basic feeling arising out of man's dependence upon and subjection to God, patience is the corollary virtue characteristic of the Christian's proper response to everything that seems to limit his exercise of lordship over the world. Ritschl makes the close connection between these two virtues clear as follows:

> Patience must be added to it [i.e., humility] as the other religious virtue. In other words, patience is religious feeling as lordship over a refractory world, and is supplementary to humility as the feeling of submission to God. Humility and patience, however, come under the conception of virtue because they are acquired frames of feeling, and at the same time powers, inasmuch as they move and rule the will.[35]

In view of his presupposition that Christianity as the true religion provides its adherents with the possibility of exercising spiritual and religious dominion and freedom over the world, the virtue of patience takes on considerable importance. In writing to his brother, Wilhelm, in 1872, Ritschl lamented that after Schleiermacher no modern theologian showed how reconciliation through Christ determined one's response toward evil and suffering in the world.[36] In Ritschl's view, patience as a universal virtue develops through man's recognition of his personal worth, enabling him to encounter and conquer outward circumstances that threaten to overcome him.

In its specifically Christian form, patience represents a heightening of the "general human exercise of patience" and it "depends on the fact that man's feeling of self and of personal worth, by being combined with the thought of the supramundane God Who is our Father, and guarantees to us salvation through dominion over the world and participation in the Kingdom of God, is raised above all natural and particular motives, even when they are the occasion of troubles."[37] Though Ritschl can define patience as the "feeling which views especially the evils of life in the light of Divine providence," patience ought also, as an acquired virtue, to assert a stabilizing effect on man's consciousness in the face of good fortune and prosperity in order that he may not become dependent upon the world.[38] In sum, Christian patience, which grows out of our belief in divine providence and our reconciliation with God, enables us to evaluate evils which may oppress us in the world as of lesser power than the "blessing of fellowship with God"; moreover, these "evils, as tests of our fidelity to God, are elevated into relative blessings. And this comes about just through the exercise of patience as the peculiar and proper manifestation of Christian freedom."[39]

The final religious virtue is prayer. Ritschl reasons, following the Reformers, that in light of God's reconciling and providential activity, thanksgiving unto God rather than petition is the ordinary form of prayer. Indeed for him prayer is, in effect, acknowledging our feeling of dependence upon God; "prayer is the expression of humility and patience, and the means of confirming oneself in these virtues."[40] Paul's injunction to pray without ceasing "denotes that transformation of prayer back into the voiceless feeling of humility and patience, which as accompanying the whole active life, is equivalent to prayer as the normal form of the worship of God."[41] Prayer in the right spirit will always be a special expression of the joy characteristic of one who relies on God's fatherly providence and reconciling love; at the same time it focuses the tone of feeling generally present in the attitude of humility. It is clear that Ritschl rejects any sharp demarcation between the Christian's general attitude of thanksgiving toward a gracious God and thanksgiving expressed through prayer. What is more, it would seem that prayer is significant not because it is possible to influence God and thereby change the divine government of the world, but rather because it reinforces the religious virtues referred to as well as man's assurance of reconciliation.[42] When exercised together, the religious virtues give rise to a feeling of blessedness or joy which is in fact "the feeling of perfection. The latter [i.e., joy] could not be enjoined as the normative accompaniment of the Christian life if the Christian religion did not give rise to the awareness that—in one's spiritual being one attains the value of a whole—to which the whole world is not comparable in worth."[43]

Up to this point we have seen how the religious virtues of Christianity encompass the whole warp and woof of man's relationship to God, the world, and to himself. The omission of any of these elements, or the failure to relate the new *Lebensführung* to the destiny of man and humanity in the Kingdom of God, would leave us with a truncated view of the former. This drive to comprehensiveness leads Ritschl to make much of the distinctiveness of the Christian *Weltanschauung*. The latter is the total perspective that results from the correlation of these religious virtues and the ethical virtues yet to be examined. In our earlier discussion of his epistemology, it became evident that he held the excellence of the Christian *Weltanschauung* to be a telling proof of the superiority and truth of this religion.[44] This high estimate of the Christian world view does not lead him into extended critiques of competing world views, but this is implicit at many points and is developed *in nuce* in the section we are considering. To begin with, Ritschl contends that there is no necessity for conflict between scientific and Christian world views; "it must be possible to harmonise the scientific study of nature and the Christian view of the world in the same mind."[45] The problem arises when the scientist universalizes laws applicable in a restricted area and attempts to make them integral to all world views without further verification.

The battle with absolutistic scientific world views is joined at several points. For example, the contention of the advocates of a mechanistic-scientific world view that modern man must get on without the "conception of the end" and especially without the presupposition of the "miraculous" attaching to the Christian *Weltanschauung* is estimated by Ritschl as "self-delusion."[46] Thus he counters: "Miracles (*Wunder*), in the sense of effects which are not produced according to law, are assumed in every philosophical or scientific theory of the universe."[47] Moreover, he argues quite cogently that apart from the conception of purpose and *telos*, no meaning whatever could be attached to the investigation of nature. Even the idea of "efficient cause" utilized in scientific investigation is not based upon empirical observation and verification, but is rather an a priori presupposition enabling the scientist to interpret changing phenomena.[48] Yet Ritschl can tolerate all of these oversights in a scientific world view by attributing them to the uncritical adoption of religious, quasi-religious, or philosophical presuppositions inherent in Western Christian culture. His ire is vented, however, when the likes of a David Friedrich Strauss develop a mechanistic world view which, if carried to its logical conclusion, would deny man his superiority to, and worth over, nature.

But in fact, Ritschl observes wryly, even advocates of a mechanistic world view—even the post-Copernican modern man—lives in a manner that contradicts his theory. "If one is in earnest with the scientific study of nature in the name of which Divine providence is denied, the consistent outcome of such a view of the world ought to be despair of that value of personal life which we destroy in ourselves by the wakeful care of every moment."[49] This is further illustrated in the case of those who hold to the evolutionary theory of "natural descent." They do not "recognise as original the specific differentiation of spiritual life and nature" and yet they "conduct themselves as though this very distinction were the fundamental rule of their existence."[50] By means of this line of argumentation, Ritschl contends that all scientific investigation of nature presupposes that man is of greater value than nature and its laws. Hence he concludes: "Thus the self-feeling of man over against the whole world must be accepted, even though unwillingly, as a fact on which every merely mechanical view of the world makes shipwreck."[51]

Against this backdrop, the charge of subjectivism and irrationalism often leveled against the Christian *Weltanschauung* is to be rejected as without foundation. To argue that the Christian world view is subjective in that it arises out of man's need of being assured of his spiritual superiority over nature and all else in the world would be tantamount to calling in question every area of scientific and spiritual activity which presupposes the distinction between spirit and nature. To be sure, the affirmation of the adequacy of a Christian or any other world view involves a value judgment. One's faith in divine providence, and therewith the belief in man's kinship with God and his superiority over nature, cannot be verified scientifically; it is a value judgment established "by our own experiences." It represents the "personal conviction of each individual, drawn from the nexus of the experiences he has made of himself."[52] The adoption of the Christian world view is therefore neither irrational nor purely subjective inasmuch as the resulting *Weltanschauung* secures man's role as spirit over nature and the world while at the same time providing a convincing and coherent perspective from which the world may be interpreted. Thus there appears to be a kind of theoretical justification of the Christian world view for Ritschl insofar as it makes sense of human life and experience.

These crucial elements are in evidence in the following typical statement:

> For in order to know the world as a totality, and in order himself to become a totality (*ein Ganzes*) in or over it by the help of God, man needs the idea of the oneness of God, and of the consummation of the world in an end which is for man both knowable and realisable. But this condition is fulfilled in Christianity alone.[53]

The fact that non-Christian world views maintain a conception of the totality of things, of order and purpose in the world, and of the uniqueness of human personality attests the pervasive though hidden influence of the Christian *Weltanschauung*. "Thus those who reject the possibility of traveling through life upon the ship of the Christian *Weltanschauung* and self-understanding nevertheless sit upon a plank taken from this ship."[54] Finally, were it not for the Christian world view informed by the understanding of the relationship between nature, man, and God which we have surveyed, it would be impossible for the Christian to achieve wholeness or perfection in the ethical sphere to which we now turn.

THE ETHICAL VIRTUES CHARACTERISTIC OF CHRISTIAN PERFECTION

In the preceding section we showed how man's reconciliation with God manifested itself in certain religious virtues synonymous with religious perfection. Ritschl's concluding statement provides us with a convenient summary:

> Religious dominion over the world, which constitutes the immediate form of reconciliation with God through Christ, is exercised through faith in the loving providence of God, through the virtues of humility and patience, and, finally, through prayer, and through this last likewise receives common expression.[56]

Though these virtues have to do primarily with inner feelings or attitudes and may therefore be referred to the realm of religious experience, it became clear that each of these virtues related to the way in which man exercises spiritual dominion over the world. Thus although in the exercise of religious virtues man points primarily in the Godward direction, this fact cannot be understood without remembering that this involves a certain stance of man toward the world. On the other hand, the ethical virtues under consideration deal in the main with man's relationship to his neighbor. The reciprocity between these two dimensions of human existence of which we spoke earlier is accentuated in the following:

> It is as certain that these two activities stand in reciprocal relation to one another (§ 37/3) as that the ends and motives in both cases have the same supramundane level. The correlation of these activities, the first religious and the second ethical, is evident in the fact that the religious duty of dominion over the world calls for the same effort of the will as the ethical duty belonging to the kingdom of God, and that this latter includes in itself religious elevation above the world. The unity of this double life-purpose is evident in the joy or blessedness springing out of

them both. This is the feeling of religious-ethical perfection. In so far, then, as blessedness is expected in the Christian life, the possibility is therein admitted of that perfection which, in the two directions of striving after the kingdom of God and its righteousness and of exercising freedom over the world, is set before us as our task.[57]

The problem facing Ritschl at this point has its antecedents in the breach between the Reformers and Rome. Although desirous of affirming that religious and ethical virtues exercise a reciprocal influence upon one another, Ritschl neither wants to equate them nor to make man's justification contingent upon his good works.[58] In contrast to Protestant orthodoxy which departed from Luther, he maintains that blessedness and eternal life obtain in the present because of man's new relationship with God.[59] They are not delayed until, or restricted to, some future eschatological vision of God, but characterize the free Christian man who exercises a spiritual power and lordship over the world as Luther rightly observed.[60] But in what sense do the good works of men lead to blessedness? How are faith and works related?

Ritschl's contention is that Protestant theology never found an adequate solution to this question though certain statements of Luther and Lutheran confessions relating to man's voluntary fulfillment of the law out of love pointed in the right direction. The impasse arose because Luther adopted Paul's dichotomy between faith and law and applied it to the Christian life as well. Yet at the same time, Luther can speak of the Christian who fulfills the law in love by doing good works, and therefore Ritschl holds that Luther did recognize the significance of Christian freedom exercised without compulsion.[61] Orthodox Lutheranism followed Luther in teaching that the works of the regenerate may be in harmony with the law, "but they contribute nothing to blessedness. On the other hand, by the Christian law James means the law of freedom, in so far as personal disposition and attention and fidelity are devoted to it. Blessedness for him, therefore, is a feature which accompanies the fulfillment of the moral law under these conditions; for it springs from free acquiescence in God's final end."[62]

Ritschl's positive solution, hinted at in the preceding quotation, intends to provide a more satisfying explanation of the relationship of faith and works and why the latter are necessary at all. Luther and James—and perhaps even Kant—can be harmonized! Though Reformation confessions speak variously of the necessity for good works because of the divine commandment, in terms of the work of the Holy Spirit and the response of living faith, as a means of promoting God's glory, and finally in order to evidence gratitude for one's salvation and to arrive at subjective certainty thereof, Ritschl finds no satisfying coordination of these reasons. Yet the answer lies close at hand in the conception of the Kingdom of God and its relationship to the Christian's activity in the realization of his freedom over the world. We have seen that the religious relationship of the believer to God through Christ gives rise to the awareness of spiritual dominion and freedom over the world. In the ethical sphere, the Christian exercises freedom over the world when the motive and goal of his action is the Kingdom of God. However, whenever man's acts or good works are dictated by the desire for self-preservation or even with reference to the highest human norms conceivable, he gives himself to something less than God and his Kingdom. The end result of the elevation of finite goals into the place of the infinite goal leads to enslavement to the world rather than dominion over it. If on the contrary the Kingdom of God as "God's supramundane final end in the world" is the personal goal in life and one acts in love toward all men, then lesser moral goals or aims such as fellowship with family and friends, etc., can be guided by this "supreme motive."[63]

True freedom, therefore, exists when men act not in accord with penultimate goals, but in terms of God's ultimate goal in the Kingdom of God, which is at one and the same time the goal of humanity and of each man. Christian freedom is misinterpreted if understood to mean that one is free from determination by any power outside of the self. "For within Christianity experience teaches that it is just in and through a special kind of dependence on God that we possess freedom to do good."[64] It is thus essential to recognize that the "highest stage of freedom" is that which is "manifested in practical life in the Kingdom of God."[65] The comprehensive manner in which one's allegiance to the Kingdom of God is determinative of man's individual and corporate action in the world is set forth as follows:

> The universal ground of all moral conduct towards our fellowmen is that the Christian religion has for its end the Kingdom of God. This association of mankind, of the most comprehensive nature both extensively and intensively, cannot be realised otherwise than through works, concrete action, and speech. These works are good in so far as they are directed towards the universal end which guarantees the usefulness of all the members of the fellowship. Now, the moral law is the system of those ends, dispositions and actions, which necessarily arise out of the universal end of the Kingdom of God. Love is the pervading motive of this organisation of law-determined action; but it is also the impulse which leads to the knowledge of all those ends which are comprehended in the moral law.[66]

We may note in passing certain points at which Ritschl engages the thought of Kant. He supports Kant's affirmation that man and his will are autonomous and free so long as he acts in accordance with the moral law, but criticizes Kant for regarding freedom solely as a regulative idea by which we judge human action, which, in fact, is not free but conditioned by the motive from which it springs. Though Ritschl agrees that acts necessarily arise out of certain motives, "yet in varying measure those actions are free whose motive is the universal conception of an end which lays a restraining hand on the very impulse it has aroused."[67] This view is somewhat similar to contemporary "situation ethics" in the contention that only because of the subjective feeling of freedom is it possible for men to determine particular actions in response to the pressure of the moral law. The latter "cannot be codified" so as to determine in advance what each appropriate decision would be. Ritschl writes: "Without the acquisition of moral freedom in the form of a good general disposition and of a development of special virtues, therefore, the moral law not only cannot be carried out, but cannot even in its whole range be known and objectively fixed."[68] Kant was further in error in holding that the Christian subjection to God involved a false heteronomy which did violence to the autonomy of the absolute moral law.

It does not follow, as Kant charged, that the acknowledgment of God and the Kingdom of God by Christians necessitates that the moral law take on statutory form. The moral law for Christians always receives its content from its final end, namely, the Kingdom of God, and the ordinary form of the moral law is universal love toward all men. Regarding its form, Ritschl affirms: "The law of universal love to our neighbour is altogether incapable of being drawn out into a statutory series of general commandments, for it is addressed, in the first place not to our actions, but to our disposition."[69] Man's general moral disposition and the virtues to which it gives rise are created and re-created by the will that is directed toward, and obedient to, man's universal moral goal in the Kingdom of God. Indeed, the will so directed is free and the sign of this freedom is that it produces both "knowledge of the moral law, and therewith the law itself; for the law does not exist for us apart from our knowledge of it."[70]

Up to this point we have shown how man's ethical acts must be seen in terms of their relationship to the Kingdom of God as their goal, and the manner in which they attest man's ethical freedom over the world. In the process we have observed a close homogeneity between man's religious and ethical functions which is due, in part, to the fact that both give rise to man's exercise of freedom or dominion over the world. Whereas the former arise as subjective feelings resulting from man's new relationship to God, man's moral dominion over the world results from action determined in accordance with God's final end in the Kingdom of God. The manner in which religious and ethical virtues are rooted in God and together provide a complete picture of Christian freedom and perfection is expressed in the following vein:

One cannot practice action motivated by the law of freedom without, in the religious functions, attesting his freedom over the world; and one cannot assure oneself of forgiveness, without exercising love in deed and in truth (I John 3:18–19. . .). All this goes to fill out the extent of Christian freedom; so also it forms the content of Christian perfection.[71]

It is important for understanding Ritschl's position to remember that actions in the ethical as well as in the religious spheres issue in the experience of blessedness or joy. The apostle James is not quite right in teaching that the man who "fulfills the law of freedom is *blessed in his deed*. But what he does express quite precisely in these words is the truth that blessedness accompanies a good deed which springs from the supreme motive, and not from a calculation of the result."[72] For whenever our action is predicated upon achieving eternal life or some result less than that dictated by the Kingdom of God, neither the feeling of blessedness nor that of freedom obtains.[73] The close correlation between the religious and ethical spheres and the manner in which each issues in blessedness is apparent in the following:

> The homogeneity of both aspects of the Christian life rests, too, upon a single ground, namely, on the commanding importance of the idea of God as supramundane, gracious, and benevolent. Since, therefore, eternal life and blessedness (*Seligkeit*) are experimentally enjoyed in this elevation of the feeling of self (*Selbstgefühl*) over the world, the motivation of action by the supramundane end of the Kingdom of God is [also] necessarily reflected in blessedness.[74]

In the preceding ways, Ritschl seeks to hold the religious and ethical poles of Christianity together. The Christian's good works in the ethical realm are more closely related to eternal life and the realm of faith than traditional Lutheranism realized. That is not to say that good works merit eternal life, or even that they are a "concomitant cause" of it.

> As the disposition which finds its motive in the supramundane end of the Kingdom of God itself comes within the compass of eternal life, therefore *good* works are, for one thing, manifestations of eternal life; but further, according to the law that the exercise of a power serves to strengthen and maintain it, they are organs of eternal life.[75]

Thus the believer's experience of spiritual freedom over the world which enables him to look even on evil with equanimity serves to reinforce action motivated by the final end of the Kingdom of God; conversely, action in the service of the Kingdom of God provides the experience of blessedness which validates the "religious feeling of self" that eternal life is, in fact, a present possession.[76] Ritschl finds this approach a better solution to the problem of the relation of faith and works. "Love, therefore, follows from faith in reconciliation only because the God in whom we put our faith has for His final aim the union of men in the Kingdom of God."[77] In this way, the religious and ethical poles of Christianity are once again seen in their interrelationships.[78]

Having set the ethical life in the larger context of the universal moral law and the Kingdom of God, we must now examine the particular ethical virtues that are of importance for Ritschl. The latter—along with the right actions relating to their exercise—grow out of the goal of the Christian community in the Kingdom of God; they represent the unfolding of the basic law of love which is to characterize all activity in the Kingdom of God, encompassing both the corporate and individual actions of all of its members. Since this law involves loving even the enemy, Christian love transcends doing good for one's neighbor which lies at the root of human society in general.[79] Though it can be said that in one sense the actualization of the life of love and the development of Christian character marked by the ethical virtues represents true fulfillment of man's justification and reconciliation, Ritschl does not accord the ethical virtues the space commensurate with their importance in the final division of *Justification and Reconciliation*. One needs to turn from the latter to *Instruction in the Christian Religion* and *Christian Perfection* in order to see their full import. The ethical virtues, as we have observed, do not flow automatically from the religious. They do constitute, however, their complement and without the ethical virtues no mature Christian character could be developed, and therefore the Protestant *Lebensführung* and Christian perfection would be incomplete.

The relationship between the good will and ethical virtues and actions is defined in these terms:

> Ethical virtues, and actions regulated by the conception of duty, are the products of a will directed toward the highest purpose. The difference between the two is that actions in accordance with duty proceed forth from the will, while virtues are acquired in the will itself; the former have relation to intercourse or association with others, and the latter belong to the individual as such.[80]

Christian ethical virtues, therefore, derive from the good will, or develop in the formulation of those duties which represent the right response to the law of love. On the other hand, Ritschl can say that the very way "virtues are acquired is by constant dutiful action."[81] Thus a reciprocity exists between Christian virtues and actions; virtues can be said to give rise to actions, and actions, in turn, reinforce Christian virtues.

In *Instruction in the Christian Religion,* he depicts all the virtues that arise out of the various areas of the will's activity. When all are present, the human will is whole or complete. It is sufficient to indicate these with little or no comment upon them. When all work in concert, they issue in the full development of the will and Christian character. The first group of virtues, "namely, self-control and conscientiousness, gives rise to the independence and worth of character."[82] The virtue of self-control (*Selbstbeherrschung*) should be seen in conjunction with man's independence of, and dominion over, the world and arises when the "will subjects the impulses of the individual disposition to the good end."[83] The customary way in which self-control is engendered is through the conscientious fulfillment of one's vocation. The second group of virtues, namely, "wisdom, discretion, determination, constancy, is founded upon clearness and energy of character."[84] Their presence attests a well-ordered existence in which individual actions are in keeping with one's ultimate purpose in life. The final group of virtues, "kindliness, thankfulness, justice, is founded upon a good disposition or amiability of character."[85] Here the disposition is good because it is motivated by love. The exercise of all of these virtues issues in the ethical maturation of the individual, and Ritschl avoids the error of certain forms of individualistic existentialism by holding that it is "utterly inconceivable" that these can obtain apart from "social intercourse with other persons."[86]

At this point we need to recall that affirmations of the movement toward, or the attainment of, ethical perfection have not met with much acceptance in Protestant history. In the first place, the Reformation *sola fide* appears to require man to look away from his imperfect works to Christ as the ground of his salvation, and Ritschl can concur in this stance if man's works are interpreted as meriting his salvation. However, he observes that such a position could be misconstrued so as to encourage quietism or retreat from the quest for perfection. He writes: "The idea of ethical perfection both in our action as well as in the development of our own character is not necessary simply in order to establish our imperfection, but rather has its value for us in what we believe is our destiny in relationship to it."[87] Unless ethical perfection is held out as an attainable goal, the will cannot be motivated to strive persistently toward it.

A second difficulty arises with respect to the manner in which ethical perfection is ordinarily conceived. A prevalent tradition in Protestantism has disallowed any conception of ethical perfection because the latter is viewed in quantitative and legalistic terms. The problem is falsely posed by assuming that the universal moral law obligates man to do the good in every area of life. No man can achieve this because the possibilities for good action are endless. Yet this inability to fulfill the moral law is construed as man's sin or imperfection. Ritschl proposes as an alternative a qualitative understanding of ethical perfection. Just as he is unwilling to admit that religious perfection marked by trust in the fatherly benevolence of God is invalidated by occasional moments of spiritual doubt and mistrust, so analogously Christian ethical perfection is not called in question because "we still continue to be conscious of the quantitative imperfectness and defectiveness even of those functions in which our Christian faith is expressed."[88] Legalistic views of perfection err in viewing man's imperfection in terms of his failure to observe all the statutes of the law. A qualitative view of perfection along the lines of Ritschl's proposal sees man as an ethical whole and therefore perfect in the light of a good disposition, or *Lebensführung*, or true inner freedom—all of which are in keeping with man's destiny in the Kingdom of God.

1. *Perfection and Vocation.*   The manner in which Ritschl relates ethical perfection to vocation has been anticipated in his analysis of the importance of Jesus' vocation for interpreting his ministry correctly. There he provides this definition of vocation: "A man's vocation as a citizen denotes that particular department of work in human society, in the regular pursuit of which the individual realises at once his own self-end and the common ultimate end of society."[89] Jesus' vocation focused in the establishment and pursuit of the Kingdom of God which is simultaneously the climax of God's purpose for himself, Jesus, and mankind. In pursuit of this goal, Jesus lives in accordance with the universal moral law, which derives from the Kingdom of God. The religious virtues that marked Jesus' fulfillment of his vocation, namely, trust in God's providence evidenced in the virtues of patience, humility, and prayer, serve as the paradigm of the Christian's religious perfection already delineated. The exercise of these virtues led the disciples to the same dominion over, and independence of, the world characteristic of Jesus. If we turn to the sphere of ethical perfection, Jesus once again serves as the model for subsequent generations. He is such because his entire vocation is the realization of the law of love that marks the fulfillment of the moral law directed toward the Kingdom of God.

Since Jesus serves as Ritschl's norm for defining Christian perfection, it is not surprising that he returns to the idea of vocation in the important final section of *Justification and Reconciliation* entitled "Action in Our Moral Calling." Once again he desires to extend a position affirmed in the Reformation, and particularly by Luther, in citing the Augsburg Confession on vocation: "In the Augsburg Confession *moral action in one's civic vocation* is reckoned as one of the features of Christian perfection, and this is intelligible from the opposition felt to monasticism."[90] The significance of one's vocation as it relates to the Kingdom of God is tied in with the principle that the whole cannot be achieved without the proper functioning of its constituent parts. Applied to the realization of the goal of humanity in the ethical Kingdom of God, this means that man must first fulfill his duties in the "narrower circles of life conditioned by nature (married life, family life, social life, national life)."[91] Activity in these areas is brought into relationship to the overarching goal of human existence through the discharge of one's vocation. Ritschl continues: "Conduct in the narrower and naturally conditioned circles is subordinated to the common end of the Kingdom of God and brought into direct relation to the same, when the regular activity incumbent upon each one in these circles is exercised in the form of one's ethical calling for the common good."[92]

The designation of vocation as the locus in which ethical perfection is realized commends itself to Ritschl for several other reasons. It will be recalled that the quantitative and legalistic view of perfection found both in Catholicism and Protestantism denied the possibility of the attainment of perfection because man could not realize all the possibilities of good dictated by the moral law. Here the center of life from which all could be understood is missing. The conception of vocation provides him with such a center as well as with a perspective from which to judge other views of perfection. Thus the quest for sanctification in Methodism seems at first glance to receive Ritschl's blessing because it is understood as the proper response to the divine love. However, the view of santification and perfection developed in Methodism is quantitative and legalistic and undermines that "moral sensibility" which is a true hallmark of ethical and religious perfection. It did this, in part, by inculcating the "idea of a fruitless search for actual sinlessness of conduct in all the details of life."[93] Ritschl's qualitative understanding of perfection is opposed to such a quest and finds expression as follows: "It [i.e., the concept of moral perfection] rather means that our moral achievement or life-work in connection with the Kingdom of God should, however limited in amount, be conceived as possessing the quality of a whole in its own order."[94] If the attainment of perfection, therefore, is seen neither in terms of actual sinlessness nor in terms of realizing all the possibilities for good, but rather in terms of the faithful discharge of one's vocation, a meaningful view of perfection can be developed. "The fact that good action is conditioned by one's calling invalidates the apparent obligation we are under at each moment of time to do good action in every possible direction."[95] Therefore, in faithful dedication to our vocation—which does not have as its primary goal doing good works—a unified life-work is developed which simultaneously is the fulfillment of Christian personality and each man's contribution to the common good, and therewith to the Kingdom of God. Ritschl summarizes this succinctly: "Moral action in our calling is, therefore, the form in which our life-work as a totality is produced as our contribution to the Kingdom of God, and in which, at the same time, the ideal of spiritual personality as a whole in its own order is reached."[96]

According to Ritschl, the charge that every man could realize more fully the potential of his particular vocation does not undermine the truth that man experiences blessedness and therewith perfection in terms of his total lifework in his vocation. Therefore, the faithful pursuit of one's vocation—and thus ethical perfection—carries in its train that same feeling of the inestimably greater value of the spiritual self over the world and nature which we found to be the end result of the religious virtues. Indeed, Ritschl interprets Paul with approval in teaching that the "ultimate standing of a person in the Kingdom of God depends on the goodness and the rounded completeness of the life-work he achieves in his moral vocation."[97]

Now that we have Ritschl's view of Christian perfection in focus, it is readily apparent why he disassociates himself from certain other conceptions of perfection and sanctification developed during the history of the church. The Roman Catholic conception of perfection developed in terms of the monastic style of life is the most objectionable theory. It is no accident that the Reformers so adamantly opposed the prevailing Roman Catholic doctrine according to which the pathway to perfection was obtained by the few who withdrew from the world and took the vows of poverty, chastity, and obedience. For the Reformers and Ritschl, the position of the Roman Church is predicated upon untenable distinctions between clergy and laity, monks and ordinary Christians, perfect and imperfect. The Reformation's emphasis upon the "priesthood of all believers" made such a hiatus impossible, and therefore Ritschl commends the Reformers for reasserting the applicability of Jesus' injunction to perfection to all his followers. Even more reprehensible as a part of the Roman Catholic view is the supposition that religious and ethical perfection are attainable only by negating the world and the ordinary relationships of life which provide occasions for sin and disobedience. Ritschl's reading of the history of monasticism leads him to conclude that withdrawal from life in the world and the adoption of the ascetic life leads to the demise of the ethical and religious life rather than to its development. Thus he can say:

> Life in the family, the quest for private property, the enjoyment of personal honor without anxiety, are not simply and necessarily occasions for sin, but are rather the unavoidable conditions of, and motivations to, the attainment of the ethical life. For the family is the school for developing social sensitivity; property and honor are the bulwarks of independence without which one can contribute nothing to the common good.[98]

One may surmise that such statements caused Barth to complain about Ritschl's bourgeois mentality and his domestication of Christianity. Be that as it may, it is clear that he held that the *Lebensideal* of the Reformers correlated faith in the divine providence and related virtues with a high estimate of one's vocation as the place in which Christian love is manifested. He writes: "This evaluation of secular vocation is therefore also a specific fundamental of Protestantism; it is the practical expression of the fact that Christianity is not conceived as a denial of the world, but rather as completing and permeating it."[99] With this emphasis, Ritschl appears as one of the true modern prophets of a "secular Christianity" in the tradition of the Reformation and it is no wonder that he exerted considerable influence upon the rise of the "social gospel" both in Europe and America.

A final erroneous tenet of the Roman Catholic view of perfection has been discussed in connection with its Protestant counterpart, namely, its legalistic and quantitative view of perfection. According to the Catholic *Lebensideal,* the believer's attitude toward God is marked by guilt and fear because of the multiplicity of God's commandments. In order to avoid transgressing the divine law and eliciting God's displeasure, Roman Catholicism encourages withdrawal from the world which provides occasions for temptation and sin. The Reformers take a much more positive stance toward the world, and Ritschl follows them in seeing progress toward perfection in terms of man's free response to the "law written on the heart" in the midst of the ordinary round of daily life.

In turning to Protestant perversions of perfection that meet with Ritschl's disfavor, let us look first at Pietism.[100] The latter is reminiscent of Catholicism at many points, and we have shown that he was convinced of the historical relationships between the development of Protestant Pietism and certain forms of medieval piety. Thus he accuses Pietists of making the same kind of division between the perfect and the imperfect in their distinction between Pietists and non-Pietists as Catholicism does in distinguishing monastics from the laity. This led Pietists to establish conventicles of the pious distinguished from the larger church. Like their medieval precursors among mystics and monastics, Pietists followed the precedent of a non-Christian Hellenism in their negative attitude toward the world and the inculcation of an ascetic and otherworldly *Lebensführung.*

Though Ritschl is willing, in part, to excuse such a stance both in Catholicism and Protestantism, given the secularization of the church to which they reacted, the depreciation of "aesthetic culture" and "time-honoured means of social recreation" gave rise to a type of overbearing humility that he found quite distasteful.[101] Even more reprehensible is the fact that the Pietists' quest for perfection did not result in that healthy estimate of self which issues from man's trust in divine providence. Instead, Pietists engaged continuously in a kind of morbid analysis of their spiritual psyches in a manner more akin to the mystic temperament than to the Christian worldliness of the Reformers. This led, in turn, to the misconception that blessedness was reserved for an eschatological vision of God, rather than seeing it obtaining in the present by virtue of man's justification and the faithful pursuit of one's vocation.[102]

Among those opposing Ritschl at this juncture was Martin Kähler. He disagreed with him at two critical points. First, he held that Ritschl erred in claiming that the doctrine of perfection played an important role in the theology of the Reformers; their statements concerning perfection were highly polemical and fragmentary, since they were directed against the Catholic view of perfection as it came to expression in monasticism. Therefore, it is illegitimate to make them the basis of a Protestant *Lebensideal*. Ritschl wrote Wilhelm Herrmann that Kähler's leaning toward Pietism's version of perfection made his negative response predictable. He wrote in the same vein to Adolf von Harnack in 1878:

> If one gives in to him [Kähler] at this point, one would have to view the religion of the Reformers as a compilation of fragments—a position which would preclude making any more sense of them than did some of my predecessors. And given his presupposition, it follows that [Protestantism] was in need of the reform effected by Pietism with its view of perfection involving scrupulosity, refraining from dancing, etc.—all of which supposedly represent an improvement over the fragments of the blessed Melanchthon. . . . But if I am to follow the Reformers, I must understand them in terms of that idea which gives their thoughts and intentions the impression of wholeness, even if in the process I understand them better at many points than they understood themselves. Otherwise my concept of religion requires me to look about for a comprehensive system and I would find this not in the Pietism being praised, but rather only in Catholicism. We can therefore suppress that development [i.e., Pietism] and justify the Reformation only if we can hold high the discovery of the idea of perfection in the *Confessio Augustana* (also art. 16; cf. art. 2). And if the orthodox, including Spener, had been aware of the latter, they would have been able to strangulate Pietism at its birth.[103]

In concluding our review of positions on Christian perfection which Ritschl opposed, we must turn our attention to that enigmatic and prophetic church historian of the University of Basel, Franz Overbeck. A year prior to the appearance of the final volume of *Justification and Reconciliation,* Overbeck published *Über die Christlichkeit unserer heutigen Theologie.* Like Friedrich Nietzsche, his contemporary and colleague at the University of Basel, Overbeck challenged the prevailing shape of Christianity in Europe, but whereas Nietzsche's attack came from outside the church, Overbeck spoke from within. He charged that all schools of Protestant theology were accommodating Christianity to culture while overlooking that "at bottom . . . Christianity is merely *negation of the world.*" This learned historian buttressed his thesis with the contention that primitive Christianity was marked by the expectation of an imminent Parousia and that both

Jesus and Paul laid down the "demand for ascetic negation of the world." In Overbeck's estimate, monasticism and its denial of the world was responsible for everything good achieved in the first fifteen centuries of Christian history.

Ritschl's response acknowledges the significance of monasticism, but distinguishes between the world view of its Eastern and Western types. In its Eastern form Ritschl sees a negation of the world that is essentially Buddhist in outlook and of no value for a Christian *Weltanschauung*. However, Western monasticism—though characterized by "certain world-negating motives"—"applied itself to ordered labour in many forms, i.e., to the task of world-mastery in the sense of technical and intellectual culture."[104] Furthermore, he concedes that the primitive church anticipated an imminent Parousia, but argues—anticipating later demythologizers—that this expectation was even for the early church a part of the "shell" and not the "kernel" of their teaching. He continues: "And there the matter will rest, for that anticipation has not acted prejudicially on any of the positive social duties which follow from Christianity."[105] In sum, Overbeck's eschatological interpretation of Christianity remained wholly incongruous to Ritschl and to many others in late nineteenth- and early twentieth-century theology. To adopt it was tantamount to succumbing to a pessimistic world view more Buddhistic than Christian, which led to "dominion of the world over man" rather than the reverse. For Ritschl, therefore, it remains axiomatic that "there attaches to Christianity only so much world-negation as belongs to world-mastery.[106] The path to Christian perfection involves the faithful exercise of the aforementioned religious and ethical virtues here and now in the daily round of one's vocation and life.

The feeling of blessedness that accompanies the individual's state of perfection is not construed by Ritschl to point to an actual state of sinlessness. Nor ought the individual experience of perfection and the development of a religious-moral character to a degree surpassing that of one's fellow Christians lead to the sectarian pattern of establishing a society of the perfect within the larger church. Indeed, those who have progressed farther along the path toward Christian perfection are, in Ritschl's estimate, those more conscious of their sin and imperfection. All Christians should realize that perfection always involves the grace of God and a corresponding activity of man, and the experience of each binds every man to his neighbor. "For we are blessed not only in fellowship with God," he writes, "but also in fellowship with all the blessed. For the former we have only God to thank; the latter we produce through our personal contribution to the common weal of the Kingdom of God."[107] Thus a higher level of achievement in one's lifework and in the maturation of a full-orbed Christian character than is the case for one's neighbor does not bring with it a feeling of complete satisfaction. There must be always the drive toward a fuller and more complete realization of one's vocation and ethical duties as well as one's trust and confidence in God. Occasional lapses should not be construed as signs that one has lost sight of the goal if one is still moving toward it. Indeed, the honest acknowledgement of these lapses and failings may be the inducement to ever greater striving. This is the note on which Ritschl concludes his pamphlet on *Christian Perfection.* "It is surely only that religious faith which is complete in itself which cries out in life's extremity: 'Lord, I believe, help my unbelief.' "[108]

CHAPTER V

Conclusion

THE PRESENT STATE OF RITSCHL STUDIES

It is not surprising that the current attempt to reassess the theology of the nineteenth century has necessitated a renewed encounter with Ritschl's thought. Until about the year 1945, however, the kerygmatic theologies of Barth and Bultmann so dominated the theological landscape that questions concerning their theological antecedents received little attention. Furthermore, Barth's polemic against Neo-Protestantism was so forceful that an entire generation interpreted it from his perspective. Nevertheless, Barth deserves credit for keeping some of the issues of the past century before us even though his interpretation is being subjected to ever more careful scrutiny. Barth's account of the history of theology in the eighteenth and nineteenth centuries is based on lectures delivered in 1932–1933 and published in book form in 1947.[1] Nothing approximating it has yet appeared in English, though of late, American theologians and historians have begun to make important contribution to the analysis of the theology of the nineteenth century.[2]

THE NEO-ORTHODOX CRITIQUE OF RITSCHL

We noted above that the dominant influence exercised by the theology of Ritschl and his followers from about 1875 until the close of World War I came to an abrupt end with the rise of the dialectical theology associated with the names of Barth, Bultmann, and Brunner. One of the factors contributing to the final eclipse of the Ritschlian theology was the radical polemic to which it was subjected, especially at the hands of Barth and Brunner. The latter's *Die Mystik und das Wort*, published in 1924, discredited Schleiermacher by associating his theology of feeling with mysticism. Although this interpretation did not meet with Barth's approval, Brunner did not retract his thesis in the second edition. He warned against the appearance of new syntheses between theological idealism and the

145

Christian faith. "The either/or which exists between speculative Idealism or mysticism and the Christian faith, between a monologue of the soul with its own divinity and faith in the divine act of revelation and of the word of reconciliation in Jesus Christ, is even today in acute danger of being weakened to a position of both/and."[3]

A year earlier, Brunner had attacked the theological liberalism of the nineteenth century and Schleiermacher and Ritschl in particular in his important work *The Mediator*. The rising *Religionsgeschichtliche Schule* (history of religions school) was pictured as standing at the end of the long tradition in the nineteenth century which had denied the centrality of the Mediator, Jesus Christ.

> Here one faith confronts the other; the belief in "general" revelation, religion without a mediator, the faith of mysticism and Idealism, stands over against the religion with a Mediator, the faith of the Scriptures and of the Christian Church. The one thing this proves is that a theology which refuses to admit the existence of this contradiction is not Christian.[4]

Ritschl fared no better in Brunner's hands than did Schleiermacher! Though admitting that Ritschl's intention differed from his performance, Brunner cites approvingly the "acute theological critic of the Idealist and Liberal school [who] once said of Ritschl, that he adorned a building constructed wholly in the Rationalistic style with a supernatural gateway."[5] Brunner's estimate concurs completely: The "Ritschlian theology is a Rationalistic system clad in scriptural garments. . . . It is an almost perfectly unified Rationalistic building of simple design."[6]

The radical critique of theological liberalism was developed especially by the Swiss fellow countrymen, Brunner and Barth. Though their analyses respecting its deficiencies were essentially the same, Barth's voice predominated. As is so often the case in life as well as in theology, the sons of a new generation often cannot understand their fathers, and in turn the fathers cannot comprehend their sons. This became apparent in Barth's growing disenchantment with the Ritschlian theology of his teacher, Adolf von Harnack. The latter—the single most influential theologian of Barth's student days—found in turn Barth's developing theological viewpoint virtually incomprehensible! In their public correspondence in 1923, Harnack addresses Barth as the leader of the "despisers of scientific theology." The questions and responses between them—intended to initiate a dialogue— served only to accentuate their differences. Barth acknowledges that his initial response to Harnack's questions only served to reveal more clearly the great chasm between their respective positions. Harnack warns Barth that he should be careful not to speak so much in terms of "either/or" in theology; "Would it not be better if he acknowledged that he plays *his* instrument, but that God might have yet other instruments?"[7] Harnack's final lament concerning the direction of the dialectical theology is from a letter to Martin Rade, editor of *Die christliche Welt*.

Our present theology is highly motivated and pays attention to main problems—and that is salutary. But how weak it is as science, how narrow and sectarian its horizons, how expressionistic its method, and how short sighted its representation of history! . . . Ritschl is today the most betrayed, although in my estimation he offers a great deal with which the Barthians could comply.[8]

Though Barth was never wholly unappreciative of nineteenth-century theological liberalism, his more recent statements are more moderate. Yet even in his lecture on *The Humanity of God* in 1956 the analysis of the theology of the nineteenth century at whose end Ritschl stood is one with his statements of the twenties. Nineteenth-century theology was "anthropocentric," "religionistic," and "humanistic." He continues:

For this theology, to think about God meant to think in a scarcely veiled fashion about man, more exactly about the religious, the Christian religious man. To speak about God meant to speak in an exalted tone but once again and more than ever about this man—his revelations and wonders, his faith and his works. There is no question about it: here man was made great at the cost of God—the divine God who is someone other than man, who sovereignly confronts him, who immovably and unchangeably stands over against him as the Lord, Creator, and Redeemer.[9]

In the lecture just cited the "old man of Basel" admits that some of his earlier barbs against his predecessors in the nineteenth century—uttered in the heat of battle—were too sharp.

How we cleared things away! And we did almost nothing but clear away! Everything which even remotely smacked of mysticism and morality, of pietism and romanticism, or even of idealism, was suspected and sharply interdicted or bracketed with reservations which sounded actually prohibitive! What should really have been only a sad and friendly smile was a derisive laugh![10]

The more irenic tone of this and similar judgments of the later Barth cannot change the fact that his earlier attack upon nineteenth-century theology in general, and Ritschl in particular, contributed greatly toward the jaundiced eye through which the nineteenth century was viewed in the period between the World Wars. Barth's wholesale rejection of the theology of his spiritual forefathers in the nineteenth century was stated quite forcefully in 1928.

> If I today became convinced that the interpretation of the Reformation
> on the line taken by Schleiermacher-Ritschl-Troeltsch . . . was correct;
> that Luther and Calvin really intended such an outcome of their labours;
> I could not indeed become a Catholic tomorrow, but I should have to
> withdraw from the evangelical Church. And if I were forced to make a
> choice between the two evils, I should, in fact, prefer the Catholic.[11]

Statements from Barth's early writings show that he always evidenced
respect for Schleiermacher's contribution—despite the harshness of judgments like the preceding—and very little for Ritschl. In his lectures on the
history of modern theology delivered in Bonn in 1932–1933 at the time of
Hitler's rise to power, Barth spoke of Ritschl in disparaging terms in
marked contrast to his recognition of Schleiermacher's greatness. "Ritschl
has the significance of an episode in more recent theology, and not,
indeed that of an epoch."[12] Though acknowledging some admiration for
Ritschl's comprehensive theological system and certain of his emphases,
most readers of Barth remember the following characterization of Ritschl's
accommodationist and cultural Christianity, an analysis with which Paul
Tillich also concurred. "[Ritschl] stands with incredible clearness and firm-
ness (truly with both feet) upon the ground of his 'ideal of life,' the very
epitome of the national-liberal bourgeois of the age of Bismarck."[13]

In spite of the polemical tone of Barth's critique of Ritschl, it cannot
be taken lightly. His central thesis regarding Ritschl's deficiency can be
paralleled in several other critics. In Barth's eyes, Ritschl's bold elevation
of a practical ideal of life to the center of his theology represents the culmination of modern theology stemming from the Enlightenment, whose real
concern was man—not God. Barth joins the chorus of earlier critics of
Ritschl who found the latter's exegetical and historical findings subservient
to, and supportive of, a prior commitment to his conception of the Christian
ideal of life. Barth writes:

> We must not allow ourselves to be blinded by sight of the extensive
> material Ritschl drew from the Bible and the history of dogma to the fact
> that this [i.e., the Lebensideal—the practical ideal of life], and ulti-
> mately this alone, was his chief concern. Nobody either before or since
> Ritschl . . . has expressed the view as clearly as he, that modern man
> wishes above all to live in the best sense according to reason, and that
> the significance of Christianity for him can only be a great confirmation
> and strengthening of this very endeavor.[14]

Barth's negative estimate of Ritschl and his school above all others in the
nineteenth century poses some peculiar problems. How could Barth repeatedly speak such appreciative words for his "revered teacher" Wilhelm
Herrmann—whom many regarded as Ritschl's most faithful disciple—

and yet be so opposed to Ritschl? Is it wholly without foundation that Ferdinand Kattenbusch, a Ritschlian and author of *German Evangelical Theology Since Schleiermacher,* could interpret Barth's early theology as bringing the best of Ritschl to fulfillment?[15] The answer to these questions would lead us too far afield. They may serve, however, to apprise us of the fact that contemporaries of the early Barth saw more lines of continuity between his thought and the theology of the nineteenth century and Ritschl in particular than he himself observed or admitted. This is due no doubt, in part, to a kind of myopia which often afflicts prophetic figures such as Barth in the throes of establishing new theological frontiers—something that we noted Barth himself admits. Our own historical distance from the events surrounding the attack of the dialectical theologians on Ritschl and his successors makes possible more balanced estimates of his contribution. We must now turn to some of these interpretations of Ritschl, asking in the process where the focus of Ritschl's theology lies.

OTHER TWENTIETH-CENTURY CRITIQUES OF RITSCHL

Violent controversies were precipitated by the rise of Ritschl's theology to a place of influence in the period following the completion of his magnum opus in 1874. A veritable flood of literature both for and against Ritschl—in addition to more moderate mediating studies—appeared from about 1875 until about 1900. Thereafter it abated somewhat in Germany as Anglo-Saxon authors in Britain, Scotland, and America interacted with Ritschl and the Ritschlian school. By about the year 1910, full-scale studies had appeared in German, French, English, Danish, and Swedish—in itself a tribute to his pervasive influence.[16] With the dawn of the twentieth century in Europe and Germany, however, a new cultural and sociopolitical era came into being in which Ritschl's somewhat secular and optimistic theology seemed reminiscent of an age of stability that was never to return. The new mood in Germany was less hopeful regarding the alliance of Christianity and culture and the inevitable progress of society. Acute social problems, a rising proletariat, and rampant nationalism effected a radically changed climate. The dire predictions of Schopenhauer and Nietzsche struck a responsive chord and many capitulated to a pessimistic world view. Also contributing to the demise of the idealistic philosophy and theology of the nineteenth century was a rising empirical and materialistic bent encouraged by the advance of the natural sciences—a movement Ritschl found ominous. The outbreak of World War I marked the real end of the more optimistic world view maintained by many, including Ritschl, during the last half of the nineteenth century. Though he had formulated his theology with one eye fixed on the *Zeitgeist,* his problems were not those of the new century. Horst Stephan, author of a history of Evangelical theology in Germany, wrote of the decline of Ritschl's influence in 1935:

> Those of us belonging to the generation educated during the latter part of the past century began to find the Ritschlian theology too fixed. We experienced ever more clearly that the problems of theology could not be resolved in the isolation in which Ritschl had viewed the Christian faith, the Bible and the Reformation. Thus we felt ourselves drawn to Troeltsch, who—though in Ritschl's tradition—had experienced quite deeply in his own person the shattering effects of the dissolution of the common cultural consciousness and was thereby able to point many theologians to newer horizons.[17]

In turning to interpretations of Ritschl's thought written since 1940 and to some earlier pre-Barthian appraisals, we note that one thing is immediately apparent. Critics past and present acknowledge the complexity of his thought, and more recent studies are as divided as earlier ones in locating the center of his theology.[18] Ritschl's vocational involvement in Biblical studies, patristics and the history of dogma, Reformation theology, dogmatics and ethics—not to mention subsidiary disciplines—has led interpreters to find the clue to his thought either in his exegetical findings, or historical research, or philosophical and especially epistemological presuppositions, or in specific doctrines, or in quite divergent combinations of the foregoing.

Philip Hefner draws attention to the "almost malicious treatment" accorded Ritschl in "recent critical literature" and attempts to redress the balances. He finds Ritschl's historical research and judgments to be the most fruitful avenue for unlocking the key to his constructive conclusions. "The argument suggests that it is the historical factors in Ritschl's thought rather than the psychological, philosophical, or philosophical-theological factors that are really the system-shaping factors in his theological achievement."[19] Like Barth, Hefner designates the concept of *Lebensführung,* or the ideal life-style, as the clue to Ritschl's thought, but he disagrees with Barth as to the grounds for Ritschl's viewpoint. Hefner contends that Ritschl's exegetical studies and understanding of the history of the church led to his view that the clue to the continuity within the church's history was to be found in the manner in which different epochs, under the impact of the Christian revelation, fashioned their conception of the Christian *Lebensideal.* Thus Ritschl's historical judgments are supposedly the key to understanding the subsequent center of his theological system.

We have observed that Barth accuses Ritschl of adopting the picture of the ideal Christian man in the age of Bismarck as his norm apart from historical and Biblical considerations—proceeding thereafter to make his historical judgments accord with his chosen norm. In fairness to Hefner it must be noted that he finds Ritschl guilty of violating his intention to take history more seriously than the idealists. By utilizing the category that he has supposedly extracted from an analysis of Christian history—the *Lebensideal*—as the norm by which various epochs in Christian history are evaluated, Ritschl robs history of its dynamic movement and diversity.[20] Thus in a sense there is some underlying agreement in the conclusions of Hefner and Barth. Their viewpoint for interpreting Ritschl is not new, however. Less than a year after Ritschl's death Wilhelm Herrmann located the essence of Ritschl's theology in his view of faith and the type of piety to which it gives rise.[21]

It will facilitate our review of other twentieth-century interpretations of Ritschl's theology if we organize them in terms of their prevailing perspectives. The divergence of opinion respecting the key to Ritschl's system derives in part from the range and complexity of his thought. In 1903, Professor Orr reminded his readers that Ritschl "in his own spirit passed through all the phases of the theological thought of his time."[22] Perhaps more important is the fact that he "undertook to develop theology at numerous points in a new manner and mode in opposition to antiquated dogmatic methods."[23]

Although the center of Ritschl's theology has been identified differently on the basis of which of his characteristic emphases received primary attention, we may subsume most analyses under four headings.[24] First, some regard Ritschl's epistemology and theological method as the key to the unlocking of the mysteries of his theology. This category must be understood rather broadly to include implicit or explicit philosophical, psychological, logical, and other presuppositions determinative of Ritschl's procedure. A second group, and by far the largest, finds the clue to his theology in his understanding of the Christian religion as an ellipse with two foci, namely, the religious pole (justification and reconciliation) and the ethical pole (the Kingdom of God). Within this group there is disagreement as to which pole is dominant. Some thinkers find the religious pole predominant; others the ethical and teleological pole. Still others find Ritschl's theology most comprehensible if due weight is given to both foci in his thought much in the manner in which Ritschl depicted his procedure. A third group views Ritschl's theology as decidedly anthropocentric; it concentrates on the human situation and anticipates emphases of more recent Christian existentialism. A final group locates the clue to Ritschl in a doctrine other than the doctrines of justification and reconciliation and the Kingdom of God. Let us turn to the rationale behind each of these choices in the attempt to discover which is most plausible.

1. *The Key to Ritschl: Epistemology?* Ritschl's publication of *Theology and Metaphysics* in 1881 marked the beginning of a lively dispute concerning the role that philosophical and epistemological presuppositions

play in his theology. Subsequently, we shall consider some of the ramifications of Ritschl's epistemology in his system. Our purpose here is more limited. We may put it thus: Did his epistemology play a decisive role both in the form and content of his theology? Otto Pfleiderer gave an affirmative reply to this question in an article published shortly after Ritschl's death. His concern was not so much to debate whether the latter's analysis and use of epistemological ground rules laid down by Kant and Lotze was accurate, but rather to show that their application involved a theological reductionism leading to the surrender of the reality of the supernatural and therefore of God.[25] A year earlier Stählin had written an extensive monograph comparing Ritschl's epistemology with those of Kant and Lotze, his acknowledged sources, and concluded that Ritschl was a Neo-Kantian. More significantly, Stählin anticipated Pfleiderer's conclusion. He held that Ritschl's adoption of Kant's axioms that we cannot know phenomena in and of themselves and further that no theoretical knowledge of the transcendent world is possible at all, ruled out the independent reality of God.[26]

Friedrich Traub also addressed himself to this problem, indicating certain inadequacies in Ritschl's understanding of the epistemologies of Kant and Lotze. Like Pfleiderer, he observed Ritschl's vacillation in matters epistemological in successive editions of *Justification and Reconciliation* and saw this as a sign that he never achieved a fully satisfactory statement of his epistemology. But Traub differed from preceding critics in maintaining with some cogency that Ritschl's theological conclusions were dictated, not by epistemological considerations, but by his Biblical and historical research; indeed, Ritschl's attempts to buttress these with the aid of a Kantian epistemology represented an afterthought. Kant's epistemology commended itself to him because it provided the possibility of distinguishing the spheres of faith and theoretical knowledge. Traub concludes: "Ritschl's starting point does not lie in epistemological considerations and therefore it is understandable that what he offers us in this area gives us the impression of being incomplete and unfinished."[27] Otto Ritschl supports Traub's conclusion in maintaining a few years later and throughout his lifetime that Ritschl's epistemology determined to some degree the structure of his theology, but not its content. The latter was derived from his understanding of God's revelation perceived in the witness of Scripture and the history of the church.[28]

Although Otto Ritschl wished for an end to the discussion of Ritschl's epistemology on the grounds that it represented a subsidiary interest and served to detract from his father's larger theological contribution, the debate continues. Even interpreters past and present who focus upon the religious or ethical poles of Ritschl's theology recognize the far-reaching effects of his epistemology upon his construction of doctrine. Paul Wrzecionko's recent book, *The Philosophical Roots of the Theology of Albrecht Ritschl,* has injected the epistemological issue back into the discussion. In marked contrast to Hefner's contention that sufficient studies of Ritschl's epistemology were extant, Wrzecionko affirms that apart from the earlier work of Stählin and Fr. H. R. von Frank virtually no serious work on Ritschl's philosophical and epistemological presuppositions had been done.

According to Wrzecionko, the *Sitz im Leben* in which Ritschl developed his theology was a median position between the objectivism of Hegel on the one hand and the subjectivism of Schleiermacher on the other. Though impressed by Hegel's comprehensive system and the vision of the idealist tradition, Ritschl's Biblical orientation caused him to be critical of their speculative treatment of Christian history. Schleiermacher's starting point in man's finitude and therewith in the human situation enabled him to accord man's subjectivity an important place in his theology. To be sure, he also sought to do justice to the objective pole by seeing man's feeling of dependence in the light of his derivation from God; moreover, this universal feeling of dependence is informed by the believer's relationship to the historical revelation in Jesus. Yet Wrzecionko contends that Ritschl's Hegelian trappings made him dissatisfied with Schleiermacher's treatment of historical revelation. In attempting to relate the historical pole seen in the events of revelation on the one hand and the believing subject on the other, Ritschl found the Neo-Kantian epistemology of his colleague Lotze to be the needed catalyst. From Lotze he derives the thread basic to his whole epistemology, namely, the principle of the correlation between cause and effect (*Wirken und Gewirkwerden*), or between activity and receptivity, and in this manner he integrated faith and historical revelation.

The way in which Ritschl brought these varying influences into a workable epistemology is summarized by Wrzecionko as follows:

> In harmony with the tendency toward historical positivism in the post-Hegelian period, Ritschl makes the decisive move of reaching back to the events of revelation attested in the Scriptures; Ritschl utilized the epistemology of Lotze . . . especially the concept of the dynamic correlation between cause and effect; and under the impression of the Kantian ethic in its neo-Kantian dress, Ritschl evaluated the reality of the Christian faith and its statements—in accordance with the nature of the practical reason—in terms of ideal contents and values. And all of these motives point to a decidedly anti-metaphysical tendency.[29]

American interpreters of Ritschl have not neglected the epistemological issues and have identified Ritschl's lineage and intention in much the same way as their European counterparts. Paul Lehmann's comparative study of the understanding of forgiveness in Ritschl and Barth pinpointed the difficulty precipitated by Ritschl's adoption of a Kantian epistemology to ensure the relevance of Christian doctrine. The result was that the question of the truth of theological statements was virtually equated with their psychological relevance. "Only that theology is reliable which conforms to the general laws of human conduct and knowledge, for apart from these, i.e., a right theory of knowledge and voluntary activity, it could never be understood."[30] Similar statements can be documented in many other critics of Ritschl, but they must suffice to show that his epistemological considerations exercise a considerable influence both upon the shape and content of his theology.

2. *The Key to Ritschl: Redemption and/or the Kingdom of God?*   A second school of thought interprets Ritschl primarily as a theologian rather than as an epistemologist or philosopher of religion. The clue to his system is to be found in his view that Christianity must be understood in the light of its two foci, namely, redemption and the Kingdom of God. Yet even a hasty perusal of the secondary literature makes it apparent that there is marked disagreement as to which pole predominates, and part of the confusion at this point is attributable to Ritschl himself. A fairly good case can and has been made for the centrality of each of these poles and the outcome is to some extent determined by which edition of *Justification and Reconciliation* is used. In our treatment, we have attempted to show how both of these poles constitute and determine the structure of Ritschl's theology and the manner in which he sought to balance them.[31]

Our concentration upon justification and reconciliation in Ritschl's theology and therewith upon the religious rather than the ethical pole could be interpreted as a failure to accord sufficient attention to the teleological dimension of his thought symbolized by the Kingdom of God.[32] However, our purpose was not to minimize the latter, but to show that Ritschl intends to accord the redemptive pole of the Christian faith its rightful place in his system. Accordingly, we argued that one cannot accuse him of succumbing to a simple moralism and of neglecting the meaning of the believers' reconciliation with God. But whereas the redemptive pole had played an important role in Protestant life and thought from Luther to Ritschl, the teleological dimension had not. Thus Ritschl saw his task to be that of bringing the redemptive pole into proper harmony with God's destiny for mankind in the Kingdom of God.

An important step in resolving the problem of interpreting Ritschl at this point was made by Fabricius in the year 1909 in his study of the development of Ritschl's theology from 1874 to 1889 in the light of the various changes Ritschl effected in the three editions of *Justification and Reconciliation*. He asks this question: Which edition of the work enables the thrust of Ritschl's theology to be seen most clearly? On the basis of a careful synoptic comparison of the three editions, Fabricius concludes that the second and third editions give the priority to the religious pole represented by justification and reconciliation whereas the first edition accorded the ethical and teleological pole the place of preeminence. Which is the "real" Ritschl? Fabricius has no doubts: "Ritschl's total view of Christianity was never more complete, consistent, or harmonious than it was in the first edition of his main work [J. R.]. In it everything was correlated with the final purpose of the ethical Kingdom of God."[33] In subsequent editions, however, the changes that minimized the centrality of the Kingdom of God brought confusion and disharmony into the whole so that at many points the argument becomes incomprehensible. Thus Fabricius felt forced to conclude that though the later editions of *Justification and Reconciliation* were perhaps more Christian, they were less authentic and characteristic of Ritschl's original intention.[34]

Though some writers subsequent to Fabricius have failed to take notice of his important contribution, a goodly number both before and after him have contended for the priority of the ethical or teleological pole in Ritschl's theology as the clue to interpreting it correctly. When seen in this light, justification and reconciliation are subordinated to the Kingdom of God as means are to ends. One of the earliest studies maintaining this position is of special significance inasmuch as it received Ritschl's approval as a true expression of his intention. A former student, Julius Thikötter, wrote a series of articles in 1883 entitled *Analysis and Critique of the Theology of Albrecht Ritschl* in which he argued that the Kingdom of God was the leading principle of his theology. Thikötter's studies pleased Ritschl so much that he was instrumental in getting his publishers to circulate them in book form.[35] Otto Ritschl also finds the teleological thrust to be the most significant for comprehending the structure and content of his father's theology.

> Thus the concept of the Kingdom of God as the universal final purpose is the leading idea which enables us to understand both the nature of man and the meaning of the divine government of the world. For from the beginning the total world government is directed towards its end so that the Kingdom of God can be the unification of his disciples in mutual love in which each at the same time gains his blessedness, and the purpose of the world is attained.[36]

In maintaining this position, Otto Ritschl and others can point to the revealing statement of Ritschl to Diestel in 1871: "I am personally convinced that the idea of redemption can be conceived aright in dogmatics only if it is interpreted as a means to the highest purpose evident in the Kingdom of God."[37]

G. Hök's analysis of the evolution of Ritschl's thought finds the same tension existing between the religious and ethical poles as had Fabricius' study. Ritschl can distinguish these two spheres quite radically when he considers that the former concerns man's blessedness while the latter has to do with the destiny of humanity in the Kingdom of God. However, when he wants to emphasize that religion and ethics have to do with specific activities directed by man's will, he cannot separate them completely; then religion—which concerns man's will in relationship to God—makes concrete ethical activities possible. In this context, man's redemption tends to be viewed as a means pointing toward the establishment of the Kingdom of God. Thus Ritschl can vacillate between asserting the complete independence of the religious and ethical spheres as we have indicated above, or he can see the religious as subservient to, or as the presupposition of, the ethical. But Hök does not find a final contradiction here. It can be accounted for by recognizing that on the subjective level the independence of each of these spheres must be maintained. Neither can become a means for the other without endangering the certainty of salvation on the one hand or the autonomy of ethical action on the other. "But religion and ethics can be distinguished completely from man's standpoint and yet be in relationship to one another from God's vantage point and his view of salvation-history so that religion becomes the presupposition for ethics."[38] The problem is acute at this point because Ritschl often fails to clarify whether he is speaking from the divine viewpoint which encompasses the whole of redemptive history moving toward the Kingdom of God or from the human.[39]

The foregoing makes clear why both nineteenth- and twentieth-century critics have found Ritschl's doctrine of justification and reconciliation the key to the whole. In discussing Ritschl's theological development and his relationship to Reformation and post-Reformation modes of thought, we are aware that he came to see the question of reconciliation as the decisive issue for Protestant theology in his day. The major portion of his research and writing was directly related to this theme and we do not misconstrue Ritschl's intention if we depict it as the attempt to present an adequate doctrine of justification and reconciliation for the Christian church in his time.

Over against those who minimize the importance of this doctrine in maintaining the primacy of God's purpose in the Kingdom of God in Ritschl's system, three things must be remembered. First, it is indubitable that Ritschl viewed the sinner's justification to be the basis for understanding the Christian life. Secondly, his Christocentrism necessitates that all knowledge of God must begin with the revelation in Jesus Christ and man's new relationship to God which derives from him. There is thus no possibility of discussing God's final purpose in the Kingdom of God unless this is first illuminated through God's forgiving love in Jesus Christ. Thirdly, there can be no knowledge of God's ultimate purpose in the Kingdom of God apart from one's participation in the church, the community that is everywhere and always to be understood as the community of forgiveness. Critics past and present have therefore concentrated upon Ritschl's exposition of this doctrine, and a considerable number make it their major concern.[40]

No matter what the estimate of Ritschl's doctrine of justification and reconciliation may be, he and Martin Kähler are perhaps the only theologians of the nineteenth century who make it central for theological construction. In Ritschl's case this takes on added significance in view of his controversy with an antagonist and colleague at Göttingen, Paul de Lagarde. As early as 1873, Lagarde maintained that Paul's teaching concerning justification was not central in his theology, but represented a polemical doctrine directed against the Judaizers. Therefore, it should be regarded neither as the essence of the gospel nor as the central doctrine of the Reformers. Nor was it relevant in any way for Protestantism in the nineteenth century. Though Lagarde maintained this position with some vehemence during the last years of Ritschl's life and after his death, there is no indication that Ritschl felt moved to change his mind![41]

3. *The Key to Ritschl: Anthropological Theology?* A third group of critics locate the center of gravity in Ritschl in a place different from that determined by the preceding, though obviously it is difficult to view anyone as a pure representative of our models. Thus, though Wrzecionko is concerned to examine the roots of Ritschl's epistemology, it is epistemology that is intended to illuminate the entire system. He concludes that Ritschl's theology is significant for modern theology because among other things it represents an important antecedent of later existential theologies which focus on the human situation.[42] This position is similar to that adopted earlier by Barth and Brunner, who held that Ritschl's theology is rigorously anthropological in both its starting point and execution. Accordingly, this school of thought contends that no understanding of Ritschl is possible if it is forgotten that for him everything circles about man's problematic situation in the world caused by the fact that he is both part of nature and yet as spirit superior to it. All religion is concerned with man's transcendence over the natural world, and Christianity offers the most adequate solution to man's threatened existence. Viewed from this perspective, everything in Ritschl's theology can be explained as necessary to secure man's victory over the world. The issue for him is therefore not finally the relationship between man and God, but rather that of man's relationship to an

impersonal and hostile world. God and revelation become the means by which man solves the problems of human existence.[43]

4. *The Key to Ritschl: The Doctrine of God?*   Brief mention must be made of some attempts to interpret Ritschl in the light of doctrines other than the foregoing. Here again, it is difficult to single out pure types. Some find the doctrine of God the clue to his system. In discussing the presuppositions of the doctrine of justification and reconciliation, we gave special attention to his doctrine of God and the manner in which it was related to his view of the Kingdom of God.[44] Thus it is understandable that Ritschl's efforts to reinterpret the doctrine of God could provide a point of departure for understanding his theology. This viewpoint commends itself particularly if one is inclined to see him as more indebted to the idealistic tradition than he was willing to admit. Thus like the idealists, Ritschl was concerned to create a comprehensive Christian *Weltanschauung;* however, instead of building it upon an idealist ontology, he constructs it upon a Kantian ethical metaphysic. The latter, however, has its roots in the nature of God, who finally makes it possible for a unified world view to be constructed. Thus a consistent and comprehensive *Weltanschauung* derived from the understanding of God can be seen underlying Ritschl's total theological effort.[45] Yet other critics single out his conception of God as wholly love as the leading principle to which all else is related.[46] Certainly Ritschl's radical Christocentrism and rejection of all natural theology made it necessary to construct his understanding of God in the light of his love manifest in Jesus Christ.

5. *The Key to Ritschl: Christology?* Our discussion of Ritschl's theology has made his Christocentrism evident and this has led some to find it the unifying principle of the whole. No natural knowledge of God is possible; all knowledge of God derives from his revelation of himself in Jesus Christ. He reveals God's purpose respecting the Kingdom of God and is the Founder of the Kingdom; through the faithful discharge of his vocation in life and death, men are brought into a new relationship to God.[47] Even a brief statement like this of the role of Christology in Ritschl's theological construction necessitates taking seriously his understanding of the mission and ministry of Jesus and the apostolic interpretation of him. This must be said even though his critics have found his exegesis and perspective questionable at certain points.

6. *The Key to Ritschl: Christian Perfection?*   A final suggestive way to get at the intention of Ritschl's system is to find everything issuing in his conception of ethical and religious perfection visible in man's supremacy

over the world.[48] The realization of this is synonymous with the ideal mode of life that marks the reconciled man within the Kingdom of God. Timm's recent study puts this somewhat differently in contending that Ritschl's exegesis of the Gospel of Mark led him to affirm that disciples engaged in the work of the Kingdom of God represent the beginnings of the divinized humanity. Thus the pursuit of the tasks of the Kingdom of God by Jesus' disciples and subsequent followers issues in the same religious and moral perfection characteristic of the life of Jesus.[49]

PROSPECTS AND PROBLEMS IN RITSCHL'S THEOLOGY

THE SCOPE OF RITSCHL'S THEOLOGY: SOME PROSPECTS

Our examination of Ritschl's theology, though limited to its major emphases, has nevertheless made it evident that we are confronted with a theological program of considerable dimensions. This must be stated even though Ritschl practiced a kind of theological reductionism that necessitated omitting doctrines once judged essential. In the period between his death in 1889 and the present, perhaps only Barth and Bultmann have exerted so decisive an influence upon theological construction as he did in his own lifetime and thereafter.

1. *Toward a New Theology.* In his own way, Ritschl intended to develop a Christian theology that would illuminate the relationships between God, man, and the world. This required dealing adequately first with the revelation of God in history culminating in the person of Jesus. Yet such was his vision of God's historical self-manifestation that he did not restrict it to the history of the people of God within the Old and New Covenants. Indeed, the manner in which he and others in the nineteenth century wrestled with the relationship of Christianity to other religions and with the phenomenon of religion may yet prove to be suggestive for contemporary research in this area. Moreover, Ritschl's careful investigation of the history and tradition of the Christian community as fruitful for understanding its present has not been surpassed by many theologians of the twentieth century despite the advances in historical knowledge. We may conclude, therefore, that Ritschl deserves a place among the leaders of nineteenth-century theology for developing a point of view that attempted in its way to do justice to the historical basis of Christianity. In the process, he contributed to the development of a new historical hermeneutic as the basis for interpreting the Christian faith, rather than to the preservation of an ontological or metaphysical hermeneutic characteristic of earlier days.[50]

No consideration of Ritschl's theology would be adequate, however, that did not recognize the fruitful way in which he incorporated the subjective pole represented by the faith of the community and the individual within his system. If in his stress upon the historical revelation of God and therewith upon the objective pole he sought to correct a deficiency in Schleiermacher, his development of the subjective pole was consciously indebted to him. In a sense one must see Ritschl attempting to revivify the rich understanding of faith and the life of faith set forth so powerfully in Luther and Schleiermacher. However, the impetus that Ritschl's theological method gave to the development of more anthropological and existential methodologies in the twentieth century in W. Herrmann, Bultmann, and others has not yet been fully acknowledged or investigated. Moreover, it may well prove to be the case that Ritschl's ethical and existential bent is more suggestive for contemporary attempts to construct what may be called existential theologies than the more individualistic, romantic, and perhaps mystical approach of Schleiermacher. Ritschl's ethical type of "existential" theology provides a more comprehensive understanding of human existence in the world than that of Kierkegaard and the highly individualistic existential theologies stemming from him in this century. Thus Macquarrie is no doubt right in saying that though theologians may find it increasingly difficult to utilize the ontological metaphysic of idealism in theological construction, they may well find the Kantian ethical metaphysic helpful. If that should become more characteristic in the future than presently, Ritschl's theological program may prove suggestive once more.[51]

2. *Salvation and the Kingdom of God.*   In addition to the creative way in which Ritschl seeks to do justice both to the objective and historical and subjective and personal dimensions of the Christian faith, another element of his constructive effort deserves mention. We refer to the scope afforded Ritschl's theology on account of the elliptical structure evident in the twin foci of redemption and the Kingdom of God. Though his interpretation of each of these poles is not without its problems which remain to be enumerated, his vision demands respect. His intention was to bring God's eternal purpose for creation and especially for humanity evident in the Kingdom of God into meaningful relationship to the history of God's dealings with mankind culminating in the person of Jesus, who actualizes the Kingdom of God and establishes the church. Moreover, the continuing history of the church and of mankind is interpreted both in the light of the redemptive significance of Jesus Christ and in terms of the fulfillment of the Kingdom of God toward which all the purposes of God are directed.

The scope of the divine government and movement in history apparent in Ritschl's vision is in effect a philosophy of history. That he could develop such a position is surely indicative both of his understanding of the

Biblical witness to God as Creator, Redeemer, and Consummator and of his indebtedness to the grand philosophies of history characteristic of the idealistic tradition in which he was nurtured. The fact that the dimension of the future and the Christian hope evident in the theology of Moltmann and others are making such an impression currently is evidence that the teleological dimension of Ritschl's thought—with all of its deficiencies—was not taken with sufficient seriousness by his successors. Thus instead of developing a deeper understanding of the import of the Kingdom of God in the light of the investigations of New Testament eschatology in Johannes Weiss and Albert Schweitzer, Ritschl's followers such as Herrmann retreated into a more subjective and individualistic understanding of the Christian faith. We can put it thus: Whereas Ritschl at his best spoke of the relationship between God, man, and the world within the perspective of the church and the Kingdom of God, his followers such as Harnack and particularly Herrmann could speak of little else than of God and the soul or of God and man's inner experience.[52] Consequently, their vision was less Biblical, historical, and comprehensive than Ritschl's and invited Barth's polemic.

To date, Bultmann and even the post-Bultmannians have not been able to transcend fully the limitations of an existentialistic hermeneutic and its excessive individualism. Accordingly, the Christian faith has been transformed in Moltmann's terms from a *cultus publicus* to a *cultus privatus;* a subjective and individual ethic constructed upon I-Thou encounters is possible, but the basis for a social ethic is lacking.[53] Thus even though one can argue that existentialism's realized eschatology is actually not much different from Ritschl's, it is clear that his conception of the church and the Kingdom of God provided him at least with the possibility of transcending the tendency toward an excessively individualistic ethic. The teleological dimension that occupies an important place, at least formally, in Ritschl's thought is almost wholly absent in Christian existentialism. Only the soteriological moment remains and it is interpreted in such an individualistic fashion that the communal nature of Christianity fails to have constitutive importance. Thus in order to find a theology that does more justice to the eschatological and teleological dimension of the Christian faith one must move beyond Barth, Bultmann, and the post-Bultmannians to Moltmann. The latter traces the weakness in the eschatological thought of W. Herrmann, the early Barth, and Bultmann to their essentially Greek understanding of revelation according to which "the *logos* [is conceived as] the epiphany of the eternal present of being," whereas it ought to be understood in terms of the Biblical categories of promise and fulfillment.[54]

3. *A Theology of the Church.* Another area in which Ritschl's theology provided helpful insights for his successors lies in his concentration

upon the church. We observed the close correlation he maintains between theology and the Christian community; theology is "faith seeking understanding" within the church. It arises within the community brought into existence by the reconciling activity of God evident in the life, death, and resurrection of Jesus Christ, and concentrates upon explicating the meaning both of his historical existence and present Lordship for the life of the church. In opposition to theological rationalism, Ritschl maintained that the faith of the apostolic community in the saving work of Christ was predicated upon both the death and the resurrection of Christ.[55] Moreover, he always held that only within the community of faith which acknowledges the risen Lord could men gain assurance of their justification and reconciliation with God.[56] The fact that Christian existentialism in our century has little appreciation for the priority of the church over the individual believer represents a radical deficiency in their theology and a retrogression from Ritschl's viewpoint. Barth's *Church Dogmatics* no doubt was influenced by Ritschl's concentration upon the church and may be seen as a fruitful development of that emphasis.

4. *Toward a Theology of Culture.*   One dominant issue in contemporary American Christianity is the relationship of Christ and culture. For some time, increasing dissatisfaction with both what is taken to be the inadequacies of Barth's kerygmatic theology and the excessive individualism of some forms of Christian existentialism has been apparent. In addition to these changes in theological direction, a consciousness of guilt has afflicted the church because of its failure to relate the gospel to man's existence in the world. Together these factors have precipitated an almost frantic attempt to convince the world of the relevancy of the Christian faith and ethic for life in the twentieth century.

It is clear that Ritschl's influence upon American Christianity and theology lies mainly in the impetus he gave to the development of the social gospel through Rauschenbusch and others. Over against an influential pietistic mentality which encouraged withdrawal from the world as the pathway to perfection, he proposed a nineteenth-century form of "worldly Christianity." This led H. Richard Niebuhr to view Ritschl as the paradigm of the "Christ of Culture" mentality in the nineteenth century.[57] This accounts for the repeated charge of his addiction to "cultural Protestantism." In this respect he reminds us of Schleiermacher's earlier attempt to build bridges between Christianity and culture.

Ritschl's rationale for relating Christ and culture has been developed earlier, and only the essential features need be reviewed here.[58] He saw God's final purpose in terms of the Kingdom of God, the ideal ethical society marked by love of God and neighbor. The latter is founded through Christ, but its fulfillment is contingent upon man's moral activity in both his personal and corporate life. The second pillar of his approach to culture is anthropological. We noted that he views man as a spiritual personality involved in the struggle to dominate the world of nature—i.e., the impersonal and material world. Though impressed with man's technological mastery of nature, this did not represent the goal of life: indeed, this capacity was in some sense feared because of the possibilities it held for a new materialism. In the light of his reading of the New Testament and Kant, Ritschl envisaged the goal of life in terms of man's movement toward the ethical and spiritual wholeness characteristic of Jesus. This is attested in man's consciousness of dominion over nature, that is, in the awareness that nature is created and preserved in order to assure the fulfillment of individual and corporate existence in the Kingdom of God. Thus Ritschl's vision avoids a division between Christ and culture; the latter is good insofar as it can be molded to preserve those moral and spiritual values which, in Paul Lehmann's apt phrase, "make human life human."[59]

In evaluating Ritschl's contribution at this point, one could commend him for the creative manner in which he sought to relate the individual and corporate dimensions of the Christian faith to man's existence in the world. Though not alone in sounding this note in the nineteenth century, he was among the most suggestive. Bonhoeffer's movement toward a Christian ethic for the "man come of age" speaks more powerfully to us than does Ritschl. Yet both are marked by a concern to avoid the perennial tendency to bifurcate human existence into two spheres represented by the church and the Kingdom of God on the one side and the secular, natural world on the other. Bonhoeffer writes: "Whoever professes to believe in the reality of Jesus Christ, as the revelation of God, must in the same breath profess his faith in both the reality of God and the reality of the world; for in Christ he finds God and the world reconciled."[60] Of late this same note is being sounded in the existentialist tradition. Gerhard Ebeling may be regarded as typical in decrying an understanding of justification by faith issuing in a quietism or escapism that denies the reality of man's being-in-the-world. Faith's sphere is the world. "For faith lives not in the abstract, the general and the timeless, but in the concrete, the particular and the historical."[61]

Though we cannot explore the lines of continuity here, the above references are sufficient to indicate some points of similarity between Ritschl and current ethical thinking. Both Bultmann's conception of inauthentic existence marked by man's enslavement to the world and to powers less than God and of authentic existence characterized by man's realization of true selfhood through faith have antecedents in Ritschl and in the idealism that influenced both. However, Paul Lehmann's construction of a Christian ethic of freedom that derives from participation in the common life and faith of the church brings Ritschl's faith-church correlation to completion better than the more individualistic ethic of Christian existentialists. For Lehmann, man is freed from the world so that he may become free for the world in response to the will of God. Moltmann's eschatological ethic provides a corrective to the more humanistically conceived Kingdom of God in Ritschl and represents a consistent realization of the import of the teleological dimension for the totality of man's life in the world.

> The promise of the kingdom of God in which all things attain to right, to life, to peace, to freedom, and to truth, is not exclusive but inclusive. And so, too, its love, its neighbourliness and its sympathy are inclusive, excluding nothing, but embracing in hope everything wherein God will be all in all. The *pro-missio* of the kingdom is the ground of the *missio* of love to the world.[62]

PROBLEMS IN RITSCHL'S THEOLOGY

1. *Epistemology and Theological Method.* Our analysis of Ritschl's epistemology and his conception of faith enables us to comprehend both the positive and the negative reactions that they called forth. He held his view of faith to be a recovery of the best insights of the Reformation and the New Testament; accordingly, he rejected all speculative, abstract, rationalistic, and intellectualistic interpretations of faith. Faith is not to be confused with assent to the Bible's authority, the idea of God's existence, or to doctrines and creeds. Faith is never disinterested knowledge about God, but trust in God who reveals himself to be "for us" in Christ. Ritschl concurred with Kant's rejection of all metaphysics that sought to establish the existence of God via reason and he opposed speculative theology which spoke about God's existence in himself (*a se*). Faith is believing trust in the God revealed in the saving work of Jesus Christ. With this approach he felt he avoided a false objectivism characteristic of Roman Catholic, orthodox Protestant, and rationalistic definitions of faith.

Ritschl undoubtedly recovered something of the dynamic understanding of faith characteristic of the Reformation, and the entire subsequent history of Protestantism is indebted to him and to Schleiermacher in this regard. Not until Barth's relentless attack upon the theological subjectivism of the nineteenth century and of Ritschl and his followers in particular were the vulnerable points of his program fully exposed. Yet Tillich found neo-orthodoxy wanting precisely at the point at which the "experiential method" of Schleiermacher and his successors was strongest. "One of the causes for the disquieting effect of neo-orthodox theology was that it detached itself completely from Schleiermacher's method. . . . The crucial question of theology today is whether or not, or to what degree, this denial is justified."[63] Where does the truth lie in this matter? Is the understanding of faith and more particularly the nature of Christian theology problematic in Ritschl's stance?

In the first place it must be said that it is wrong to interpret Ritschl to mean that statements of faith as value judgments have no objective referent. He traced the origin of the church to the historical activity of Jesus. In the second place, his Kantian epistemology did not require the denial of the objective reality of things or persons external to us affecting us in some way; his point was rather that we do not perceive these external events or things as they are in themselves (*a se*), but only as we apprehend them in their relationship to us and in their value for us. These facts, however, do not resolve all of the difficulties in Ritschl's position. Hans Iwand maintained that Kant's principle that we know things only as we perceive them and not as they are in themselves cannot be identified with Luther's understanding of the way in which revelation is known. To be sure, Ritschl followed Luther in opposing the speculative approach to God which bypasses his revelatory acts; Luther, however, did not deny the reality of the *deus absconditus,* nor more importantly did he allow the nature of God to be reduced to, or identified with, his acts known through faith.

Ritschl's error, according to Iwand, is that he took Kant's epistemological principle and made it into a formal principle of his theological method. Thus there are two kinds of knowledge: speculative or metaphysical knowledge which does not affect me existentially and subjective knowledge which is of value to me as a person. Religious knowledge is that which is relevant to man's subjectivity; it has nothing to do with that which is objectively ascertainable in the world.[64] The three immediate and serious conseqences of this position are: First, the tendency to equate God's nature and existence with his revelatory acts; the traditional doctrine of God falls out of the picture. And secondly—though at times Ritschl appears to modify this position —there does not seem to be any surety that what we know of God is commensurate with his being-in-himself. Thirdly, the designation of religious knowledge as that which is of value for the believer tends to make God in his revelation conform to man's subjective needs and desires. Gollwitzer follows Iwand's thesis in identifying the deficiency of this approach to man's knowledge of God thus: "Here a predetermined self-exposition prior to the event of the Word of God already decides who God is, how he may encounter us, and in what sense man requires him."[65]

Let us look at each of these consequences issuing from Ritschl's epistemological program. In the first place, his theological reductionism tends to deny God any reality apart from his perceivable relationships to the world. The problem here is not so much Ritschl's restriction of knowledge of God to what is knowable through revelation, but the tendency to reduce the reality of God to his historical acts, or more properly, to the effects that they produce. One could perhaps argue that Ritschl fails to apply his epistemology consistently in his doctrine of God and that God's independent existence is never really jeopardized. Yet it is also true that the application of his epistemology led his successors and especially twentieth-century Christian existentialists to regard God as nothing but a symbol descriptive of certain dimensions of human experience.

This latter difficulty is related to the second: Is there any surety that the apprehension of God in his revelation provides us with knowledge of the true nature of God? Once again, there are statements in Ritschl—especially when interpreting New Testament texts—to the effect that God's acts are congruous with his nature in himself, but often his epistemological empiricism necessitates becoming agnostic at this point. Here again the departure from Luther and the Reformers is evident. The God for us (*pro nobis*) and the God apart from us (*extra nos*) cannot be divorced from each other without doing violence to the Christian understanding of revelation. We can put the difference thus: Whereas for the Reformers faith lives from the objective reality of God who is never equated with human existence, Ritschl, and even more his successors, tend toward a theological subjectivism that calls in question the objective reality of God and turns faith in upon itself. Ritschl followed in Scheiermacher's steps here and both reach the same impasse. Ritschl's desire was to adopt an empirical and historical theological method that would permit a kind of practical verification of theological statements.

Perhaps on account of the critical strictures of Strauss and others regarding the impossibility of verifying the facticity of much in the Gospels, Ritschl retired to what appeared to be a safe haven—the subject matter of theology was the investigation of the religious consciousness of the apostolic community of faith. But he did not stop there; to do so would leave the present reality of faith unexplained. Therefore, he moves once again in Schleiermacher's direction and weakens the revelatory pole in his thought by restricting theology to an investigation of man's religious and ethical response to God's revelation.[66] It seems, therefore, that there is a steady movement toward theological subjectivism in Ritschl's own development that issues ultimately in the loss of transcendence and agnosticism in twentieth-century Christian existentialism. To be sure, he wrote with an awareness of Feuerbach's taunt that theology is nothing but projection or disguised anthropology, but it is not at all clear that his theological program provides an adequate alternative.[67] In Ritschl's system, it is often questionable whether we are talking about Biblical faith which "lives upon the objectivity of God."[68]

Ebeling does not tire of commending the Reformers for the manner in which they succeeded in rejecting all supports for faith apart from the Word of God. For them, however, the *solus Christus, sola gratia,* and therewith the external pole of revelation were not separated from the *sola fide,* and the strength of the latter derived from the former.[69] Ebeling apparently would disagree with Iwand's charge that the subjective pole (*pro me*) is preeminent in the nineteenth century thereby giving rise to the question of the certainty of salvation in a way unknown to the Reformers. For them the certainty of salvation derived from the prior work of Christ. "Certainty [of salvation] and the *extra me* are correlates in the Reformers."[70] This viewpoint in Luther was also related to his conception of the "bound will." The nineteenth century—and Ritschl was not as guilty as some at this point—found this doctrine reprehensible, since it took salvation out of the hands of man and of human control. Therefore, the *in me* (revelation perceived by man) was made the beginning and end of theology. Thus in 1909, Schaeder could say that the dominant question for theology in the period after Ritschl was that of the certainty of salvation. Everything centered upon man, and theology was the poorer for it.[71]

A third difficulty created by Ritschl's epistemology is related to the foregoing, but deserves special mention. In the attempt to avoid a speculative doctrine of God, he insisted that true religious knowledge obtains when man acknowledges the value of God for the proper assessment of man's existence in the world. The positive response that his existential understanding of faith elicited has been noted, and his contribution at this point cannot be denied. The problem does not lie in his conception of the dynamics of faith itself, but rather in the way in which the question Ritschl raises about human existence restricts what can be said about God and his revelation from the outset. Long before Bultmann and his followers, he insisted that man's asking about God involves a certain preunderstanding concerning the nature of revelation and human existence. For Ritschl, man's self-understanding prior to receiving the revelatory answer centers in the question of the problematic nature of human existence. Man's existence in the world is threatened because of the spirit-nature split within man and because of an indifferent and hostile world. Thus to be aware of the human condition prior to any mention of God's historical revelation means to be conscious of the dilemma deriving from the spirit-nature dichotomy.

Ritschl's utilization of this preliminary understanding of human existence as a problem seeking a solution has certain obvious consequences. Only that is of value in the revelation of God which speaks to the dilemma raised by human existence in the world. Whatever in God's nature or revelation has no apparent relevance to this overriding question of human existence falls outside the theologian's purview and interest. Thus all God-talk is restricted to what is of value to the community of faith and the individual believer within it. By proceeding with this theological method, Ritschl makes himself vulnerable to the kind of criticism later directed against Bultmann's hermeneutic. Bultmann also utilizes a particular preunderstanding—not really so different from Ritschl's—which requires that the New Testament be interpreted as though its concern was always to resolve the questions of human existence. In this way both Ritschl and Bultmann are often guilty of making it appear that God is of value only insofar as he answers man's problem. God is forced to fit the mold of man's preunderstanding and therefore His sovereignty and freedom are denied from the start.

Ritschl's procedure at this point accounts for the frequent charge that his theology is strongly anthropological rather than theocentric or Christocentric. God and the Christian religion are finally intended to serve man. They assure man both of his superiority to nature and of the fact that the natural world is subordinate to the world of spirit which comes to its fulfillment in man. Interpreting Ritschl in the best possible light, one could argue that he maintains the priority of God's glory and purpose. The fact that God intends man to fulfill his destiny as spirit within the Kingdom of God is therefore not the sign of an anthropocentric theology, but rather of a theology that accentuates God's loving will. God does not realize his glory apart from man, but in the process of bringing humanity to its fulfillment in the Kingdom of God.[72] Thus what might appear to be a man-centered theology from the human perspective is, in fact, a theocentric or Christocentric theology when viewed, as it were, in the light of God's ultimate purpose for mankind in the Kingdom of God.

The ambiguity of Ritschl's theology with respect to the knowledge of God that derives from his theological method may be illustrated in another way. Though he saw himself as a foe of all natural theology that bypassed the concrete, historical revelation in Jesus Christ in its approach to God, he, in effect, operates with a natural theology in utilizing Kant's moral argument for the existence of God. This argument verifies both man's superiority as spirit to nature and the existence of a Supreme Being directing nature to spiritual and ethical ends. On this basis Ritschl affirms the following: "Now religion is the practical law of the spirit, in accordance with which it sustains its fundamental character as an end-in-itself against the restrictions it suffers from nature."[73] However, apart from the special, historical revelation giving rise to the Christian religion, man does not experience the highest possible resolution of the crisis of human existence. Ritschl, therefore, allows natural theology to define man's problematic situation on the basis of man's universal conformity with his Creator; however, it is only through special revelation that man as spirit finds the answer to the ambiguities that inhere in human finitude. Thus Ritschl writes: "This practical law [i.e., religion as the practical law of the spirit] attains its complete development in Christianity, for Christianity lays down the principle that personal life is to be prized above the whole world of nature."[74] It is therefore axiomatic for him that only in Christianity, with its conception of a purely spiritual God directing all things, can man's superiority to nature be realized and therewith human destiny be fulfilled in the Kingdom of God. Moreover, only within Christianity does a satisfactory resolution of the spirit-nature and spirit-world problem obtain.

Although Ritschl's adoption of a Kantian metaphysic or natural theology at this juncture was not intended to diminish the significance of the historical revelation affirmed in Christianity, it must be said that he does not justify sufficiently the bases for his approach. Among other things, a systematic development of a doctrine of man and the manner in which it is to be related to the universal revelation in creation is lacking. Furthermore, Ritschl does not guard himself adequately against the charge that his use of a Kantian natural theology in the description of the human problem predetermines the kind of answer that God's historical revelation must provide. It seems that whatever in God's revelation fails to relate to man's problematic situation as already defined must be left aside. This is what was intended in saying that Ritschl's theology is finally anthropological; God and the Christian religion must finally conform to man's subjective needs and desires. Expressed somewhat differently: Does Ritschl's Kantian metaphysic and epistemology determine a priori what God can and must say and do in his revelation?

Seen in somewhat broader perspective, the issue is whether the apologetic pole in his thought represented by his sensitivity to the prevailing positivism and empiricism influenced by both Kant and the rising natural sciences necessitated the reduction of the Christian faith to a version acceptable to the modern mind and the prevailing world view. To be sure, Ritschl was conscious of the dangers of subordinating the Christian faith to an alien metaphysic, but he is not always successsful in avoiding this pitfall.

2. *Epistemology and Christology.* The theological reductionism dictated by Ritschl's epistemology affects not only the doctrine of God but all other doctrines. We can illustrate this with respect to his Christology.[75] Along with others in the nineteenth century who were critical of Chalcedonian Christology, Ritschl proposes a more empirical and historical reconstruction. Only Christological statements rooted in the ministry and work of Christ and its effects attested in the New Testament are allowable. The approach must be from the historical to the suprahistorical in Christology;

therefore the Synoptic portrait of Jesus is to be preferred to the Johannine. This starting point necessitates that the ethical estimate of Jesus precede the religious evaluation. Christological statements that do not grow out of the awareness of Jesus' redemptive activity as founder of the Kingdom of God are speculative and of no interest to faith.

There is much that is suggestive in Ritschl's Christology, but certain difficulties need to be noted. Though his thesis that the deity of Jesus is to be understood in the light of his saving work has been widely accepted, it is clear that Luther—claimed by Ritschl as his model—did not derive Jesus' deity from the value attached to his person by the church. In the Reformers, the doctrine of the incarnation preserved the Christological stress of the New Testament and the early church, but Ritschl's reductionism rules out this approach.

Instead of beginning with the incarnation, Ritschl points us to what Jesus does. His unique relationship to God is seen in the perfect harmony between the divine will and his human will. He is different from all other men because he trusts perfectly in God. In this sense, he is the religious ideal of humanity. He is also the ethical ideal of mankind in that he always acts in love toward others in pursuit of establishing the Kingdom of God. In this vein, Ritschl pictures Jesus as the fulfillment of humanity and as the representative man who marks the beginning of the new humanity. Jesus' followers are ushered into the relationship with God that he enjoyed and, like him, can experience supremacy over the world. On these grounds, Ritschl can speak of the Godhead of Christ in summary as follows:

> Since the aim of the Christian life is to be attained in the form of personal freedom, the two unavoidable designations by which we interpret Jesus, namely, as the complete revealer of God and as the manifest archetype (*Urbild*) of spiritual lordship over the world, can be united in the predicate of his Godhead.[76]

3. *The Doctrine of Sin.*   Ritschl's revision of the doctrine of sin is an attempt to avoid the deficiencies of the traditional doctrine of original sin. At every point, he shows how sin derives from man's misuse of his freedom and how it affects his self-consciousness. In this way sin is directly related to man's subjectivity and therefore intelligible. Critics past and present, however, point to certain difficulties that Ritschl's reconstruction poses.

The main weakness stems from the incompatible approaches to understanding man as sinner and understanding the nature of sin. We saw Ritschl's concern to correlate the Christian knowledge of sin with its exposure through the historical revelation in Jesus Christ or with the standard of the good revealed in the Kingdom of God. Careful observation shows, however, that Ritschl is unable to restrict his understanding of sin to the light shed on its nature through what may be broadly termed God's revelation of himself in history. Thus on the one hand, Ritschl interprets man's situation in idealistic categories: Man is a spiritual being housed in a material body in the midst of an impersonal and unfriendly material world. Man's existence is further threatened because of its temporality. Man's longing is to realize his essential superiority as spirit over the world of nature and the material dimension of his existence. We have observed that Ritschl can interpret all religions as attempts to resolve the question posed by man's situation vis-à-vis the world and nature. Within this approach to understanding man, the poles of discussion are spirit (*Geist*) and nature, or man and the world. Though the development of humanity and the evolution of religion give evidence of partial solutions to man's quest for supremacy over the world, the final solution is found only in Christianity.

On the other hand, the Biblical description of man as sinner moves between the poles of man and God. To be sure, man's sin always affects his relationship to himself, nature, and the world, but the primary focus lies upon the distorted and broken relationship with God which cries out for a solution. When stated in this way, the question to be put to Ritschl is whether his conception of man's problematic situation derives from the Biblical witness or from some other source. Expressed differently, our question is whether the description of man's dilemma in terms of the spirit-nature or spirit-world polarity can be harmonized with the Biblical depiction of man as sinner in rebellion against God.

The tensions between these two approaches to the human dilemma and the nature of man's alienation are quite apparent. If the problem is man's realization of his superiority as a spiritual being over the world, it is no longer possible to speak of man's radical alienation from God in the manner of the Old Testament, the teaching of Jesus, the apostle Paul, and the Reformation. Ritschl might have shown more clearly than he did that man's sin in Pauline terminology involves the struggle between the warring factions within man referred to as flesh and spirit. Or he could have developed the analysis of sin in terms of man's perversion of his creaturehood and the universal revelation of God evident in the created order as Paul does in the first chapters of Romans and as Calvin does following him in the opening chapters of the *Institutes*.[77] Had Ritschl done so, his analysis of man as sinner would have been both more Biblical and realistic. That is not to say that his interpretation of the doctrine of sin does not include certain important elements characteristic of the Biblical understanding of man. It does, but Ritschl's dual approach in the description of man's problematic situation involves certain inconsistencies.

We may pinpoint some of the difficulties as follows: If the human situation is viewed in the light of man's quest for self-realization as spirit rather than in terms of his broken relationship to God, several consequences follow. First, it rules out the possibility of viewing sin as occasioning a radical alienation between God and man. This must be said even though certain of Ritschl's statements noted earlier might be cited in his defense. Thus his categorization of all sin apart from man's final and irrevocable rejection of God as sins of ignorance points in this direction. To be sure, he departs from the human standpoint in saying that this estimation of sin "holds good in the first place as the *standard for the judgment of God*."[78] But it is also the category by which we can estimate sin universally. We ask: Is it possible on the basis of the teaching of Jesus to estimate man's breach of God's law so lightly? Does not Ritschl minimize the gravity of sin by presupposing that it does not lead to any real opposition of God to man, since God remains eternally the loving one toward man? Or again, does not Ritschl's more psychological description of sin enable him to excise all New Testament descriptions pointing to the power of sin as something transcending man and even more powerful than man's collective sin found in Ritschl's kingdom of sin?

Furthermore, does not Ritschl's restriction of the wrath of God to his punishment of those finally recalcitrant do away with the present judgment of God of which Paul speaks in Rom. 1:18? And does not his view of God as wholly love lead both to a static view of God that denies his freedom and also to a superficial view of sin that occasions no reaction on the part of a righteous and holy God? In addition to these presuppositions and assertions we must include his contention that "there may be a sinless development of life."[79] In the light of these questions, it is clear that Ritschl can claim neither Biblical nor Reformation precedent for all aspects of his doctrine of sin.[80] He is unable to harmonize his picture of man as spirit seeking self-realization or dominion over the world with the Scriptural witness concerning man's condition as sinner. This leads Paul Lehmann to a pointed indictment of Ritschl: "Fundamentally, the most appropriate critical superscription with which to adorn the portal of Ritschl's theological reconstruction is this: *man wants forgiveness; and man forgives himself*."[81]

If the latter criticism appears excessively harsh in the light of certain statements by Ritschl, it must nevertheless be said that he internalizes and subjectivizes the doctrine of sin. In the last analysis, therefore, assertions concerning sin are descriptions of man's feelings and have no reference to an actual separation between God and man. Such a view makes it necessary to ask whether Ritschl has really left behind the idealistic approach that operates with the idea of an eternal reconciliation between God and man and therefore does not accept a radical view of man's fallenness and alienation. If this is so, then reconciliation is really man's discovery that as spirit he is in fact not alienated from God at all, but eternally one with him. If the latter is true, then man's consciousness of guilt is illusory and does not correspond with reality, since there is actually no objective state of affairs corresponding thereto.[82]

4. *Justification and Reconciliation.* It can be argued that whereas Anselmic atonement theories and all those which place the accent upon the objective work of Christ are often deficient in relating this to man's life, Ritschl's difficulty is precisely the opposite. He wants to show how man's justification and reconciliation determine man's self-consciousness and therewith his attitude toward God, others, and the world. In the process, however, it is often questionable whether the manner in which the latter is related to, and derivative from, the activity of God is convincing. We observed that his intention was to effect a balance between the objective and subjective poles of the doctrine of justification and reconciliation, but his statements about the former can be known only in the light of the latter. This explains his tendency to look more at the consequences of justification and reconciliation in man than at its basis in God's activity. This is already apparent in Ritschl's reversal of the usual reconciliation-justification sequence. Following Pauline precedent, many Protestant treatments interpret reconciliation in terms of what God does in Christ; justification, on the other hand, has to do with the believer's appropriation thereof. Ritschl reverses these terms. What God does for man's salvation is bound up with the conception of justification, but his treatment of the latter does not include the content ordinarily included within the concept of reconciliation. For this reason, critics have accused Ritschl of ending with a subjective doctrine of the atonement. He moves all too quickly to, and concentrates upon, the effects which God's redemptive activity has upon man's subjectivity.

Another weakness of Ritschl's doctrine of justification and reconciliation was anticipated in the discussion of his doctrine of sin. Man's need to realize himself as spirit over against the world and nature is the problem seeking solution; it is not that of his radical estrangement from God. Man's justification and reconciliation must therefore be construed so as to resolve his dilemma as Ritschl understood it. Accordingly, one cannot speak of God's displeasure or negative attitude toward man, the sinner; he remains the loving one even in the face of man's sin. God's purpose is always directed toward man's victory over the world evident in his realization of himself as spirit in the Kingdom of God. Elsewhere we have referred to this fulfillment in terms of Ritschl's conception of the ideal life-style.[83] In the last analysis, one cannot deny that he views the redemptive activity of God teleologically, that is, in the light of the movement of salvation history toward the Kingdom of God. This leads Garvie to comment "that while, according to the orthodox view, the sinner is forgiven for the sake of what Christ has done, according to Ritschl's view he is forgiven with a view to what he may become as a citizen of the kingdom."[84]

Ritschl's reconstruction of the work of Christ is a creative restatement of the Abelardian view. Jesus is the revealer of the divine redemptive love in his kingly and prophetic ministry whose object is the establishment of the church and the Kingdom of God: Jesus appears more as revealer than as redeemer, since his saving activity is not required to effect a radical cure. One could say with Pannenberg that Ritschl's soteriological interest is modest: along with other Neo-Protestant theologians, he is "concerned only with making possible the humanness of life on earth."[85] Jesus is the paradigm of man's victory over the world and the representative of the new humanity in the Kingdom of God whose corporate will is attuned to the Father's. Ritschl ties the reconciling work of Jesus so closely to the church that it may be said that justification is an attribute of the community. Although he thereby corrected an excessive individualism that interpreted man's salvation in isolation from the church, his position is likewise one-sided. One must affirm the priority of Christ to the church and the latter to the believing individual, but the close correlation Ritschl posits between justification and the church may lead to a dissolution of the personal dimension of faith and the individual's experience of forgiveness of sins within the fellowship.

The greatest difficulty for Ritschl comes at the point of relating his doctrine of justification and reconciliation to the death and resurrection of Jesus. Interpreting Jesus in terms of his vocation is helpful in depicting his historical ministry. However, the early church did not interpret Jesus primarily in the light of his earthly ministry before the cross and resurrection; on the contrary, the activity of God in the latter events was the basis for the church's confession of Jesus as Lord. Richard R. Niebuhr has observed quite rightly that though Ritschl's Biblical exegesis led him to recognize the centrality of the resurrection for the understanding of Jesus in the primitive church, his hermeneutic precludes attributing anything to the risen Lord that cannot be ascribed to the historical Jesus. Thus in his positive theological construction, the exalted Christ pales into insignificance. As a Biblical thelogian, Ritschl is forced to say that the early church saw Jesus victorious over the world in the light of his resurrection; as a systematic theologian, the model that is to inspire the church is the remembrance of Jesus' patience in the face of his suffering and death.[86]

Obviously, Ritschl's stress upon the life and ministry of Jesus was intended as a corrective both to atonement theories that focused solely upon his death and resurrection and to a mystical and pietistic tendency that concentrated on the present Lord while neglecting the historical Jesus. In the process, however, Ritschl creates an unbridgeable chasm between the Jesus of history and the Christ of faith. R. R. Niebuhr contends that Ritschl "cannot forge any artificial connection between the Christ of faith and the Jesus of history to replace the natural link of the resurrection, which he has now denied to the mind of the community."[87] His difficulty is therefore twofold. First, faith cannot be equated with knowledge about the historical Jesus even if it is established critically. Second, though faith is formally defined in terms of personal trust in Christ, the latter as the object of faith becomes ever more illusory. Theology therefore must necessarily restrict itself to an analysis of the effects produced by Jesus within the primitive Christian community and its successors.

Ritschl's failure to come to terms with the meaning of the resurrection for interpreting the continuing existence of the church creates real difficulties for his doctrines of God, Christology, and the church. Because his Christology has lost its ontological basis in the preexistence of the Son and in his continuing life by virtue of his resurrection, the manner in which God is present in Jesus is not adequately treated. It would seem, therefore, that a Christology divorced from the understanding of God as triune creates as many new problems for Ritschl as the former doctrine which he rejects as too speculative. This explains why he was often accused of denying Jesus' deity, though to be sure he could regard such an affirmation as a value judgment of the community.

The view of the church as the living fellowship of those who acknowledge the risen Lord is also jeopardized by his failure to develop the significance of the resurrection for comprehending its continuing existence. There is no doctrine of the *Christus praesens* in Ritschl; to speak of this smacked too much of mysticism and Pietism and therewith of an immediate relationship between Christ and believers. The alternative for Ritschl is to remind the church to look back to Jesus, the founder of the church and the Kingdom of God. To be sure, he could and did speak of the continuing influence of the historical Jesus upon the church in its subsequent life, but this must always be traced back to his historical existence.[88] Nor was he able to speak of the present Christ as Lord and Head of the church in terms of the activity of the Holy Spirit, for no doctrine of the Spirit is found in Ritschl's theology. The Spirit of God is the continuing influence of the historical Jesus within the community of faith; he is not the third Person of the Trinity. Ritschl's reticence at this point derived from his fear that to allow an immediate relationship between the Spirit and Christians would be to succumb to mysticism.

5. *The Kingdom of God.*   In earlier discussions we have attempted to show how Ritschl's view of the Kingdom of God is both formally and materially of great import for his system. Indeed, it is difficult to rebut the charge

of those who affirm that his thought is best understood when everything else—including his doctrine of justification and reconciliation—is seen as subordinate to the Kingdom of God. We cannot pursue that controversy again, but it is a historical fact that Ritschl's doctrine of the Kingdom of God continues to be influential even in the present.[89]

Here we must restrict our discussion to some of the major criticisms of Ritschl's doctrine of the Kingdom of God. One of the most telling was expressed by his son-in-law, Johannes Weiss. In 1892, just three years after Ritschl's death, Weiss wrote a pamphlet entitled *The Preaching of Jesus Concerning the Kingdom of God*. In its second edition in 1900 and in his larger work on *The Idea of the Kingdom of God in Theology* published in 1901, Weiss contended that Ritschl and his school had no right to claim the teaching of Jesus as the basis for their interpretation of the Kingdom of God.[90] Both Weiss and subsequently Albert Schweitzer held that Jesus' conception of the Kingdom was comprehensible only in the light of the prevailing Jewish apocalypticism which anticipated the imminent inbreak of the Kingdom of God, the end of the world, the Last Judgment, and the resurrection of the dead.

A recent writer finds Weiss critical of Ritschl's view of the Kingdom at three points. In the first place, Ritschl does not see the significance of the "antithesis between the Kingdom of God and the Kingdom of Satan." Secondly, he mistakenly sees the Kingdom of God being fulfilled through human effort, whereas Jesus pictured this in terms of God's radical inbreak into history. Thirdly, he errs in portraying Jesus as envisaging the evolution of the Kingdom in history as the "moral organization of humanity." Quite the contrary is the case: Jesus saw himself standing at the end of history and therefore did not anticipate any historical evolution of the Kingdom.[91] In sum, Ritschl is accused by Weiss and critics following him of adopting the Enlightenment's humanistic and evolutionary view of the Kingdom of God rather than Jesus' radically eschatological conception thereof.

Though one cannot hold that later interpretations of the Kingdom of God in the teaching of Jesus and the New Testament have vindicated Ritschl rather than J. Weiss and A. Schweitzer, recent studies by Timm and Schäfer have rescued certain of Ritschl's valuable insights. Without detailing these, several statements of a general nature may be made. First, New Testament studies since Weiss and Schweitzer make it apparent that it is far too simplistic to identify Ritschl's teaching on the Kingdom of God with that of the Enlightenment. His depiction of the Kingdom of God in the light of the Old Testament and the teaching of Jesus remains sound. The discovery of the influence of Jewish apocalyptic and Hellenism upon the New Testament by the *religionsgeschichtliche* school occurred after Ritschl's formative period. Nevertheless, he affirmed the decisive importance of the Kingdom of God. Moreover, his viewpoint is in agreement with the current apocalyptic interpretations of the Kingdom of God which maintain that the latter refers to "God's decisive intervention in history and human experience," even though no consensus exists as to when and how this is to be conceived in the light of Jesus' teaching.[92]

A second point at which Ritschl has been vindicated over against Weiss and those following him lies in his recognition that the Kingdom of God is both present and future in the teaching of Jesus.[93] This position also accords with the direction of contemporary New Testament scholarship which is critical of both the view of Weiss and others who held that Jesus conceived the Kingdom as wholly future and of the view of C. H. Dodd and the school of "realized eschatology" who contend that Jesus viewed the Kingdom as wholly present.[94] A third point at which Ritschl anticipates contemporary discussion is the manner in which he relates Jesus' teaching concerning the Kingdom of God and ethics. Although Perrin notes considerable diversity of opinion as to how these are to be correlated, his own position is not uncommon and is, in fact, not far removed from Ritschl's. Perrin writes:

> Our argument is that the ultimate purpose of the intervention of God in history and human experience is to make it possible for man to enter into a new and perfect relationship with himself, and that the ethical teaching is designed to illustrate the kind of response which man must make in order to enter into this relationship.[95]

Among the most frequent charges against Ritschl in this area is that he is guilty of a moralistic interpretation of the Kingdom of God and the Christian faith. It is undoubtedly true that he was influenced by the Enlightenment view that the superiority of Christianity derived from the purity of its ethic, but for him it is likewise to be seen in its conception of God and his redemptive activity. We have shown that Ritschl attempted to distinguish the religious and ethical moments in Christianity, and though he did not always achieve clarity at this point, he never derived justification and reconciliation from man's ethical activity in the Kingdom of God. To be sure, one can argue that the subordination of justification and reconciliation to the overarching idea of the Kingdom of God makes it appear that the moral pole finally takes precedence over the religious. This explains why some critics have held that man's activity rather than God's grace predominates in Ritschl's system.[96] Undoubtedly, certain of his statements make him vulnerable to this charge, and one can say that he fails at times to carry through the balanced treatment of the religious and ethical moments so clearly set forth in his formal statements.[97]

Timm summarizes the way in which Ritschl correlates religion and ethics, the divine and human purposes, dependence and freedom within the overarching conception of the Kingdom of God:

Ritschl understands his theology as the scientific theory of religious praxis, that is, as a world view. Accordingly, theology has the task of providing intellectual support for the religio-ethical self-realization of humanity. For the human spirit remains a creature despite its practical superiority over nature; it is therefore affected by that which is different from itself, namely, nature, which it has not created. Thus even though man may maintain his superiority over nature through his own activity, he has thereby not yet answered the question as to whether his action is true, that is, whether it is appropriate to nature's determination. A negative response to this question would issue inevitably in ethical resignation. However, God has given a positive answer to this anxious question of humanity through the life and activity of Jesus Christ; the latter [answer] must be developed scientifically by the Christian theologian. By presupposing an absolute being for whom the creation of nature as well as a universal kingdom of spirits represent two successive moments in his self-realization, the theologian is to provide the proof for the deification of humanity in the Kingdom of God which is experienced in practice. By virtue of its practical orientation, Ritschl's theology is a universal-eschatological theory of the Kingdom of God as the correlate of the purpose of God himself (*selbstzweckes Gottes*).[98]

In view of his teleologically oriented interpretation of Christianity, some critics have accused Ritschl of minimizing the significance of history. We have alluded on several occasions to this inheritance from idealism in his thought and numerous passages point in this direction. Certainly, Ritschl intended to reject all speculative thinking in theology, and there is an anthropological and practical thrust in the way in which all theological statements are grounded in the interpretation of man's religious and ethical activity. Nevertheless, in the last analysis everything that occurs in the universe derives from God's original and therewith his final purpose for the universe and particularly for man. When pushed to its limit, this perspective contradicts the primacy that Ritschl purportedly attributes to historical thinking as the foundation of all theological understanding. It empties time and man's religious consciousness of any real significance—and certainly makes it impossible to speak of man's response affecting the divine will and disposition. Interpreted in this light, he is a thoroughly theocentric thinker; ultimately, he thinks from above to below and not vice versa. He could have done the latter more effectively had he pursued the Christocentric perspective that he develops as his starting point in his programmatic statements.[99]

A possibility available for developing a more dynamic and historically informed teleology in terms of the operation of the Holy Spirit or the exalted Christ within the community of faith and the world was not utilized by Ritschl. For him, the church's perspective is always retrospective. Though it must be that, it cannot be only that. Dietrich Ritschl provides the corrective integral to the faith of the church through the ages in maintaining that "recognizing the presence of Christ means recognizing the presence of the *risen* Christ. . . . Therefore, when remembering the resurrection the Church *hopes. Memory and hope are the dimensions of the presence of Christ.*"[100] Had Ritschl developed the teleological perspective that leads the church to look to the future fulfillment of God's promise to his people more adequately, he would have been better able to counter the criticism that his doctrine of the Kingdom of God is moralistic and humanistic. In defense of Ritschl, one can point out that he did not succumb to the prevalent tendency in Western Christianity of concentrating upon justification to the neglect of sanctification.[101] His version of the latter comes to expression in the *Lebensideal,* or ideal life-style, characterized by man's dominion over the natural world—a conception, however, too narrow to encompass all the ramifications of man's reconciliation with God.[102] But his theology has something of the same retrospective perspective because he was not able to relate Christology and pneumatology in the fruitful way in which he related Christology and soteriology.

The inadequate development of the teleological pole in his thought made his theology more anthropocentric than he intended.[103] Instead of seeing creation, history, and the church moving toward the goal intended by God, Ritschl increasingly restricted his gaze to the individual's quest for self-realization. A more comprehensive perspective was available to him in the stress upon man's faith in divine providence, but there is little appreciation of God's purposive activity in man's present history.[104] This deficiency stems from Ritschl's depreciation of creation and the natural order and leads him to develop an eschatology without any cosmic dimension. This mode of thinking reaches its climax in the individualistic eschatology of later existentialists. Moltmann pictures the problematic nature of the latter as follows:

> It is not possible to speak of believing existence in hope and in radical openness, and at the same time consider the "world" to be a mechanism or self-contained system of cause and effect in objective antithesis to man. Hope then fades away to the hope of the solitary soul in the prison of a petrified world, and becomes the expression of a gnostic longing for redemption.[105]

6. *A Final Statement.* In this chapter we have looked at some of the strengths and weaknesses of Albrecht Ritschl's theology. Others could be mentioned. Our purpose has not been to trace the influence of Ritschl upon contemporary theology or to construct an alternative position. The task that we attempted was more modest: it was to listen once again to the voice of

one who is of historical significance because he stands at the end of a period of great theological ferment and development in the nineteenth century and in some ways points toward new ways of interpreting the Christian faith which are influential even in the present. Some of the problems to which he addressed himself are no longer ours, and some of his solutions have been rejected. But since the church must always reflect on the relationship between God, man, and the world, Ritschl's vision remains impressive and instructive at many points.

To be sure, today some may find his confessional, Biblical, and Christocentric orientation too traditional for an age that calls God and revelation into question. This may indeed be a prevalent contemporary mood. But if theology is responsible for doing more than addressing itself to prevailing moods in the church and the world, it must speak ever and again of man's sin and alienation, of God's redemptive love in Jesus Christ, and of man's hope for the future in the light of the fulfillment of God's purpose in the Kingdom of God. Whenever the church does this, the questions with which Ritschl struggled in his day will once again come alive. Should this not occur in the future even more than presently, it will be a sure sign that the church's understanding of man's need and God's grace does not even begin to approximate the vision of Albrecht Benjamin Ritschl.[106]

Notes

INTRODUCTION

1. Cited in G. Wayne Glick, *The Reality of Christianity* (Harper & Row, Publishers, Inc., 1967), p. 82; see Glick's summary of Ritschl's contribution to Harnack, p. 82.

2. D. Horst Stephan, "Albrecht Ritschl und die Gegenwart," *Zeitschrift für Theologie und Kirche*, N.F., 16. Jhr. (1935), p. 21.

3. James Orr, *The Ritschlian Theology and the Evangelical Faith* (Thomas Whittaker [1897]), pp. 27–28.

4. Cited in Glick, *op. cit.*, p. 53.

5. Robert Stupperich (ed.), "Briefe Karl Holls an Adolph Schlatter (1897–1925)," *Zeitschrift für Theologie und Kirche*, 64. Jhr., Heft 2 (April, 1967), p. 216.

6. *Ibid.*, pp. 227–228.

7. *Ibid.*

8. H. R. Mackintosh, *Types of Modern Theology* (London: William Collins Sons & Co., Ltd., 1964), p. 139.

9. Some biographical information about Ritschl is available in several older English studies. In addition to James Orr's *The Ritschlian Theology*, see also his *Ritschlianism: Expository and Critical Essays* (London: Hodder and Stoughton, 1903), and Robert Mackintosh, *Albrecht Ritschl and His School* (London: Chapman and Hall, 1915). The major source of biographical information remains that of Ritschl's son, Otto Ritschl, *Albrecht Ritschls Leben* (Freiburg i.B. and Leipzig: J. C. B. Mohr-Paul Siebeck, 1892; 1896), 2 vols. Cited hereafter as Otto Ritschl, I and II. He includes a complete Ritschl bibliography; see I, pp. 438 ff.; II, pp. 526 ff. This helpful biography is a carefully documented study of Ritschl's life and thought.

10. Hermann Timm, *Theorie und Praxis in der Theologie Albrecht Ritschls und Wilhelm Herrmanns* (Gütersloh: Gerd Mohn, 1967), p. 35. Cited hereafter as *Theorie und Praxis*.

11. Otto Ritschl, I, p. 428.

12. Otto Ritschl, I, pp. 1–2.

13. Otto Ritschl, "Albrecht Ritschls Theologie und ihre bisherigen Schicksale," *Zeitschrift für Theologie und Kirche*, N. F., 16. Jhr. (1935), pp. 44–47, for the following.

CHAPTER I

1. Otto Ritschl, II, p. 106.

2. Otto Ritschl, II, p. 106.

3. Otto Ritschl, II, p. 107.

4. Albrecht Ritschl, *Theologie und Metaphysik: Zur Verständigung und Abwehr* (Bonn: Adolph Marcus, 1881), p. 43; cf. pp. 38–39. Cited hereafter as *Theol. und Meta*. All citations are from the first edition. This pamphlet is the aging Ritschl's final attempt to set forth and defend his methodology. Instead of silencing his critics, it led to more concerted attacks upon him. Cf. Otto Ritschl, II, pp. 385–404.

5. Cajus Fabricius, *Die Entwicklung in Albrecht Ritschls Theologie von 1874 bis 1889 nach den verschiedenen Auflagen seiner Hauptwerke dargestellt und beurteilt* (Tübingen: J. C. B. Mohr, 1909), pp. 4, 135.

6. Albrecht Ritschl, *Die christliche Lehre von der Rechtfertigung und Versöhnung: Der biblische Stoff der Lehre* (1st ed.; Bonn: Adolph Marcus, 1874), Bd. II, p. 1. Hereafter the three volumes of this work will be cited as *R.V.* I, *R.V.* II, *R.V.* III. An arabic numeral following the volume number indicates the edition referred to. The best treatment of Ritschl's theological method and extensive bibliography can be found in Gösta Hök, *Die elliptische Theologie Albrecht Ritschls* (Uppsala: Universitets Arsskrift, 1942), and Fabricius, *op cit.*

7. *R.V.* II/1, p. 1.

8. *R.V.* II/1, p. 1.

9. *R.V.* II/1, pp. 1–2.

10. Otto Ritschl, II, pp. 167–168.

11. Otto Ritschl, II, p. 168.

12. Both Hök and Fabricius have given careful attention to this subject. See Hök's study of the evolution of Ritschl's conception of religion and the literature in Hök, *Die elliptische Theologie*, pp. 177 ff.; for a survey of the theological interpretation of religion in the nineteenth and twentieth centuries, see John Baillie, *The Interpretation of Religion* (Abingdon Press, 1956).

13. Albrecht Ritschl, *The Christian Doctrine of Justification and Reconciliation: The Positive Development of the Doctrine,* tr. of the third edition by H. R. Mackintosh and A. B. Macaulay (Edinburgh: T. & T. Clark, 1902), pp. 194–196. Hereafter cited as *J.R.* III.

14. See Immanuel Kant, *Religion Within the Limits of Reason Alone,* tr. and ed. by Theodore M. Greene and Hoyt H. Hudson (Harper Torchbook, Harper & Brothers, 1960), esp. Book III, Chs. 6–7.

15. Hök, *op. cit.,* pp. 14–15.

16. Albrecht Ritschl, *A Critical History of the Christian Doctrine of Justification and Reconciliation,* tr. by John S. Black (Edinburgh: Edmonston and Douglas, 1872), pp. 443–444. Hereafter cited as *J.R.* I. Cf. *J.R.* III, pp. 202–203; *R.V.* III/2, p. 188; *R.V.* III/1, p. 11.

17. *J.R.* III, pp. 196–197.

18. See references to literature in Hök, *op. cit.,* p. 50.

19. *J.R.* III, p. 202.

20. Albrecht Ritschl, *Instruction in the Christian Religion* included in the book on *The Theology of Albrecht Ritschl,* by Albert Swing (Longmans, Green & Company, 1901), p. 171. Cited hereafter as *Instruction.* For an extensive analysis of Ritschl's views on religion in relationship to other nineteenth-century views of the same, see Hök, *op. cit.,* pp. 5–15, and esp. pp. 178–247. The German edition of *Instruction* is entitled *Unterricht in der christlichen Religion* (6th ed.; Bonn: A. Marcus und Weber's Verlag, 1903); cited hereafter as *Unterricht.*

21. Hök, *op. cit.,* p. 247.

22. *Ibid.,* pp. 234–235.

23. *J.R.* III, p. 199.

24. Hök, *op. cit.,* pp. 234–236.

25. *Ibid.,* p. 243.

26. *Ibid.,* p. 244.

27. *Ibid.,* pp. 138–139.

28. *Ibid.,* p. 142.

29. *Ibid.,* p. 144.

30. *Ibid.,* pp. 138–177; for a summary of the nineteenth-century development, see esp. pp. 174–177.

31. *J.R.* III, pp. 197 ff.; cf. Hök, *op cit.,* pp. 139–140.

32. *R.V.* III/1, p. 171.

33. *J.R.* III, p. 203; cf. p. 25.

34. Cited in Otto Ritschl, II, p. 385.

35. Fabricius, *op. cit.,* pp. 16 ff.; cf. Hök, *op. cit.,* pp. 171 ff.

36. Fabricius, *op. cit.,* p. 16.

37. *Ibid.*

38. *Ibid.*

39. *Ibid.*

40. Otto Ritschl, II, p. 186.

41. *J.R.* III, p. 18.

42. Otto Ritschl, II, pp. 186–187.

43. *J.R.* III, p. 291.

44. *J.R.* III, p. 295.
45. *J.R.* III, p. 293.
46. *J.R.* III, p. 292.
47. *R.V.* III/2, p. 11; cf. *J.R.* III, p. 11.
48. *J.R.* I, p. 1; see pp. 1–10.
49. *J.R.* III, § 2.
50. *J.R.* III, p. 4.
51. *J.R.* III, p. 3; cf. p. 5; and Otto Ritschl, I, p. 155; II, p. 209.
52. *J.R.* III, p. 8.
53. *J.R.* III, pp. 8–11.
54. *J.R.* III, p. 11.
55. *J.R.* III, p. 12.
56. *J.R.* III, p. 13.
57. *J.R.* III, p. 13.
58. *J.R.* III, p. 14.
59. *R.V.* II/1, p. 5.
60. *R.V.* II/1, pp. 10–18.
61. *R.V.* II/1, p. 18.
62. *R.V.* II/1, pp. 20–23.
63. *J.R.* III, p. 1.
64. Fabricius, *op. cit.*, p. 121.
65. *J.R.* III, p. 7.
66. *J.R.* III, p. 1.
67. *J.R.* III, p. 1.
68. *J.R.* III, p. 3.
69. *J.R.* III, p. 3.
70. *J.R.* III, p. 5; cf. p. 6.
71. *J.R.* III, p. 8; cf. pp. 7–8; John 7:17.
72. *R.V.* II/1, p. 4; cf. Friedrich Schleiermacher, *The Christian Faith,* tr. of the second edition and ed. by H. R. Mackintosh, J. S. Stewart, *et al.* (Edinburgh: T. & T. Clark, 1956), § 19.
73. *R.V.* II/1, p. 4.
74. *The Christian Faith,* p. 76.
75. *J.R.* III, p. 49.
76. *J.R.* III, p. 22.
77. *Theol. und Meta.,* p. 51. Schneckenburger's comparative study of Lutheran and Reformed doctrine seems to have exerted some influence upon Ritschl on his first acquaintance with it in 1854. However, later examination of it in the light of the sources that engaged Ritschl made him call in question the accuracy of many of the former's conclusions. See Otto Ritschl, I, pp. 266, 407; II, p. 53; also, *R.V.* II/2, § 8.
78. See Albrecht Ritschl's *Die Geschichte des Pietismus: Der Pietismus in der reformierten Kirche* (Bonn: Adolph Marcus, 1880–1886), Bd. I.

Cited hereafter as *Pietismus* I; subsequent volumes will be referred to by Roman numerals II and III.

79. *J.R.* I, p. 523; cf. *J.R.* I, § 22; cf. *J.R.* III, § 20, 56, 59–60.

80. *Theol. und Meta.*, p. 48.

81. Hök, *op. cit.*, pp. 6–8.

82. *Theol. und Meta.*, p. 47.

83. *J.R.* III, p. 22; cf. Otto Ritschl, II, pp. 228–229.

84. *J. R.* III, pp. 34–35; cf. *J.R.* III, § 62–68.

85. Otto Ritschl, II, p. 236.

86. *J.R.* III, p. 213.

87. *J.R.* III, pp. 34, 324.

88. *J.R.* III, p. 34.

89. Ritschl opts for the understanding of faith as trust over against the orthodox stress upon faith as assent to doctrine or dogma. This existential understanding of faith characteristic of the Ritschlian school in representatives such as Wilhelm Herrmann has become normative for much Protestant theology since Ritschl. See Otto Ritschl, II, pp. 191 ff.

90. *J.R.* III, pp. 34–35.

91. *J.R.* III, p. 35.

92. *R.V.* II/1, pp. 2–3.

93. *J. R.* III, pp. 14–15.

94. Otto Ritschl, II, p. 183.

95. See, e.g., *J.R.* III, p. 9.

96. It must be remembered, however, that Schleiermacher gave careful attention to the place and function of practical theology and regarded it in one sense as the crown of theology. See Friedrich Schleiermacher, *Brief Outline on the Study of Theology*, tr. by Terrence N. Tice (John Knox Press, 1966), § 257–338.

97. *J.R.* III, p. 25.

98. *J.R.* III, p. 25; cf. *J.R.* III, § 29. See the statement, "The religious view of the world, in all its species, rests on the fact that man in some degree distinguishes himself in worth from the phenomena which surround him and from the influences of nature which press in upon him" (*J.R.* III, p. 17).

99. *J.R.* III, pp. 225–226.

100. *J.R.* III, p. 25; cf. *J.R.* III, all of § 3. Also, Hök, *op. cit.*, pp. 146 f., on Ritschl's view of religion as it relates to a *Weltanschauung;* on Ritschl's use of philosophy, see Hök, *op. cit.*, pp. 330 ff.

101. *J.R.* III, p. 15.

102. *J.R.* III, p. 24; cf. Otto Ritschl, II, p. 167. It is instructive to compare Barth's antiapologetic stance with that of Ritschl, recalling that he was schooled in the Ritschlian theology mediated through Wilhelm Herrmann, Barth's "unforgettable teacher." Both Ritschl and Barth reject

beginning with a natural theology as a vehicle for apologetics and opt instead for a Christocentric starting point.

103. *J.R.* III, p. 15.

104. *Theol. und Meta.*, p. 38. See the relevant sections below in Chapter V for the debate over Ritschl's epistemology and theological method.

105. *J.R.* III, p. 16.

106. *J.R.* III, p. 16.

107. *J.R.* III, p. 19.

108. *J.R.* III, § 30.

109. *J.R.* III, p. 19.

110. *Theol. und Meta.*, p. 31. Daniel L. Deegan views Ritschl's epistemology as a "critical empiricism" and shows something of both its strength and weakness. See "Critical Empiricism in the Theology of Albrecht Ritschl," *Scottish Journal of Theology*, Vol. 18, No. 1 (1965), pp. 40–56.

111. *J.R.* III, p. 193.

112. Cf. *J.R.* III, § 27–29.

113. *J.R.* III, p. 20.

114. *J.R.* III, p. 21.

115. *J.R.* III, pp. 543 f.; cf. Hök, *op. cit.*, pp. 8, 14–15.

116. *J.R.* III, pp. 219 f.

117. *J.R.* III, p. 19.

118. *J.R.* III, pp. 19–20.

119. One of the earliest studies of Ritschl's epistemology is by Leonhard Stählin, *Kant, Lotze and Ritschl: A Critical Examination*, tr. by D. W. Simon (Edinburgh: T. & T. Clark, 1889). For a recent critical study, see Paul Wrzecionko, *Die philosophischen Wurzeln der Theologie Albrecht Ritschls* (Berlin: Alfred Töpelmann, 1964).

120. Cf. Hök, *op. cit.*, p. 46.

121. See the instructive critique of existentialism at this point in Helmut Gollwitzer, *The Existence of God as Confessed by Faith*, tr. by James W. Leitch (The Westminster Press, 1965), esp. pp. 67–78.

122. *J.R.* III, p. 212; cf. p. 21.

123. *J.R.* III, p. 21.

124. *Theol. und Meta.*, pp. 57–62. Karl Barth's criticism of Melanchthon's method of constructing the doctrine of God is similar to Ritschl's at some points; see *Die kirchliche Dogmatik* (12 vols.; Zollikon-Zurich: Evangelischer Verlag, 1932–1967). Vol. II/Part 1 (1948), pp. 290 f.; cf. the English translation, *Church Dogmatics*, ed. by G. W. Bromiley and T. F. Torrance (12 vols.; Edinburgh: T. & T. Clark, 1936–1962), Vol. II/Part 1 (1957), pp. 259–260. References hereafter will be cited as *K.D.* for the German edition and as *C.D.* for the English edition.

125. Hök, *op. cit.*, p. 345; cf. pp. 327, 338.

126. *Ibid.*, pp. 345–346; cf. *R.V.* III/1, pp. 178 ff.

127. *J.R.* III, p. 207.

128. *J.R.* III, p. 203 (italics are mine).

129. *J.R.* III, p. 204.

130. *J.R.* III, p. 194.

131. *J.R.* III, pp. 204–205.

132. *J.R.* III, pp. 207–208.

133. *J.R.* I, p. 4.

134. *J.R.* III, pp. 440–513.

135. *J.R.* I, pp. 443–444.

136. *J.R.* I, p. 444; an extensive treatment and evaluation of Schleiermacher's theology is found in *J.R.* I, § 62–68. For Ritschl's final estimate of Schleiermacher, see *Schleiermachers Reden über die Religion und ihre Nachwirkungen auf die evangelische Kirche Deutschlands* (Bonn: Adolph Marcus, 1874).

137. *J.R.* I, p. 451.

138. *J.R.* I, p. 567.

139. *J.R.* I, p. 568.

140. *J.R.* I, pp. 522–523.

141. *J.R.* I, p. 568.

142. *R.V.* II/1, pp. 6–7.

143. *R.V.* II/1, pp. 5–7.

144. *R.V.* II/1, p. 8.

145. *R.V.* II/1, pp. 8–9.

146. *R.V.* II/1, pp. 8–9.

147. § 3 and 4 are entitled, respectively, "The Authority of Holy Scripture for Theology" and "Biblical Theology."

148. It is instructive to note that about one half of *R.V.* II deals with an analysis of such Old Testament concepts as the Kingdom of God; vicarious suffering; the holiness, grace, and love of God; the justice and wrath of God; the idea of sacrifice; etc.

149. *R.V.* II/1, p. 18.

150. For a résumé of Ritschl's views on early Christianity and New Testament literature, see Otto Ritschl, II, pp. 172–177.

151. *R.V.* II/1, p. 13.

152. *R.V.* II/1, p. 11.

153. *R.V.* II/1, pp. 17–18.

154. *R.V.* II/1, pp. 20–21. Ritschl's concern to see the documents of the New Testament as expressions of the faith of the community in Jesus anticipates in some ways the position of Martin Kähler in his epoch-making work of 1892, *Der sogenannte historische Jesus und der geschichtliche, biblische Christus* (2d ed.; Munich: Chr. Kaiser Verlag, 1956).

155. *R.V.* II/1, p. 18.

156. *R.V.* II/1, pp. 24–25.

CHAPTER II

1. *J.R.* III, p. 8.
2. *J.R.* III, p. 27.
3. *J.R.* III, p. 27.
4. *J.R.* III, p. 29.
5. In a subsequent exposition of the doctrine of justification, we shall observe how significant the consequences of justification are for man's manner of life in the world in Ritschl's system.
6. *J.R.* III, pp. 28–29.
7. *J.R.* III, p. 10; *J.R.* III, § 2, is important for this emphasis. For a recent analysis of Ritschl's interpretation of apostolic Christianity, see Philip Hefner, *Faith and the Vitalities of History* (Harper & Row, Publishers, Inc., 1966), pp. 12–44. The most important books for interpreting Ritschl's view of primitive Christianity in the New Testament and the early church are *Die Entstehung der altkatholischen Kirche* (2d ed.; Bonn: Adolph Marcus, 1857), cited hereafter as *Entstehung,* and *R.V.* II.
8. Among others who hold this thesis are Alfred Garvie, *The Ritschlian Theology* (Edinburgh: T. & T. Clark, 1899), pp. 237 ff., and Fabricius, *Die Entwicklung . . . ,* esp. pp. 71–88.
9. *J.R.* III, pp. 8–13.
10. *J.R.* III, pp. 11–12.
11. *J.R.* III, p. 9.
12. *J.R.* III, p. 10. *R.V.* II, § 5, "The Proclamation of the Kingdom of God," contains Ritschl's interpretation of Jesus' view of the Kingdom.
13. Cited in Otto Ritschl, II, p. 107.
14. *J.R.* III, p. 326.
15. Otto Ritschl, II, p. 196.
16. See Ritschl's article on "Reich Gottes" in *Realencyklopädie für protestantische Theologie und Kirche,* ed. by Albert Hauck and others (2d ed.; Leipzig: J. C. Hinrichs'sche Buchhandlung, 1883), Vol. 12, pp. 605–606.
17. A comparative analysis of the way in which the concept of the Kingdom of God is determinative of the structure and content of the *Unterricht* may be found in Fabricius, *op. cit.,* pp. 6–21.
18. See *J.R.* III, Chs. 4, 6.
19. *R.V.* II/1, p. 90. Ritschl's earliest studies of God's righteousness, love, and wrath are incorporated in *R.V.* II/2, Ch. 2, and in *J.R.* III. This important section (*R.V.* II/2, Ch. 2) is a comparative analysis of these divine attributes in the Old and New Testaments and is crucial for understanding Ritschl's systematic conclusions in *J.R.* III.
20. See *J.R.* III, § 29–30.

21. *J.R.* III, p. 228.

22. *J.R.* III, pp. 228–238; cf. *Theol. und Meta.*, pp. 13–22; cf. also *J.R.* III, § 34, for the understanding of God as love. For Ritschl's brief and negative estimate of German idealism, see *J.R.* I, Ch. II.

23. The most relevant sections are found in *J.R.* III, Ch. 4, esp. § 27–30, 34.

24. *J.R.* III, pp. 214–215.

25. *J.R.* III, p. 225.

26. *J.R.* III, pp. 219–220.

27. Cf. Immanuel Kant, *Critique of Judgment,* tr. by J. H. Bernard (Hafner Library of Classics; Hafner Publishing Company, 1964), pp. 330–334.

28. Cf. Ritschl's argument, *J.R.* III, pp. 224–225.

29. *J.R.* III, p. 225.

30. *J.R.* III, pp. 219–225.

31. *J.R.* III, pp. 214–218.

32. Fabricius, *op. cit.,* p. 117; see the discussion, pp. 112–117.

33. *J.R.* III, p. 325.

34. *J.R.* III, pp. 324–325.

35. *J.R.* III, pp. 324–325.

36. *J.R.* III, pp. 324–325.

37. The title of § 34 in *J.R.* III is "Love as Determination of the Nature of God in Relation to the Son and the Kingdom of God." The first and second editions of *J.R.* III did not include the reference to the Son, indicating perhaps a growing Christocentrism in Ritschl's thought; cf. also *J.R.* III, § 39.

38. *R.V.* II/1, § 12–13.

39. *R.V.* II/1, p. 100; cf. pp. 90–101.

40. *J.R.* III; see esp. § 30, 33–34, 36.

41. *J.R.* III, pp. 277–278.

42. *J.R.* III, pp. 271–272.

43. *J.R.* III, pp. 11–12.

44. *J.R.* III, p. 272.

45. *J.R.* III, p. 326; cf. pp. 279–280.

46. *J.R.* III, p. 306.

47. *J.R.* III, p. 312; cf. § 35 in its entirety.

48. *J.R.* III, p. 281.

49. *J.R.* III, p. 281. The opening definition of the Kingdom of God in § 5 of *Instruction in the Christian Religion* reads: "The Kingdom of God is the divinely vouched-for highest good of the community founded through His revelation in Christ; but it is the highest good only in the sense that it forms at the same time the ethical ideal, for whose attainment the members

of the community bind themselves together through their definite reciprocal action" (*Instruction*, pp. 174–175).

50. *J.R.* III, p. 290; cf. pp. 283, 290–291, 468 ff.

51. *J.R.* III, p. 282.

52. *J.R.* III, p. 326; Otto Ritschl provides useful summaries of the doctrines of God and Christology in Albrecht Ritschl; see Otto Ritschl, II, pp. 192–199, 208–221.

53. *J.R.* III, § 44, 47–48.

54. *J.R.* III, pp. 416–417; cf. § 44–45. Among the merits of Rolf Schäfer's book is the careful attention he gives to Ritschl's Christological starting point and his interpretation of Jesus in addition to an analysis of Ritschl's positive Christology. See his *Ritschl* (Tübingen: J. C. B. Mohr [Paul Siebeck], 1968), esp. pp. 44–67, 101–114. Since I received this book after the completion of my study, it is necessary to restrict my references to it.

55. *J.R.* III, pp. 397–398.

56. *J.R.* III, p. 398. Daniel L. Deegan has shown that Ritschl's interpretation of Jesus avoids the error of the original quest which attempted to understand Jesus apart from the faith of the community and the later error of opposing the Jesus of history to the Christ of faith. See his "Albrecht Ritschl on the Historical Jesus," *Scottish Journal of Theology*, Vol. 15, No. 2 (1962), pp. 133 ff.

57. *J.R.* III, pp. 445–446.

58. *Instruction*, § 21, p. 195; cf. *J.R.* III, p. 445.

59. *J.R.* III, pp. 442–445.

60. *J.R.* III, p. 452. For Ritschl's view of the centrality of the Kingdom of God for Jesus, see also *Entstehung*, pp. 27–51; and *R.V.* II, § 5.

61. *J.R.* III, pp. 442–452. The heading of § 48 is "The Ethical Estimate of Christ According to his Vocation Carries with It the Religious Recognition of Him as Revealer of God."

62. *Instruction*, § 21, p. 195; cf. *R.V.* II/2, § 5–7. Ritschl interpreted Jesus as the founder of the Kingdom of God as early as 1857; see *Entstehung*, pp. 27–51.

63. *J.R.* III, p. 12. The original German title of § 44 in *R.V.* III/1 reads: "Die specifische Bedeutung des Stifters in der christlichen Religion," which may be translated as follows: "The Specific Significance of the Founder of the Christian Religion."

64. *J.R.* III, p. 386.

65. *J.R.* III, p. 469; for Ritschl's doctrine of election, see especially *J.R.* III, § 22.

66. *J.R.* III, p. 468; cf. the statement in *Instruction*, p. 197. "Therefore, as the original type of the humanity to be united into the kingdom of

God, He is the original object of the love of God (§ 12), so that the love of God for the members of His kingdom also is only mediated through Him (§ 13)."

67. J.R. III, p. 469.

68. J.R. III, pp. 469–470.

69. J.R. III, p. 471.

70. J.R. III, p. 471; but cf. the more typical and normative statements on pp. 451–452. Timm, *Theorie und Praxis*, p. 32, n. 8, has shown that many studies of Ritschl follow the lead of Otto Ritschl in seeing a radical discontinuity between the early Ritschl prior to 1857 under the influence of Hegel and idealism and the mature Ritschl of *Justification and Reconciliation*. It will be apparent in this study that there are points of continuity as well as of discontinuity between Ritschl and the heritage of idealism.

71. J.R. III, p. 471. On the basis of his analysis of Ritschl's lectures in dogmatics in 1881–1882 and in other years, Rolf Schäfer comes to a conclusion similar to ours in maintaining that Ritschl regarded the doctrine of the Trinity as the final and comprehensive statement of Christian doctrine; see his *Ritschl*, pp. 150–153.

72. J.R. III, p. 472.

73. J.R. III, pp. 471–472; in this section on election, Ritschl avails himself of a kind of speculation about the Absolute reminiscent of certain forms of German, and especially Hegelian, idealism mediated to him through J. E. Erdmann, Richard Rothe, and F. C. Baur.

74. *Instruction*, § 22, pp. 196–197; cf. the statement in J.R. III, p. 454: "For in the characteristic activity of Christ in the discharge of His vocation, the essential will of God is revealed as love, since Christ's supreme aim, namely, the Kingdom of God, is identical with the supreme end of the Father."

75. John 4:34.

76. J.R. III, pp. 446–449.

77. There is a consistent mistranslation of the German word *Treue* by the English word "truth" throughout J.R. III, in order, it would seem, to make it accord with the customary English translation of the Johannine passage. It is much better to render the German *Treue* as "faithfulness" or "fidelity," and it is the latter virtue that stands out in Ritschl's analysis of Jesus' attitude toward his vocation.

78. J.R. III, p. 454.

79. J.R. III, pp. 463–464.

80. Otto Ritschl, II, p. 213.

81. J.R. III, pp. 464–466.

82. J.R. III, p. 460; cf. p. 480; and *Instruction*, § 22, p. 196.

83. *J.R.* III, pp. 448–450.

84. For this emphasis, see *Instruction,* § 23–24, pp. 197–199.

85. *J.R.* III, p. 292.

86. Cf. *J.R.* III, § 36.

87. See *J.R.* III, § 49–50; esp. pp. 454–470.

88. *J.R.* III, pp. 467–468.

89. *J.R.* III, p. 468. Ritschl agrees at this point with Kant, who likewise stressed the volitional aspect of human existence, and finds Schleiermacher's preoccupation with feeling a mark of Romanticism and a retrogression from Kant.

90. *J.R.* III, pp. 483–484.

91. Cf. *J.R.* III, § 27–50.

92. *J.R.* III, p. 1.

93. Karl Barth, *C. D.* IV/1 (1956), pp. 38–91.

94. *J.R.* III, § 40.

95. *J.R.* III, pp. 331 ff. For a recent illuminating study of the relation of law and gospel in Ritschl within the context of the nineteenth-century debate, see Gerhard O. Forde, *The Law-Gospel Debate* (Augsburg Publishing House, 1969), pp. 96–119.

96. *J.R.* III, pp. 328 ff.; cf. especially § 40. Note the similarity between Ritschl's statement concerning the centrality of Jesus Christ for the construction of every doctrine and that of Karl Barth. "But if . . . in the Christian religion, Jesus Christ is the standard of . . . [the] believers' view of the world and estimate of self, then in Dogmatics His Person must be regarded as the ground of knowledge to be used in the definition of every doctrine" (*J.R.* III, p. 331). Cf. the following programmatic statement of Karl Barth: "Jesus Christ in his *self-revelation* is the *basic text* (*Grundtext*) . . . of all theology" (*K.D.* IV/2 [1955], p. 136). Or: "If it [i.e., Jesus Christ] were a principle and not a name indicating a person, we should have to describe it as the epistemological principle of the message" (*C.D.* IV/1 [1956], p. 17).

97. *Instruction,* p. 202, § 26. Cf. *Instruction,* § 26–33, for the above-mentioned topics.

98. *J.R.* III, p. 27; cf. *Instruction,* § 28.

99. *J.R.* III, p. 328.

100. *J.R.* III, p. 336.

101. *J.R.* III, p. 328.

102. *J.R.* III, p. 340.

103. This stress on man as a volitional being is important for Ritschl's psychology, anthropology, and his understanding of man's activity in the Kingdom of God, and thus of his ethics.

104. For the preceding paragraph, see *J.R.* III, § 40–41.

105. *J.R.* I, § 45–46.
106. *J.R.* I, p. 366.
107. *J.R.* I, Chs. 7–8.
108. *J.R.* I, p. 387.
109. *J.R.* I, p. 387.
110. *J.R.* I, p. 388.
111. *J.R.* I, p. 390.
112. *J.R.* I, p. 390.
113. *J.R.* I, p. 394.
114. *J.R.* I, p. 394.
115. *J.R.* I, p. 389; see, for example, how similar Ritschl's positive statement is to Kant's in *J.R.* III, § 57–58.
116. Cf. *Religion Within the Limits of Reason Alone,* esp. Books I and II.
117. *J.R.* III, p. 344; cf. *Instruction,* § 30. We shall return to this concept later in Ritschl's doctrine of sin.
118. *J.R.* I, pp. 410, 434; *J.R.* III, p. 319.
119. For Ritschl's most extensive interpretation of Kant, see esp. *J.R.* I, § 56–58.
120. For Ritschl's interpretation of Schleiermacher set forth above, see *J.R.* I, § 62–64; *J.R.* III, § 40–43.
121. *J.R.* III, pp. 334, 350.
122. *J.R.* III, p. 329.
123. *J.R.* I, p. 180; cf. pp. 143, 193.
124. *J.R.* III, p. 334.
125. *J.R.* III, p. 333.
126. *J.R.* III, p. 334.
127. *J.R.* III, pp. 333–334; cf. *Instruction,* § 27.
128. *J.R.* III, p. 380; cf. Otto Ritschl, II, p. 200.
129. *J.R.* III, pp. 348–349.
130. *J.R.* III, p. 334.
131. *J.R.* III, p. 333; cf. pp. 334–335.
132. *J.R.* III, p. 335.
133. *J.R.* III, p. 335.
134. *J.R.* III, p. 335.
135. *J.R.* III, pp. 336–337.
136. *J.R.* III, p. 337.
137. *Instruction,* § 28, p. 204; cf. § 30.
138. *J.R.* III, p. 349.
139. *J.R.* III, p. 338.
140. *J.R.* III, p. 338.
141. *J.R.* III, p. 350; cf. pp. 338 ff.

142. *J.R.* III, pp. 383–384.

143. *J.R.* III, p. 353.

144. *J.R.* III, p. 351.

145. *J.R.* III, p. 353.

146. *J.R.* III, pp. 360 ff.; cf. *J.R.* III, § 9–10, 30.

147. *J.R.* III, pp. 350–358.

148. *J.R.* III, p. 365; cf. *Instruction*, § 31, 33.

149. On this point, Ritschl follows Kant in writing: "That which the tradition of the Church desires to express in the notion of original sin cannot be apprehended as guilt by anyone who does not draw a distinction between *himself* (himself as he should be under the idea of freedom, and under the obligation of the moral law), and the empirical course of his own life in itself, and along with the life of the race" (*J.R.* I, p. 395).

150. *J.R.* III, p. 365; cf. *Instruction*, § 33.

151. *J.R.* III, § 10–11.

152. *J.R.* III, p. 54.

153. *J.R.* III, p. 384.

154. *J.R.* III, p. 58.

155. *J.R.* III, p. 59.

156. *J.R.* III, p. 369; *J.R.* III, § 43, is entitled "Sin and the Possibility of Its Forgiveness."

157. *J.R.* III, p. 369.

158. *J.R.* III, p. 376; cf. esp. *R.V.* II/2, § 28.

159. *J.R.* I, pp. 406 f.

160. *J.R.* III, p. 383; cf. p. 379.

161. *J.R.* III, p. 384.

162. *J.R.* III, p. 383.

Chapter III

1. *J.R.* I, p. 1.

2. *J.R.* III, p. vii.

3. Hefner, *Faith and the Vitalities of History,* pp. 1–11.

4. *R.V.* II/1, pp. 24–25.

5. Otto Ritschl, I, p. 294.

6. Otto Ritschl, II, pp. 302–304, 386–390.

7. *J.R.* III, p. 36.

8. *J.R.* III, p. 37; cf. pp. 21, 54. For Ritschl's discussion of various Roman Catholic views of justification, cf. also *J.R.* I, Chs. 1–3; also *J.R.* I, § 21, and *Unterricht*, § 45.

9. *J.R.* III, p. 487.

10. *J.R.* III, p. 527.

11. *J.R.* III, p. 527.

12. *J.R.* III, p. 531.

13. *J.R.* I, pp. 433–434. For Ritschl's extended treatment of Kant, see *J.R.* I, esp. § 56–58. Ritschl regarded Socinianism as a radical departure from normative Reformation Christianity and gave careful attention to this movement from the time of his early article "Die Rechtfertigungslehre des Andreas Osiander" (1857) to the period during which he wrote concerning it in *J.R.* I, Chs. 5 and 6, and *J.R.* III, Chs. 4, 7, and 8, esp. § 31, 51, 54, 55, 59.

14. *J.R.* III, § 59.

15. *J.R.* I, Ch. 11. For one account of Ritschl's breach with Baur and the Tübingen School, see Otto Ritschl, I, Ch. 8. Ritschl's essay, "Über geschichtliche Methode in der Erforschung des Urchristenthums," *Jahrbücher für deutsche Theologie*, VI (1861), pp. 429–459, provides a summary of some of his differences with Baur and the Tübingen School. See Otto Ritschl, I, pp. 393–398, for a discussion of this article. For Ritschl's disagreement with Baur, see also *J.R.* I, pp. 10–16. For a recent comprehensive study of F. C. Baur, see Peter C. Hodgson, *The Formation of Historical Theology* (Harper & Row, Publishers, Inc., 1966), esp. pp. 86 ff. on Baur and the Tübingen School. Stephen D. Crites provides an analysis of the concept of reconciliation in Hegel in "The Problem of the 'Positivity' of the Gospel in the Hegelian Dialectic of Alienation and Reconciliation" (unpublished doctoral dissertation, Department of Religion, Yale University, 1961).

16. *J.R.* I, pp. 571–573. It is noteworthy that Ritschl utilizes all these emphases in his positive reconstruction.

17. *J.R.* I, p. 573.

18. *J.R.* III, p. 27; cf. *R.V.* III/1, § 5, and *J.R.* III, § 5.

19. Cf. *R.V.* III/1, § 22, and *J.R.* III, § 20.

20. *J.R.* III, Chs. 2–3. Though Barth's doctrine of election has certain antecedents in the Reformed tradition, the parallels to Ritschl's structure of the doctrine of justification are instructive; cf. *C.D.* II/2 (1957); this also applies to the formal structure of the doctrine of justification, *C.D.* IV/1 (1956), § 61.

21. *J.R.* III, p. 113.

22. *J.R.* III, p. 548.

23. *J.R.* III, p. 110; cf. pp. 548 ff., 577. Among other sections making this emphasis, see *J.R.* I, § 22; *R.V.* II, § 37; *J.R.* III, § 56, 59–60.

24. Otto Ritschl, II, p. 47.

25. *J.R.* III, p. 549; cf. Schleiermacher, *The Christian Faith*, § 24, p. 103.

26. *J.R.* III, p. 549; the heading of § 40–45 in *Unterricht* makes this point strongly: "Christus als Versöhner der Gemeinde." See *Instruction,* § 40–45.

27. *J.R.* III, p. 31; see § 6.

28. *J.R.* III, p. 35.

29. For a typical example of the charge of subjectivism in Ritschl, see Otto Weber, *Grundlagen der Dogmatik* (2 vols.; Neukirchen Kreis Moers: Verlag der Buchhandlung des Erziehungsvereins, 1955 and 1962), Vol. II, pp. 208–209.

30. See, for example, Ritschl's review of J. C. K. von Hofmann's method in Otto Ritschl, I, pp. 307 ff. For comparative studies of Hofmann and Ritschl, see Bernhard Steffen, *Hofmann und Ritschls Lehren über die Heilsbedeutung des Todes Jesu* (Gütersloh: Verlag Bertelsmann, 1910), and Christoph Senft, *Wahrhaftigkeit und Wahrheit: Die Theologie des 19. Jahrhunderts zwischen Orthodoxie und Aufklärung* (Beiträge zur historischen Theologie, Bd. 22; Tübingen: J. C. B. Mohr [Paul Siebeck], 1956), pp. 87–171.

31. The priority of the objective pole over the subjective pole is seen in *J.R.* III, Chs. 1–2, where § 8–18 discuss the objective pole prior to the systematic exposition of the "subjective aspect," which is first developed in § 19 ff.; however, the latter comes into focus only in Ch. 3, § 23–26. The same sequence obtains in the "proof" of the doctrine where Ch. 8, "The Necessity of Basing the Forgiveness of Sins on the Work and Passion of Christ," precedes the analysis of the "Religious Functions" that arise out of man's justification and reconciliation in Ch. 9.

32. Cited in Otto Ritschl, I, p. 298. This citation is from the article "Die Rechtfertigungslehre des Andreas Osiander," *Jahrbücher für deutsche Theologie* (1857), Heft 4, p. 828. See *J.R.* III, p. 124, and elsewhere for this emphasis.

33. *J.R.* III, p. 25.

34. *J.R.* I, p. 159.

35. *J.R.* I, p. 157. Ritschl criticizes F. C. Baur and I. August Dorner for overlooking the significance of the correlation between justification by faith and the understanding of the nature of the church in the Reformers, thereby contributing to a continuing misconstruing of the Reformation view of justification in a subjectivistic direction. See *J.R.* I, pp. 10–19, 157–159.

36. Albrecht Ritschl, *Gesammelte Aufsätze* (Freiburg i.B. and Leipzig: J. C. B. Mohr-Paul Siebeck, 1893), Vol. I, p. 247; cf. pp. 244–247. In defense of I. A. Dorner, it should be noted that he, too, stresses the priority of the objective work of Christ against all types of synergism; cf. *A History of Protestant Theology Particularly in Germany, Viewed Accord-*

ing to Its Fundamental Movement in Connection with the Religious, Moral, and Intellectual Life, tr. by George Robson and Sophia Taylor (Edinburgh: T. & T. Clark, 1871), Vol. II, pp. 163 ff.

37. *J.R.* I, p. 157.

38. Cited by Ritschl, *J.R.* I, p. 158, n. 1.

39. *J.R.* I, § 22, esp. pp. 129, 133.

40. *J.R.* III, p. 85.

41. *J.R.* III, pp. 38–39.

42. *J.R.* III, § 8; cf. *Instruction,* § 36–38.

43. *J.R.* III, p. 1.

44. *R.V.* II, § 5–11.

45. *R.V.* II/2, pp. 26–27.

46. *R.V.* II/2, § 5–6.

47. Cf. Chapter II, the section "The Doctrine of the Person and Life-work of Jesus Christ and Justification and Reconciliation."

48. *J.R.* III, pp. 439, 442; cf. § 47–48.

49. *J.R.* III, pp. 2–3.

50. *J.R.* III, p. 442.

51. See esp. Wilhelm Herrmann, *The Communion of the Christian with God,* tr. by J. Sandys Stanyon and R. W. Stewart (G. P. Putnam's Sons, 1906). For a recent analysis of Herrmann, see Robert T. Voelkel, *The Shape of the Theological Task* (The Westminster Press, 1968). Gerhard Ebeling's interpretation of Jesus as the "witness of faith" is similar to the approach characteristic of Ritschl and Herrmann; see *The Nature of Faith,* tr. by Ronald G. Smith (London: William Collins Sons & Co., Ltd., 1961), Ch. 4.

52. *J.R.* III, p. 443.

53. *J.R.* III, p. 451; cf. p. 472.

54. *J.R.* III, p. 546; cf. all of § 50, 55, 56; also *Instruction,* § 26–45.

55. Cf. above Chapter II, the section entitled "The Love of God Revealed in the Son and the Kingdom of God." Barth's strictures with respect to Ritschl's doctrine of God are instructive at this point; see *C.D.* II/1 (1957), pp. 364 ff., 382.

56. *J.R.* III, p. 473.

57. See above Chapter II the section entitled "The Doctrine of God and Justification and Reconciliation."

58. *J.R.* III, pp. 483–484.

59. *J.R.* III, pp. 473–474. This assertion is based on Ritschl's conclusions concerning the meaning of the "righteousness of God" in the Old Testament and the New Testament; see *R.V.* II, Ch. 2, § 14–15.

60. *R.V.* II, § 16–19.

61. *R.V.* II/2, § 21, p. 154, cf. esp. pp. 135–137; 153–156. For a

study of the eclipse of the concept of the wrath of God in modern theology and in Ritschl, see James P. Martin, *The Last Judgment* (Wm. B. Eerdmans Publishing Company, 1963), esp. pp. 196–208.

62. *J.R.* III, p. 474.

63. *J.R.* III, pp. 473–474.

64. *J.R.* III, pp. 474–475.

65. Schleiermacher, *The Christian Faith*, e.g., § 94; cf. *J.R.* III, pp. 474–476.

66. *J.R.* III, p. 475.

67. *J.R.* III, pp. 474–476.

68. *J.R.* III, pp. 478–479.

69. *J.R.* III, p. 479.

70. *R.V.* II, § 7; *J.R.* III, § 49; cf. *Instruction*, § 41.

71. *J.R.* III, § 55; cf. *Instruction*, § 39–40.

72. *J.R.* III, Ch. 8; cf. esp. § 55–56; also *R.V.* II, § 22.

73. Ritschl puts the matter thus at the outset of an important section with the title "Proof [i.e., for the necessity of basing the forgiveness of sins on the work and passion of Christ] Derived from the Intention of Christ to Found His Religious Community." "As Christ connects the bestowal of *forgiveness* with the prophecy of Jeremiah, forgiveness is to be regarded as the common fundamental *attribute of the community to be founded by Him*" (*J.R.* III, p. 543).

74. See the discussions above in Chapter II under the headings "Justification and Reconciliation and the Kingdom of God" and "The Vocation of Jesus as the Founder of the Kingdom of God." Schäfer makes much of Ritschl's view that Jesus' death is to be understood as the particular and unrepeatable sacrifice of the New Covenant which effects forgiveness of sins once and for all; see his *Ritschl*, pp. 53–59.

75. *J.R.* III, p. 607.

76. *J.R.* III, p. 547.

77. *J.R.* III, pp. 542–543; in *R.V.* II, Ch. 3, "Die Bedeutung des Todes Christi als Opfers zum Zwecke der Sündenvergebung," one finds a good discussion of the use of the term "sacrifice" in both the Old and the New Testament. "Paul" (§ 27) and The Letter to the Hebrews provide the best New Testament precedent for holding that the forgiveness of sins is the immediate result of the sacrificial death of Christ. Further development of Paul's equation of justification with the forgiveness of sins is found in *R.V.* II, § 37.

78. *J.R.* III, p. 477.

79. *J.R.* III, p. 71. Cf. *Instruction*, § 42.

80. *J.R.* III, p. 546; cf. *Instruction*, § 41–45; *R.V.* II, § 11, 22.

81. *J.R.* III, pp. 607–608.

82. *J.R.* III, pp. 64–67.

83. *J.R.* III, pp. 49–52.

84. *J.R.* III, p. 58.

85. See the caption of § 12 in *J.R.* III, p. ix.

86. *J.R.* III, p. 85.

87. *J.R.* III, pp. 63–64.

88. *J.R.* III, p. 74.

89. Otto Ritschl, I, p. 298. This is the total emphasis of our section entitled "Justification as the Act of God: The Objective Pole of the Doctrine of Justification."

90. *J.R.* I, p. 179.

91. *J.R.* I, p. 179.

92. *J.R.* I, p. 179.

93. *J.R.* III, pp. 79–80; cf. § 16.

94. *J.R.* III, p. 80.

95. *J.R.* III, § 17–18.

96. *J.R.* III, p. 84.

97. *J.R.* III, pp. 84–85.

98. *J.R.* III, § 15, 18.

99. *J.R.* III, p. 77; cf. *R.V.* III/4, p. 75.

100. *J.R.* III, p. 78.

101. *J.R.* III, p. 78.

102. *J.R.* III, p. 79; cf. *Instruction,* § 37.

103. *J.R.* III, pp. 69, 74, 98.

104. *J.R.* III, pp. 76–77.

105. *J.R.* III, p. 96; cf. § 18.

106. *J.R.* III, p. 85.

107. See above, Chapter I, the sections "The Church and Christian Theology," "The Faith of the Church as the Object of Theological Investigation," and "Religious Assertions as Value Judgments."

108. I have dealt with Ritschl's approach to the problem of relating divine activity and human freedom and responsibility above, Chapter I, "Religion: The Divine-Human Relationship."

109. *J.R.* III, p. 34.

110. Cited by Otto Ritschl, II, p. 191.

111. *J.R.* III, p. 100.

112. In *J.R.* III, pp. 577–578, Ritschl writes: "Certainly there is in no case either a mechanical or a logical necessity laid upon individuals to join themselves in faith to the existing Christian community. Faith begins in harmony with the law of freedom. It cannot be calculated beforehand whether Christ will find faith, and the fact that He found it was not more determined beforehand than the purpose in general guarantees the result."

113. *J.R.* III, Ch. 9, for the "Consequences" of justification. Apart from *J.R.* III, Ch. 3, "The Subjective Aspect of Justification Considered in Detail," the discussion concerning the nature of faith is found scattered in Ch. 2 and in § 59–61.

114. *J.R.* III, p. 607.

115. *J.R.* III, p. 107; cf. pp. 577–578.

116. *J.R.* III, pp. 103–107.

117. *J.R.* III, pp. 107–108.

118. In addition to the sections cited in n. 107 above, see above in this chapter the section "Justification, the Church, and the Individual."

119. *J.R.* III, p. 591; this is an important point for Schleiermacher, Ritschl, and Barth, and it is to be preferred to the excesses of religious individualism characteristic of much recent Christian existentialism.

120. *J.R.* III, § 20.

121. *J.R.* III, p. 577.

122. *J.R.* III, p. 103.

123. See above, Chapter I, "Religion: The Divine-Human Relationship."

124. *J.R.* III, p. 101.

125. For a positive appraisal of this understanding of faith, see John Baillie, *The Idea of Revelation in Recent Thought* (Columbia University Press, 1958); for a critique of certain aspects of this tradition as it finds expression in theological existentialism, see Gollwitzer, *op. cit.*, pp. 66–67.

126. *J.R.* III, pp. 591–592.

127. The following sections in Ritschl's systematic exposition are the most significant for this problem; *J.R.* I, Ch. 4; *J.R.* III, § 19–20, 23–26, 59–61, 67.

128. *J.R.* III, p. 593.

129. *J.R.* III, p. 596.

130. *J.R.* I, p. 238.

131. *J.R.* I, p. 121.

132. Ch. V treats the consequences of justification. The manner in which Ritschl's idea of the *Lebensführung* or *Lebensideal* derives from his interpretation of justification and represents its full amplification can be seen in the recent work on Ritschl by Philip Hefner, *op. cit.*, esp. Chs. 2–3.

133. *J.R.* I, p. 242.

134. *J.R.* I, § 41.

135. See *J.R.* I, § 42: "The Doctrine of the *applicatio gratiae* or *efficacia meriti Christi*. Divergence of the Two Confessions." Further variations concerning the appropriation of justification in the branches of orthodoxy cannot detain us here. See the full discussion in *J.R.* I, § 34–47.

136. *J.R.* III, p. 142.

137. *J.R.* III, p. 142.

138. *J.R.* III, pp. 142–143.

139. *J.R.* III, p. 146; cf. pp. 150, 154, 168 and *J.R.* I, p. 122.

140. *J.R.* III, pp. 152 ff.

141. *J.R.* III, p. 653.

142. *J.R.* III, pp. 148 ff., 179 ff.

143. *J.R.* III, p. 148; cf. pp. 655 ff.

144. *J.R.* III, pp. 149–150.

145. *J.R.* III, p. 150.

146. *J.R.* III, pp. 151, 649 ff.; cf. § 25, 67; cf. also *Pietismus* II, pp. 5–6. For Luther's attitude toward penance, see *J.R.* I, § 24.

147. *J.R.* III, p. 180.

148. *J.R.* III, p. 151.

149. *J.R.* III, p. 151.

150. We cannot enter here into the distinctions Ritschl makes between the "older Pietism" of Halle associated with the names of Spener and others in the eighteenth century and "modern Pietism" at the beginning of the nineteenth century. The latter is characterized by a more churchly orientation and is, in fact, one of the streams that fed into the "repristination of Lutheran Orthodoxy" (*J.R.* I, p. 513); see the extended discussion of Pietism in Ch. 10 of *J.R.* I and in *Pietismus*. In the discussion in *J.R.* III, Ritschl seems to have the older, more authentic Pietism in mind in most instances.

151. Ritschl writes against orthodoxy in *J.R.* III, p. 159, thus: "Now feeling is simply that function of mind in which the Ego is present to itself; and reconciliation with God must imply a modification of the feeling of self, if the assurance thereof is to occupy the mind at every moment and become a motive impelling the will."

152. Ritschl's *Pietismus* (3 vols.) appeared during the years 1880–1886 and was the product of his later years. Its publication intensified the attack of Pietists upon Ritschl's theology; during this period in his career, Ritschl always had his gaze fixed upon the Pietist perversion of the true faith of the Reformers.

153. *J.R.* I, p. 155.

154. *J.R.* III, p. 191.

155. *Pietismus* II, pp. 9–10.

156. *J.R.* I, § 59.

157. *J.R.* III, p. 598.

158. *J.R.* III, pp. 601, 604.

159. *J.R.* III, p. 603.

160. *J.R.* III, p. 603.

161. *J.R.* III, pp. 605–606.

162. *J.R.* III, p. 607; cf. pp. 654–655. Althaus holds a view similar to Ritschl's in proposing the thesis that whereas the Reformers taught that man understands himself in relationship to the events of *Heilsgeschichte,* Pietism taught the necessity of the recapitulation of the *Heilsgeschichte* within the individual; Paul Althaus, "Die Bekehrung in reformatorischer und pietistischer Sicht," *Neue Zeitschrift für Systematische Theologie,* Bd. I, Heft 1 (1959), p. 17.

163. *R.V.* III/2, p. 554.

164. *J.R.* III, p. 162.

165. *J.R.* III, p. 160; pp. 166 ff.

166. *J.R.* III, p. 176.

167. *J.R.* III, p. 595; see the references to *R.V.* I and *R.V.* II for historical materials.

168. *J.R.* III, p. 595; cf. pp. 593–594.

169. *J.R.* III, p. 594.

170. *J.R.* III, pp. 595–596.

171. *J.R.* III, pp. 595–597.

172. *J.R.* III, p. 579.

173. *J.R.* III, p. 579.

174. *J.R.* III, pp. 581–583.

175. *J.R.* III, p. 583.

176. *J.R.* III, pp. 583–584.

177. *J.R.* III, Ch. 9, § 62–68.

178. *J.R.* III, § 25–26.

179. *J.R.* III, p. 168.

180. *J.R.* III, pp. 174–175.

181. See the discussion above in Chapter I on Ritschl's methodology.

182. *J.R.* III, pp. 22–23.

183. *J.R.* III, p. 191.

CHAPTER IV

1. Johannes Wendland, *Albrecht Ritschl und seine Schüler im Verhältnis zur Theologie, zur Philosophie und zur Frömmigkeit unserer Zeit dargestellt und beurteilt* (Berlin: Georg Reimer Verlag, 1899), p. 125.

2. Fabricius, *op. cit.,* pp. 74 ff.

3. Otto Ritschl, II, pp. 124–125; see *R.V.* II, Ch. 4, esp. § 37–40.

4. Albrecht Ritschl, *Die christliche Vollkommenheit: Ein Vortrag* and *Unterricht in der christlichen Religion,* with an introduction by Cajus Fabricius (Leipzig: J. C. Hinrichs'sche Buchhandlung, 1924), p. xiv. Hereafter this critical edition of the above two works will be cited as *Christliche Vollkommenheit* and *Unterricht* II respectively. B. B. Warfield refers

to an English translation of *Christian Perfection* in *Bibliotheca Sacra,* October, 1878, which the present writer has not consulted; see Warfield's *Perfectionism,* Vol. I (London: Oxford University Press, 1931), n. 46, p. 72. He also provides a bibliography of works dealing with Ritschl's view of perfection; see n. 114, pp. 109–110.

5. Otto Ritschl, II, p. 156.

6. Otto Ritschl, II, p. 143

7. *Instruction,* p. 279.

8. For a helpful analysis of Ritschl's use of the category of *Lebensführung* or the "ideal life-style" as the key for interpreting his evaluation of the historical development of Christianity, see Hefner, *op. cit.,* esp. pp. 12–90.

9. *Pietismus* I, p. 41; cf. *Christliche Vollkommenheit,* pp. 1–8; *J.R.* III, p. 656.

10. For materials relevant to the above discussion, the reader is referred to: *J.R.* I, § 23–24; *R.V.* II, § 30–40; *J.R.* III, esp. § 25–26, 63, 67; and *Christliche Vollkommenheit.*

11. *Instruction,* § 50, pp. 232–233.

12. Fabricius, *op. cit.,* e.g., pp. 75–78 ff.

13. *J.R.* III, p. 609.

14. In *Christliche Vollkommenheit,* Ritschl deals first with the ethical aspects of perfection evidenced in one's vocation, etc., since these appear to be closer to everyday experience; see pp. 10–13.

15. Cited in *Christliche Vollkommenheit,* p. 7; my translation of the quotation from the Augsburg Confession.

16. *Christliche Vollkommenheit,* p. 7.

17. *J.R.* III, § 25; cf. § 26 and *R.V.* II, esp. § 37–39; *J.R.* I, § 24, 26.

18. *Christliche Vollkommenheit,* p. 13.

19. *J.R.* III, § 63.

20. *J.R.* III, p. 168.

21. *J.R.* III, p. 169; cf. p. 591.

22. *J.R.* III, p. 475.

23. *J.R.* III, p. 476; in *J.R.* III, § 44–45, Ritschl is more willing to speak about the unique relationship that Jesus enjoyed with God, or of a religious estimate of his Person; in § 47–48, the ethical estimate of his Person predominates, and this is the approach Ritschl favors.

24. Otto Ritschl, II, pp. 312–313; later, under pressure, Scholz aligned himself with the Lutheran Church (*ibid.,* p. 314).

25. *J.R.* III, § 38 and 64, esp. pp. 625–627; cf. *Instruction,* § 51.

26. *Christliche Vollkommenheit,* pp. 8–9.

27. *J.R.* III, § 44, 49, 53; the framework for this point is provided above, Chapter II, the section entitled "The Doctrine of the Person and Lifework of Jesus Christ and Justification and Reconciliation."

28. *J.R.* III, p. 457; cf. p. 502.

29. Cf., for example, *J.R.* III, p. 457.

30. *J.R.* III, p. 617.

31. *J.R.* III, p. 611; cf. p. 458; *Instruction,* § 51.

32. *J.R.* III, p. 635.

33. *J.R.* III, p. 637; Fabricius has shown that in the first edition of *R.V.* III, Ritschl often defined religion in terms of "dependence upon God," i.e., in terms of *Abhängigkeit* as understood by Schleiermacher. In the second edition, as noted earlier, he substituted less distinctly Schleiermacherian language and spoke of subjection or submission (*Unterordnung*), etc., to God. See Fabricius, *op. cit.,* pp. 75–88.

34. *Christliche Vollkommenheit,* p. 17.

35. *J.R.* III, p. 637.

36. Otto Ritschl, II, p. 143.

37. *J.R.* III, p. 628.

38. *J.R.* III, p. 627; cf. *Instruction,* § 53.

39. *J.R.* III, p. 629.

40. *J.R.* III, p. 646.

41. *J.R.* III, p. 646.

42. *J.R.* III, pp. 626, 644–645, 670; *Instruction,* § 54–55. For Ritschl's attitude toward miracle, see Otto Ritschl, I, pp. 293–298.

43. *Christliche Vollkommenheit,* p. 17.

44. See the sections in Chapter I above entitled "Religion as *Weltanschauung*" and "The Movement of Theology toward a System and a *Weltanschauung.*" Also, *J.R.* III, esp. § 28.

45. *J.R.* III, p. 616.

46. *J.R.* III, p. 616.

47. *J.R.* III, p. 616.

48. *J.R.* III, p. 616.

49. *J.R.* III, p. 621.

50. *J.R.* III, p. 621.

51. *J.R.* III, p. 620.

52. *J.R.* III, p. 618.

53. *J.R.* III, p. 200; cf. pp. 590–593, 616–625.

54. *Christliche Vollkommenheit,* p. 10.

55. See the earlier discussions on the Kingdom of God above in Chapters II and III.

56. *J.R.* III, p. 670.

57. *Instruction,* pp. 228–229.

58. In order to understand Ritschl's discussion of the ethical virtues, one should consult carefully *J.R.* III, § 51–54.

59. *J.R.* III, § 52.

60. *J.R.* III, § 52; the close connection between justification and eternal life or blessedness is evident in the following: "Accordingly eternal life, in the Christian sense, is that spiritual independence, possible in the realm of Divine grace, which, in harmony with God's providence, subdues all things to itself, so that they become means to blessedness, even when viewed externally they run counter to it" (*J.R.* III, p. 507).

61. *J.R.* III, p. 509.

62. *J.R.* III, pp. 509–510.

63. *J.R.* III, p. 512.

64. *J.R.* III, p. 292; cf. pp. 512–523; in this connection, see esp. *J.R.* III, § 36.

65. *J.R.* III, p. 514.

66. *J.R.* III, p. 511.

67. *J.R.* III, p. 514.

68. *J.R.* III, p. 515; cf. p. 667; and *Instruction,* pp. 252–253.

69. *J.R.* III, p. 526.

70. *J.R.* III, p. 515.

71. *J.R.* III, pp. 668–669.

72. *J.R.* III, p. 517.

73. *J.R.* III, p. 517.

74. *J.R.* III, p. 517; cf. pp. 518, 522, 527, 668–670.

75. *J.R.* III, p. 518.

76. *J.R.* III, p. 518.

77. *J.R.* III, p. 520.

78. That Ritschl intends to absorb Luther's valid insights is indicated in his analysis of the relationship of faith and moral action in Luther; cf. *J.R.* I, § 23.

79. *Unterricht* II, § 26, pp. 54–55.

80. *Instruction,* pp. 246–247.

81. *Instruction,* p. 247.

82. *Unterricht* II, § 66, p. 90; cf. *Instruction,* p. 249.

83. *Instruction,* p. 248.

84. *Instruction,* p. 250.

85. *Instruction,* pp. 250–251.

86. *Instruction,* p. 248.

87. *Christliche Vollkommenheit,* p. 4; cf. *J.R.* III, pp. 661–663.

88. *J.R.* III, p. 651.

89. *J.R.* III, p. 445. For the relation of perfection and vocation, see *J.R.* III, § 48; also above, Chapter II, the section "The Doctrine of the Person and Lifework of Jesus Christ and Justification and Reconciliation."

90. *J.R.* III, p. 661.

91. *Instruction,* pp. 239–240.

92. *Instruction,* p. 240.

93. *J.R.* III, p. 665.

94. *J.R.* III, p. 665; cf. *Instruction,* pp. 262-263.

95. *J.R.* III, p. 666.

96. *J.R.* III, p. 668.

97. *J.R.* III, p. 669; cf. *Christliche Vollkommenheit,* p. 12.

98. *Christliche Vollkommenheit,* p. 6.

99. *Pietismus* I, p. 41; Ritschl remarks that the Reformer's view of vocation caused some Catholic opponents to accuse Protestantism of giving rise to Epicureanism and heathenism (*ibid.,* p. 42).

100. See the discussion above, Chapter III, the sections entitled "Justification by Faith and Assurance of Salvation" and "In Pietism" for other aspects of Ritschl's critique of Pietism.

101. *J.R.* III, pp. 639–640.

102. For the above analysis, see especially: *Pietismus* I, pp. 38 ff.; *Pietismus* II, Ch. 27; *J.R.* III, pp. 639–640.

103. Otto Ritschl, II, pp. 324–325; cf. *Pietismus* I, pp. 41 ff.

104. *J.R.* III, pp. 612–613.

105. *J.R.* III, p. 613.

106. *J.R.* III, p. 613; Karl Barth was among the first to take seriously Overbeck's unheeded attack upon the acculturated Christianity of the nineteenth century; cf. his early essay on Overbeck, "Unerledigte Anfragen an die heutige Theologie" in *Die Theologie und die Kirche,* Vol. II (Munich: Chr. Kaiser Verlag, 1928), and the later essay in *Die Protestantische Theologie im 19. Jahrhundert* (2d ed.; Zollikon-Zurich: Evangelischer Verlag, 1952), cited hereafter as *Prot. Theol.* The smaller English version translated by Brian Cozens was published with the title *From Rousseau to Ritschl* (London: SCM Press, Ltd., 1959).

107. *J.R.* III, p. 669.

108. *Christliche Vollkommenheit,* p. 18.

CHAPTER V

1. Barth, *Prot. Theol.* The most extensive study of the history of modern theology remains that of Emanuel Hirsch, *Geschichte der neuern evangelischen Theologie im Zusammenhang mit den allgemeinen Bewegungen des europäischen Denkens,* 5 vols. (Gütersloh: Verlagshaus Gerd Mohn, 1949–1954).

2. See the Harper & Row series Makers of Modern Theology edited by Jaroslav Pelikan; studies of Schleiermacher, F. C. Baur, Kierkegaard, and Albrecht Ritschl have been published.

3. Emil Brunner, *Die Mystik und das Wort* (2d ed.; Tübingen: J. C. B. Mohr-Paul Siebeck, 1928), pp. iii-iv.

4. Emil Brunner, *The Mediator*, tr. of the second German edition by Olive Wyon (The Westminster Press, 1947), p. 71. This book remains an important historical document in assessing the breach between dialectical theology and nineteenth-century liberalism. The analysis of Ritschl as an exponent of a radically anthropocentric theology is also characteristic of D. Erich Schaeder's estimate which first appeared in 1909; *Theozentrische Theologie* (3d ed.; Leipzig and Erlangen: A. Deichertsche Verlag, 1925), Part I, pp. 118–143.

5. Brunner, *The Mediator*, p. 56.

6. *Ibid.*, p. 57.

7. Karl Barth, *Theologische Fragen und Antworten, Gesammelte* Vorträge, Vol. III (Zollikon: Evangelischer Verlag, 1957), p. 31. See Glick, *op. cit.*, pp. 222 ff., for a review of this debate.

8. Cited in Glick, *op. cit.*, p. 225.

9. Karl Barth, *The Humanity of God* tr. by John Newton Thomas and Thomas Wieser (John Knox Press, 1960), pp. 39–40. For an initial attempt to assess Barth's relationship to his predecessors, see my "The Theology of Karl Barth and the Nineteenth Century," *Religion in Life*, Vol. XXXIV (Winter, 1964–1965), pp. 81–94. The most extensive treatments of Barth's theological evolution are found in James D. Smart, *The Divided Mind of Modern Theology: Karl Barth and Rudolf Bultmann, 1908–1933* (The Westminster Press, 1967), and T. F. Torrance, *Karl Barth, An Introduction to His Early Theology* (London: SCM Press, Ltd., 1962).

10. Barth, *The Humanity of God*, p. 43.

11. Karl Barth, *Theology and Church, Shorter Writings 1920–1928*, tr. by Louise P. Smith (Harper & Row, Publishers, Inc., 1962), p. 314, n. 1.

12. Barth, *From Rousseau to Ritschl*, p. 390.

13. *Ibid.*, p. 392; see Paul Tillich, *Perspectives on 19th and 20th Century Protestant Theology*, ed. by Carl E. Braaten (Harper & Row, Publishers, Inc., 1967), p. 218.

14. Barth, *From Rousseau to Ritschl*, p. 391.

15. Ferdinand Kattenbusch, *Die deutsche evangelische Theologie seit Schleiermacher* (Giessen: Verlag Alfred Töpelmann, 1934), Part II, p. 3. For a recent study illuminating the theology of W. Herrmann as an important link between the theology of Ritschl and that of Barth and Bultmann, see Peter Fischer-Appelt, *Metaphysik im Horizont der Theologie Wilhelm Herrmanns* (Munich: Chr. Kaiser Verlag, 1965); also Voelkel, *op. cit.*

16. Hök, *op. cit.*, pp. xviii-xxxiv, in an incomplete bibliography lists approximately two hundred and eighty books, articles, and reviews relating to Ritschl, dating roughly from the period 1880–1940; most of these appeared, however, prior to 1910. See Rolf Schäfer, *Ritschl*, pp. 209–215,

for a list of the most important secondary works on Ritschl and for more recent literature. For a complete Ritschl bibliography see Otto Ritschl, I and II.

17. D. Horst Stephan, "Albrecht Ritschl und die Gegenwart," *loc. cit.,* pp. 34–35; see the entire article for one description of the demise of Ritschl's theology.

18. For literature, see Hök, *op. cit.,* n. 2, p. 2, and Schäfer, *Ritschl,* pp. 209–215.

19. Hefner, *op. cit.,* p. 6; cf. esp. pp. 1–11; 88–111.

20. *Ibid.,* pp. 95–111.

21. Wilhelm Herrmann, *Faith and Morals,* tr. by D. Matheson and R. Stewart (Williams and Norgate, 1904), esp. pp. 35–36; for Herrmann's development of this point, see Fischer-Appelt, *op. cit.,* pp. 194 ff.

22. Orr, *Ritschlianism,* p. 34.

23. Otto Ritschl, "Albrecht Ritschls Theologie und ihre bisherigen Schicksale," *loc. cit.,* p. 43.

24. For Otto Ritschl's list of these emphases, see above, Introduction n. 13.

25. O. Pfleiderer, *Die Ritschl'sche Theologie kritisch beleuchtet* (Braunschweig: C. A. Schwetschke und Sohn, 1891), pp. iv–v; also, the first essay on Ritschl's epistemology.

26. Stählin, *Kant, Lotze and Ritschl,* esp. Ch. 3; Stählin writes from the perspective of the Erlangen School and especially under the influence of Hofmann.

27. Fr. Traub, "Ritschls Erkenntnistheorie," *Zeitschrift für Theologie und Kirche,* 4. Jhr. (1894), esp. pp. 120–129.

28. Otto Ritschl, II, pp. 390–392; and "Albrecht Ritschls Theologie und ihre bisherigen Schicksale," *loc. cit.,* pp. 47–48.

29. Wrzecionko, *Die philosophischen Wurzeln der Theologie Albrecht Ritschls,* p. 33; for the above discussion, see pp. 9–33.

30. Paul Lehmann, *Forgiveness: Decisive Issue in Protestant Thought* (Harper & Brothers, 1940), p. 93.

31. See above, Chapter III.

32. The teleological thrust of Ritschl's understanding of justification and reconciliation is made evident above, esp. in Chapters II and IV.

33. Fabricius, *op. cit.,* p. 88; cf. esp. pp. 75–88.

34. *Ibid.,* pp. 75 ff.; cf. *Christliche Vollkommenheit,* p. xxvi.

35. Otto Ritschl, II, p. 414; J. Thikötter, *Darstellung und Beurteilung der Theologie Albrecht Ritschls* (Bonn: Adolph Marcus, 1883).

36. Otto Ritschl, II, p. 196; he makes this same point emphatically in 1935 in speaking of a "rigorous teleological viewpoint" characterizing his father's system. Dogmatics is constructed in the light of "the final end of

the divine government of the world, which final and highest purpose is revealed by Jesus to be the Kingdom of God." Or again, he can speak of a "thoroughly religiously grounded teleological pragmatism" ("Albrecht Ritschls Theologie und ihre bisherigen Schicksale," *loc. cit.*, pp. 48–49; cf. p. 45).

37. Otto Ritschl, II, p. 107; cf. p. 324; among the numerous critics in addition to those cited who have opted for the priority of the Kingdom of God in Ritschl, the following may be named: Richard Wegener (1897); Alfred Garvie (1899); Martin Kähler (ca. 1900); B. B. Warfield (1931); Paul Lehmann (1940); Christian Walther (1961); Hermann Timm (1967). The latter work has just come to the writer's attention. It is the most recent careful study in which Ritschl's theology is interpreted as "The Teleological System of the Kingdom of God."

38. Hök, *op. cit.*, pp. 280–281; cf. pp. 271–282.

39. *Ibid.*, p. 281. Some recent commentators have defended Ritschl against the charge of Barth and others that he transformed religion into ethics. Hans Vorster says: "But Ritschl does not speak of ethical judgments in order to put them in the place of religious judgments. Ethical judgments are to be seen much more as an aid to interpretation with the sole purpose being to make religious judgments scientifically comprehensible." See his "Werkzeug oder Täter," *Zeitschrift für Theologie und Kirche,* 62. Jhr., Heft I (1965), p.54. Rolf Schäfer follows a view similar to Hök's in holding that the concept of the Kingdom of God is first of all a religious conception for Ritschl inasmuch as it is directly related to God's revelation and grace. Thus in order to understand Ritschl, the priority accorded the religious pole (gospel) over law must be kept in view. See "Das Reich Gottes bei Albrecht Ritschl und Johannes Weiss," *Zeitschrift für Theologie und Kirche,* 61. Jhr., Heft 1 (1964), pp. 68–88.

40. Virtually all critics of Ritschl deal at some point with his doctrine of justification and reconciliation, but the following are among those who make it central in their interpretation. Dates of publication are in parentheses. Th. Häring (1888); E. Bertrand (1891); A. Dieckmann (1893); B. Steffen (1910); K. Gräder (1922); W. Weber (1940); P. Lehmann (1940); G. Hök (1942); P. Hefner (1966); full bibliographical data on most of the authors is available in G. Hök.

41. For an account of this controversy, see Karl Holl's essay "Die Rechtfertigungslehre im Licht der Geschichte des Protestantismus," in *Gesammelte Aufsätze zur Kirchengeschichte* (Tübingen: J. C. B. Mohr, 1928), Vol III, pp. 525–557; esp. pp. 526, 552 ff. Lagarde's treatment of the doctrines of justification and reconciliation as myths was reiterated by the *religionsgeschichtliche* school around 1900.

42. Wrzecionko, *op. cit.*, pp. 248 ff.

210 INTRODUCTION TO THE THEOLOGY OF ALBRECHT RITSCHL

43. In addition to Barth, Brunner, and Schaeder, recent critics sharing this perspective include: Christoph Senft, *Wahrhaftigkeit und Wahrheit;* Ernst Haenchen, *Gott und Mensch: Gesammelte Aufsätze* (Tübingen: J. C. B. Mohr, 1965)—see the essay on "Albrecht Ritschl als Systematiker," pp. 409–475.

44. See above, Chapter II, the section, "The Doctrine of God and Justification and Reconciliation." Among recent writers giving special attention to Ritschl's doctrine of God, see: Wrzecionko, *op. cit.;* Timm, *Theorie und Praxis;* P. Th. Jersild, *The Holiness, Righteousness and Wrath of God in the Theologies of Albrecht Ritschl and Karl Barth* (unpublished dissertation, Münster/Westphalia, 1962, N.V.); Walter Schlosser, *Orthodoxe Tradition und kritischer Neuansatz in der Gotteslehre Albrecht Ritschls* (unpublished dissertation, Göttingen, 1962, N.V.); see Schäfer, *Ritschl,* pp. 27–30, for a review of Schlosser, and pp. 70–91, for his analysis of Ritschl's doctrine of God.

45. See, for example, the recent study by Timm, esp. on "Ritschl's Speculative Doctrine of God," pp. 62–68, and 69–74; also, Wrzecionko's statement that the consequences of Ritschl's epistemology are crucial for the doctrine of God which appears to be the center of his system; esp. the section on the doctrine of God, *op. cit.,* pp. 199–246.

46. Some critics regard Ritschl's rejection of the traditional Lutheran view of the relationship of law and gospel to be responsible for many of his deficiencies; see, for example, Robert C. Schultz, *Gesetz und Evangelium* (Berlin: Lutherisches Verlagshaus, 1958), pp. 168–178; see also the important study of Gerhard O. Forde, *The Law-Gospel Debate.*

47. See the sections above, Chapter II, "The Love of God Revealed in the Son and the Kingdom of God," and "The Doctrine of the Person and Lifework of Jesus Christ and Justification and Reconciliation." Among recent works giving special attention to Ritschl's Christology, see: Bruno Berndt, *Die Bedeutung der Person und Verkündigung Jesu für die Vorstellung vom Reiche Gottes bei Albrecht Ritschl* (unpublished dissertation, Tübingen, 1959, N.V.); see Schäfer's analysis, *Ritschl,* pp. 20–24. Schäfer himself makes much of Ritschl's "christological starting-point" and of the role that Christology plays in his system; cf. esp. pp. 44–67; 101–114.

48. See the discussion above, Chapter IV, Introduction, for those making this emphasis. Also, B. B. Warfield's *Perfectionism,* Vol. I, pp. 3–109; see also R. Newton Flew, *The Idea of Perfection in Christian Theology* (London: Oxford University Press, 1934), pp. 374–393. Some who interpret Ritschl as an advocate of "Anthropological Theology," Chapter V above, may also be brought into the picture at this point.

49. Timm, *Theorie und Praxis,* pp. 43–48; cf. Ritschl, *Instruction,* § 24.

50. For a current statement on the need for a historical hermeneutic, see Carl Michalson, *Worldly Theology* (Charles Scribner's Sons, 1967), esp. pp. 217 ff. For contemporary discussion of this point, see James M. Robinson and John B. Cobb, Jr. (eds.), *The New Hermeneutic* and *Theology as History* (New Frontiers in Theology, Vols. 2 and 3; Harper & Row, Publishers, Inc., 1964 and 1967). See also Carl E. Braaten, *History and Hermeneutics* (New Directions in Theology Today, Vol. II; The Westminster Press, 1966).

51. John Macquarrie, *God and Secularity* (New Directions in Theology Today, Vol. III; The Westminster Press, 1967), p. 12.

52. See W. Herrmann, *The Communion of the Christian with God,* and Adolf von Harnack, *What Is Christianity?* tr. by Thomas Bailey Saunders (G. P. Putnam's Sons, 1923).

53. Jürgen Moltmann, *Theology of Hope,* tr. by James W. Leitch (Harper & Row, Publishers, Inc., 1967), pp. 310 ff.; Hefner, *op. cit.,* pp. 153–177, speaks of "The Current Retreat from the Vitalities of History" evident in the theological existentialism of James M. Robinson and Gerhard Ebeling.

54. Moltmann, *op. cit.,* p. 40; for Moltmann's critique of the eschatological thought of these theologians see pp. 37–94.

55. Richard R. Niebuhr locates an unresolved tension between Ritschl's exegetical conclusions affirming the centrality of Jesus' resurrection—in addition to the redemptive import of his death—for the apostolic church and his own inability to see its significance for understanding the church's continuing existence. His failure to do so makes it impossible for him to find a satisfactory solution to the problem concerning the relationship of faith and history; see *Resurrection and Historical Reason* (Charles Scribner's Sons, 1957), pp. 35–42. Van A. Harvey's *The Historian and the Believer* (The Macmillan Company, 1966) is a careful analysis and critique of various positions on the faith/history problem in twentieth-century theology.

56. *J.R.* I, p. 2; *R.V.* II/2, p. 158.

57. H. Richard Niebuhr, *Christ and Culture* (Harper & Brothers, 1951), pp. 91-101.

58. See above, esp. the discussion in Chapter II in the section entitled "The Doctrine of the Person and Lifework of Jesus Christ and Justification and Reconciliation."

59. Paul Lehmann, *Ethics in a Christian Context* (Harper & Row, Publishers, Inc., 1963), p. 366.

60. Dietrich Bonhoeffer, *Ethics,* ed. by E. Bethge and tr. by N. H. Smith (The Macmillan Company, 1955), p. 67; for a more recent influential statement of "worldly holiness" indebted to Bonhoeffer's understanding of Jesus as "the man for others," see John A. T. Robinson, *Honest to God*

(The Westminster Press, 1963), Chs. 4–5. For a balanced statement and survey of the present development of a more positive Christian anthropology, see Roger L. Shinn, *Man: The New Humanism* (New Directions in Theology Today, Vol. VI; The Westminster Press, 1968); for an analysis of the rising secular theologies, see Macquarrie, *God and Secularity*.

61. Ebeling, *The Nature of Faith*, p. 152.

62. Moltmann, *op. cit.*, p. 224.

63. Paul Tillich, *Systematic Theology* (The University of Chicago Press, 1951), Vol. I, p. 41.

64. Hans J. Iwand, "Wider den Missbrauch des 'pro me' als methodisches Prinzip in der Theologie," *Evangelische Theologie*, Bd. 14 (1954), pp. 120–125; Gollwitzer, *op. cit.*, pp. 207–209, summarizes Iwand's position.

65. Gollwitzer, *op. cit.*, p. 208; see the chapter, "Existentializing of the Talk of God Since Kant," pp. 67–78.

66. *J.R.* III, pp. 4, 20, 607; see above Chapter I, the section entitled "The Faith of the Church as the Object of Theological Investigation."

67. Although Feuerbach's reductionism was radical and complete, he might have pointed Ritschl to a weakness in his position had he heeded these words: "Religion is satisfied only with a complete Deity, a God without reservation; it will not have a mere phantasm of God; it demands God himself. Religion gives up its own existence when it gives up the nature of God; it is no longer a truth when it renounces the possession of the true God. Scepticism is the arch-enemy of religion; but the distinction between object and conception—between God as he is in himself, and God as he is for me—is a sceptical distinction, and therefore an irreligious one" (Ludwig Feuerbach, *The Essence of Christianity*, tr. by George Eliot [Harper Torchbook, Harper & Brothers, 1957]), p. 17.

68. Barth, *C.D.* II/1 (1957), p. 13.

69. Gerhard Ebeling, *Word and Faith*, tr. by James W. Leitch (Fortress Press, 1963), p. 36.

70. Hans J. Iwand, *Um den rechten Glauben*, ed. by K. G. Steck, *Gesammelte Aufsätze* (Munich: Chr. Kaiser Verlag, 1959), Bd. 9, p. 266.

71. Schaeder, *Theozentrische Theologie*, Part I, pp. 88, 113–114; cf. Iwand, *Um den rechten Glauben*, pp. 247–268.

72. *J.R.* III, p. 282.

73. *J.R.* III, p. 223.

74. *J.R.* III, p. 223.

75. For a fuller discussion of his Christology, see above Chapter II.

76. *R.V.* III/4, p. 367; cf. *J.R.* III, p. 389.

77. *Calvin: Institutes of the Christian Religion*, ed. by John T. McNeill; tr. by Ford Lewis Battles, 2 vols. (The Library of Christian Classics; The Westminster Press, 1960).

78. *J.R.* III, p. 379.

79. *J.R.* III, p. 378.

80. This must be said despite the positive merits of his doctrine of sin alluded to above in Chapter II.

81. Lehmann, *Ethics in a Christian Context,* p. 81.

82. Pfleiderer, *op. cit.,* pp. 69-70; it is instructive to compare the position of Hegel with Ritschl's exposition of his view in *J.R.* I, pp. 595–605.

83. See above, Chapter IV, the section, "Christian Perfection or the Protestant *Lebensideal*," for Ritschl's positive statement; for critiques of Ritschl's view, see Chapter V, above, the sections, "The Neo-Orthodox Critique of Ritschl" and "The Key to Ritschl: Anthropological Theology?"

84. Garvie, *op. cit.,* p. 317.

85. Wolfhart Pannenberg, *Jesus—God and Man,* tr. from the second German edition by Lewis L. Wilkins and Duane A. Priebe (The Westminster Press, 1968), p. 45. Pannenberg continues: "They [i.e., Neo-Protestant theologians] are no longer concerned with the conquest of death and with the theme of resurrection, and they deal with the question of the forgiveness of sins only in the sense that the possibility for every individual's overcoming sin derives from Jesus" (*ibid.*). Pannenberg's frequent references to Ritschl indicate that his position is receiving serious consideration once again.

86. Richard R. Niebuhr, *op. cit.,* pp. 41 ff.

87. *Ibid.,* p. 42.

88. *J.R.* III, pp. 406 ff., 431.

89. See Rolf Schäfer, "Das Reich Gottes bei Albrecht Ritschl und Johannes Weiss," *loc. cit.,* pp. 68–88.

90. *Ibid.,* p. 68, for this literature.

91. Norman Perrin, *The Kingdom of God in the Teaching of Jesus* (The Westminster Press, 1963), p. 17. A brief statement of the Weiss-Ritschl controversy is available in Perrin, though his treatment of Ritschl's contribution is sketchy. Schäfer's article offers a fuller assessment of the position of Weiss and also an indication of the relevance of Ritschl's position for contemporary discussions of the Kingdom of God in the teaching of Jesus; see above n. 39.

92. Perrin, *op. cit.,* p. 184.

93. *R.V.* II/2, pp. 26–34.

94. Perrin, *op. cit.,* p. 159; pp. 185 ff.

95. *Ibid.,* p. 201.

96. For example, Garvie, *op. cit.,* p. 245.

97. Ritschl can say: "Dogmatics . . . comprehends all of the conditions of Christianity within the scheme of the divine operation; ethics, which presumes this knowledge, comprehends the area of personal and social

Christian life according to the scheme of personal activity" (*R.V.* III/4, p. 14; *J.R.* III, p. 14; see also the rest of this statement).

98. Timm, *Theorie und Praxis,* pp. 73–74.

99. See Ritschl's discussion of the eternity of God in *J.R.* III, § 37, for Ritschl's speculative perspective.

100. Dietrich Ritschl, *Memory and Hope* (The Macmillan Company, 1967), p. 62.

101. *Ibid.,* pp. 102–140.

102. For an analysis of contemporary theology in terms of various conceptions of freedom, see Robert T. Osborn, *Freedom in Modern Theology* (The Westminster Press, 1967).

103. One critic argues that Ritschl's increasing minimization of the teleological dimension actually encouraged a more mystical and individualistic understanding of Christianity. See Fabricius, *op. cit.,* pp. 80–83.

104. Ritschl affirms trust in what might be called God's general providence, but he has little to say about the special providence of God. This is apparent in his understanding of prayer.

105. Moltmann, *op. cit.,* p. 69.

106. In addition to sources indicated in the course of our study which point to a renaissance of interest in Ritschl and the issues that concerned him, contemporary Catholic studies of the conception of justification in Protestant theology deserve notice. The most extensive dialogue at this point is that between Hans Küng and Karl Barth. See the former's *Justification: The Doctrine of Karl Barth and a Catholic Reflection,* tr. by T. Collins, E. E. Tolk, and David Granskou (Thomas Nelson & Sons, 1964).